BYRON

—— AND ——

THE SHELLEYS

THE STORY OF A FRIENDSHIP

BYRON

— AND —

THE SHELLEYS

THE STORY OF A FRIENDSHIP

JANE BLUMBERG

A JULIET GARDINER BOOK

C&B

COLLINS & BROWN

First published in Great Britain in 1992
by Collins & Brown Limited
Mercury House
195 Knightsbridge
London SW7 1RE

British Library Cataloguing-in-Publication Data:
A catalogue record for this book
is available from the British Library.

ISBN 1 85585 110 5 (hardback edition)
ISBN 1 85585 129 6 (paperback edition)

Filmset by Falcon Graphic Art Ltd,
Wallington, Surrey
Printed and bound in Great Britain by The Bath Press

CONTENTS

*For M. J. T. Thompson
with much love and thanks*

AUTHOR'S NOTE

The following editions of the poetry of Byron and Shelley have been used throughout:

The Works of Percy Bysshe Shelley, comprising *The Poetical Works* and *Essays, Letters From Abroad, Translations and Fragments*, ed. Mary Shelley (London: Edward Moxon, 1854).

The Poetical Works of Lord Byron, Collected and Arranged with Notes by Sir Walter Scott, Lord Jeffrey, Professor Wilson, William Gifford, Rev. George Crabbe, Bishop Heber, J. G. Lockhart, Lord Broughton (John Cam Hobhouse), Thomas Campbell (London: John Murray, 1870).

The following editions of letters and journals have been used throughout:

The Letters of Mary Wollstonecraft Shelley, 3 volumes, ed. Betty T. Bennett (Baltimore: The Johns Hopkins University Press, 1980–88).

The Journals of Mary Shelley, 2 volumes, eds. Paula Feldman and Diana Scott-Kilvert (Oxford: O.U.P., 1987).

The Letters of Percy Bysshe Shelley, 2 volumes, ed. Frederick L. Jones (Oxford: O.U.P., 1964).

Byron's Letters and Journals, 11 volumes, ed. Leslie Marchand (London: John Murray, 1973–81).

I have endeavoured to include reference dates within the body of the text. Where this is not possible, references can be found in the chapter notes.

I wish to thank John Murray Publishers, the Oxford University Press and the Johns Hopkins University Press for permission to quote from their publications.

I would also like to thank my editor, Juliet Gardiner, for her excellent guidance and encouragement.

LIST OF ILLUSTRATIONS

CHAPTER I
GENEVA

O<small>N A NIGHT IN MAY</small> 1816, a small group of young English travellers watched from the shore as a spectacular summer storm of thunder and lightning sped across the surface of Lake Geneva. The event was recorded in a letter to England on 1 June:

> The thunder storms that visit us are grander and more terrific than I have ever seen before. We watch them as they approach from the opposite side of the lake, observing the lightning play among the clouds in various parts of the heavens, and dart in jagged figures upon the piny heights of Jura, dark with the shadow of the overhanging cloud, while perhaps the sun is shining cheerily upon us. One night we *enjoyed* a finer storm than I had ever before beheld. The lake was lit up — the pines on Jura made visible, and all the scene illuminated for an instant, when a pitchy blackness succeeded, and the thunder came in frightful bursts over our heads amid the darkness.

The party, who had taken up residence on the lake, loved drama in nature above all but they listened too, in the voices of the storm, and for all of that wet and unsettled summer, for a corresponding quiver and growl from beyond: they sought the supernatural; they revelled in the sublime.

Mary Wollstonecraft Godwin, soon to turn nineteen, was deeply impressed by the violence that she described in the letter to her half-sister. So too were her remarkable companions. She shared the spectacle with her lover Percy Bysshe Shelley and her impulsive and antagonistic stepsister Claire Clairmont. Another also brooded over the scene. Shelley had just met, on the shores of the lake, George Gordon, the sixth Lord Byron. Though still resident at the Hotel d'Angleterre across the lake in the Geneva suburb of Secheron, Byron rowed across to spend every evening with his new friends no matter what the weather was like. And the weather that they shared, in the 'year without a summer', was unprecedented. Thousands of miles away, in Indonesia, on the island of Sumbawa, the great volcano Tambora had erupted with a violence and magnitude far exceeding any twentieth-century volcanic eruption. The fall-out of its massive ash plume, in addition to that of two other cataclysmic eruptions in other parts of the world in 1812 and 1814, affected the weather throughout the northern hemisphere for much of 1816.[1]

Byron wrote the third canto of *Childe Harold's Pilgrimage* later in the summer, and continued the epic poem which had, on the publication of Cantos I and II in 1812, made him famous overnight. He drew upon that evening in May and its memorable storm, and his perspective — the heights of the Jura flickering in the background — suggests that he observed it from the same spot as Mary:

XCII

The sky is changed! — and such a change! Oh night,
And storm, and darkness, ye are wondrous strong,
Yet lovely in your strength, as is the light
Of a dark eye in woman! Far along,
From peak to peak, the rattling crags among
Leaps the live thunder! Not from one lone cloud,
But every mountain now hath found a tongue,
And Jura answers, through her misty shroud,
Back to the joyous Alps, who call to her aloud!

XVC

Now, where the quick Rhone thus hath cleft his way,
The mightiest of the storms hath ta'en his stand:
For here, not one, but many, make their play,
And fling their thunder-bolts from hand to hand,
Flashing and cast around: of all the band,
The brightest through these parted hills hath fork'd
His lightnings, — as if he did understand,
That in such gaps as desolation work'd,
There the hot shaft should blast whatever therein lurk'd.

But it was Mary who made the most resounding use of the tempest; in her novel *Frankenstein* (1818), Alpine storms rage round the hapless Victor and flashes of lightning reveal the fleeing Monster to his horrified creator. Nature in tumult characterizes Mary's novel but, ironically, no storm heralds the Monster's birth. Instead, the night of his creation is still, with a dismal winter rain. In fact, it is surprisingly gentle: 'my candle was nearly burnt out, when, by the glimmer of the half-extinguished light, I saw the dull yellow eye of the creature open; it breathed hard, and a convulsive motion agitated its limbs.' Despite Mary's emphasis on the anticlimax — and poignancy — of the birth, in almost all the adaptations and Hollywood representations a stroke of lightning electrifies the prone being into life. But such adaptations are not completely insensitive to the underlying reality of the story. In fact, many have discovered the true spirit of the Monster's birth in another, perhaps unconscious way; coming out of the Geneva summer of 1816, he was born as a consequence of a dazzling meeting of three minds, ignited and powered by nature at her most exuberant. The storm vivified a potent friendship between Mary, Byron and Shelley.

Byron moved from the hotel and joined the Shelley party ten days after the storm when he took up the lease of the Villa Diodati a few hundred yards from their modest cottage. To them he represented, at least in print, the very incarnation of the exuberant energy that they lived and breathed for. And Byron shared this vitality, describing the emotions of that summer in Canto III of *Childe Harold* again:

XCIII

...Most glorious night!
Thou wert not sent for slumber! let me be
A sharer in thy fierce and far delight, —
A portion of the tempest and of thee!
How the lit lake shines, a phosphoric sea,
And the big rain comes dancing to the earth!
And now again 'tis black, — and now, the glee
Of the loud hills shakes with its mountain-mirth,
As if they did rejoice o'er a young earthquake's birth.

The summer was to be a creative highpoint for all three writers, heightened in Mary's memory by her own achievement. It was recollected as the bright zenith of her happiness; she was never to be as carefree again. All three were so young and so full of promise. Even Byron, so deliciously world-weary that he signed his age as '100' in the hotel register, was only twenty-eight.

Percy, Mary, their four-month-old son William and Claire had made for Switzerland immediately on leaving England on 3 May 1816. Shelley had originally intended to take his family to Italy, but Claire persuaded them to go to Geneva. She was determined to rendezvous with Byron and resume the distinctly one-sided relationship that she had initiated in London that spring, when the poet, in the teeth of a scandal and separated from his wife, was preparing for exile. To Byron, the liaison that they had formed was purely sexual but to Claire their secret couplings were vested with intense emotional meaning.

When the Shelley party reached the Hotel d'Angleterre Claire had to wait a further twelve days for her reluctant lover's arrival on 25

May. Her self-interest had historic consequences. When Byron and Shelley met for the first time on the 27th — Byron evidently studiously avoided Claire for as long as possible — they were delighted with one another. The volume of Mary's life-long journal which contains her daily entries for May 1815 to 21 July 1816, in which she would presumably have recorded her impression of their meeting, has been lost, but John Polidori, Byron's querulous young travelling companion and physician, recorded the event. Byron, indulging in a favourite pastime, had been sailing on the lake all day and, as his boat drew up to the hotel dock, he noticed three figures idling by the water:

> Getting out L.B. met M. Wollstonecraft Godwin, her sister, and Percy Shelley ... Dined: P.S., the author of *Queen Mab* came: bashful, shy, consumptive, twenty-six [sic]: separated from his wife; keeps the two daughters of Godwin, who practise his theories; one L.B.'s.[2]

Polidori, who grew jealous of Shelley's easy entry into Byron's usually hard-won esteem, had obviously relished the rumours surrounding the young man and two women. The same gossips who whispered of Byron's unnatural desire for his half-sister Augusta and of his cruelty to his wife believed that Shelley, grandson of a baronet and son of a Member of Parliament, had purchased, for the sum of £1,000, the two daughters (both of questionable parentage) of the impecunious William Godwin. Their first joint exploit, the six-week 'elopement' across Europe in 1814, had given visitors from England a taste for more news of their illicit adventures. Tourist telescopes were trained upon Byron's Villa Diodati from across the lake; to have two notorious black-hearts joined together in common purpose on foreign soil was a situation almost too rich for even the most salacious gourmand of gossip.

Though Shelley never achieved fame in his own lifetime for his poetry — rather, he was infamous for his exploits — Byron probably knew the younger poet's radical poem *Queen Mab*, which Shelley had sent to him in 1814. He had also met Mary very briefly when Claire brought her to see her recent conquest, though Mary did not know the true nature of their connection at the time. Still, Shelley was eager to get his party away from the English tourists staying at the Hotel d'Angleterre and conserve his dwindling funds. On 3 June he took a small house known as the Maison Chapuis on the opposite shore of the lake, near the village of Montalegre, and on 10 June Byron and Polidori moved into the Villa Diodati.

Whole days (or as much of the day as was left after Byron's late rising) — and often nights — were spent in each other's company. Talk of ghosts and the telling of macabre tales often occupied such nights, as driving rain besieged the house. Polidori had something to say about these conversations and gives a graphic, not to say comical example:

> ... Twelve o'clock. Really began to talk ghostly. LB repeated some verses of Coleridge's Christabel, of the witch's breast; when silence ensued, and Shelley, suddenly shrieking and putting his hands to his head, ran out of the room with a candle. Threw water in his face, and after gave him ether. He was looking at Mrs S, and suddenly thought of a woman he had heard of who had eyes instead of nipples, which taking hold of his mind, horrified him ... (17 June)

Byron and Shelley sailed most days, often twice, usually accompanied by the ladies in the evenings. Mary relates to Thomas Moore, Irish poet and lyricist and Byron's biographer, that during one excursion, Byron's spirits were particularly high, the wind was brisk and waves rocked the boat. 'I will sing you an Albanian song,' he cried, 'now, be sentimental and give me all your attention.' The assembled company, expecting to hear an intriguing 'Eastern melody', were shocked by Byron's serenade — 'It was a strange, wild howl that he gave forth; but such as, he declared, was an exact imitation of the Albanian mode.' He laughed at their consternation, enjoying their shocked sensibilities.

When Moore came to write his biography of his friend, Mary provided information about Byron's daily routine:

> At Diodati, his life passed in the same regular round of habits and occupations into which, when left to himself, he always naturally fell; a late breakfast, then a visit to the Shelleys' cottage and an excursion on the Lake; — at five, dinner (when he usually preferred being alone), and then, if the weather permitted, an excursion again ... when the weather did not allow of their excursions after dinner, — an occurrence not unfrequent during this very wet summer, — the inmates of the cottage passed their evenings at Diodati, and, when the rain rendered it inconvenient for them to return home, remained there to sleep. 'We often', says one, who was not the least ornamental of the party, 'sat up in conversation till the morning light. There was never any lack of subjects, and, grave or gay, we were always together'.[3]

There were probably two reasons for Byron's reluctance to dine in company; he hated to see women eat, unless it were lobster salad and champagne — suitably feminine food. And Byron was also an inveterate dieter, favouring a periodic and drastic means of keeping his weight down by strenuous dieting and the consumption of powerful purgatives. He was embarrassed by his tendency to put on weight — reports of his health and appearance from friends invariably mention whether he was fat or thin — and his regime that summer was particularly severe:

> His system of diet here was regulated by an abstinence almost incredible. A thin slice of bread, with tea, at breakfast — a light vegetable dinner, with a bottle or two of Seltzer water, tinged with vin de Grave, and in the evening, a cup of green tea, without milk or sugar, formed the whole of his sustenance. The pangs of hunger he appeased by privately chewing tobacco and smoking cigars.[4]

But the summer was to pass agreeably, despite Claire's awkward presence. In fact, Mary's gratitude to Byron must have been profound; at last her difficult stepsister had her own poet and would leave Mary's alone. The tension at Maison Chapuis was at least temporarily eased. Byron enjoyed the sexually compliant Claire and he was also practical enough to employ her in the tedious job of copying out his verse from his rough drafts, a task that he himself despised. Claire eagerly fair-copied the third canto of *Childe Harold's Pilgrimage*, as well as *The Prisoner of Chillon*, copies that Shelley took back to London to give to John Murray, Byron's publisher. Claire often sent notes to Byron asking if he wished her to spend the night, but always couched as requests to do more copying.

Claire was probably aware of her pregnancy by this time, even if she chose to ignore Byron's studied indifference, though he still exploited her availability. She frequently stole up the pathway from Chapuis late at night. Byron confessed as much to his half-sister Augusta Leigh, but he denied the rumours that had found their way back to England of outrageous licentiousness at Diodati — the white table-cloths hung out to dry in his garden were *not* ladies' petticoats, as observers at the other end of the telescopes reported. He blamed the talk of '*promiscuous intercorse*' [sic] and incest surrounding the Godwin girls on Southey — the Poet Laureate and his political and ideological arch-enemy. To Augusta, Byron admitted to having only one mistress that summer, and that she was taken only half-heartedly. He wrote on 8 September:

> a foolish girl — in spite of all I could say or do — would come after me — or rather went before me — for I found her here — and I have had all the plague possible to persuade her to go back again — but at last she went. — Now — dearest — I do most truly tell thee — that I could not help this — that I did all I could to prevent it — & have at last put an end to it. — I am not in love — nor have any love left for any, — but I could not exactly play the Stoic with a woman — who had scrambled eight hundred miles to unphilosophize me — besides I had been regaled of late with so many 'two courses and a *desert*' (Alas!) of aversion — that I was fain to take a little love (if pressed particularly) by way of novelty.

Anxious as he was to guard his reputation, Byron could not resist the desire to shock. One night at Diodati, perhaps bored with the unchanging routine, he claimed to have had an unfaithful mistress murdered at Constantinople. Byron said that the unhappy girl, whom he had seduced and by whom he had fathered two children, was sewn into a sack and thrown into the sea, a method of assassination that disposed of the hapless Thirza in *The Giaour*. His mistress had been of 'mean birth', he explained, and deserved her fate.

Amongst his other dark crimes, Byron liked to hint at his incestuous affair with his half-sister Augusta. In a letter written many years later to Edward Trelawny, an adventurer and later member of the Shelley circle, Claire claimed that Byron had shown her Augusta's letters. Parts of each letter, she maintained, were written in a code that only they could understand. Byron almost certainly did sleep with his half-sister and many, including his estranged wife, believed that Byron was the father of Augusta's daughter Medora. Byron often swore that his sister was the only woman that he ever truly loved. She was shallow and amongst the least intelligent of the women that he knew but the fact that their liaison was illicit, rather than a relationship of ideal love, helped to lend Byron his much-cherished 'criminal' credibility. He valued Augusta because she helped to enhance his self-image and lend authenticity to his diabolical persona.

If Claire seemed oblivious of her degradation, John Polidori was aggressively jealous that summer of his own ponderous dignity. He dogged events at the periphery of the close-knit group. Though only twenty-one when Byron hired him as his personal doctor, he was something of a prodigy, having qualified as a physician at nineteen. But his aspirations — and grandiloquence — went much further; he fancied himself a writer and was not shy of advancing his own literary claims or of competing with Byron himself.

Moore records a piquant and characteristic conversation between Byron and his employee:

> 'After all', said the physician, 'what is there you can do that I cannot?'
> — 'Why, since you force me to say', answered the other, 'I think there are three things I can do which you cannot'. Polidori defied him to name them. 'I can', said Lord Byron, 'swim across that river — I can snuff out that candle with a pistol-shot at the distance of twenty paces — and I have written a poem of which 14,000 copies were sold in one day'.[5]

Byron's accurate assessment of his athletic skills and comment about his poem *The Corsair*[6] (1814) would have left a humbler man contrite, but Polidori was undeterred. When, dissatisfied with the result of a sailing competition, he challenged Shelley to a duel Byron silenced him: 'Recollect, that though Shelley has some scruples about duelling, I have none; and shall be, at all times, ready to take his place.'[7]

And Polidori's reputation did not improve with the years. A kinsman could not rehabilitate his legendary bad character. William Michael Rossetti, son of Polidori's sister, edited his uncle's diary in 1911. In his introduction he wrote:

> Dr. Polidori figures not very advantageously in the books concerning Byron and Shelley. He is exhibited as overweening and petulant, too fond of putting himself face to face with those two heroes of our poetical literature, and too touchy when either of them declined to take him at his own estimation. I will allow that this judgement of Polidori is, so far as it goes, substantially just; and that some of the recorded anecdotes of him prove him deficient in self-knowledge, lacking prudence and reserve, and ignoring the distinction between a dignified and quarrelsome attitude of mind.[8]

But 'Pollydolly's' presence was not completely unwelcome that summer. He inadvertently obliged the party by acting as a butt for jokes. One afternoon, Byron and the doctor watched as Mary struggled up the wet path from Chapuis to Diodati. Knowing that Polidori was attracted to Shelley's mistress, Byron suggested that to jump off the balcony and assist her progress would be a noble and memorable gesture. Polidori did so; he slipped in the mud and, twisting his ankle, howled with pain. Mary came to *his* assistance and he was carried unceremoniously into the house where he lay upon the sofa, provoking his employer's ire with his litany of complaints.

On another occasion he was persuaded to allow his play, *Cajetan*, to be read to the assembled company. To his great delight, Byron began the reading, but it soon became clear that Byron was accompanying his exaggerated gestures with sly winks to the audience. The devastated Polidori realized in a flash that his tragedy was moving those assembled to tears of laughter rather than sorrow. He fled sobbing from the room though Byron dissuaded him — on that occasion — from suicide.[9] Polidori was able to reflect, in a more philosophical moment, about his play's reception. 'Shelley etc. came in the evening,' he wrote in his diary, 'talked of my play etc., which all agreed was worth nothing.'

The doctor was further piqued when Byron and Shelley made a tour of the opposite end of the lake in their boat, leaving him behind. His jealousy of the younger poet had begun to irritate Byron who seized the opportunity offered by the sprained ankle for escape. On 23 June, under Byron's direction, the poets set off to tour the countryside where Rousseau had lived and which he had used as a setting for his novels.

Rousseau would long fascinate and frustrate the two poets; he represented both the height of enlightenment culture and the utter failure of the French Revolution to achieve its enlightened goals. With his *La Nouvelle Héloïse* in hand, a novel that Byron had introduced to Shelley, they sought out the countryside its characters had trod. In a long letter to his friend Thomas Love Peacock, Shelley described their journey. They passed through Evian, 'wretched, diseased and poor'; Meillerie, 'the well known scene of St Preux's visionary exile . . . inchanted [sic] ground', and the mountains of La Valais and the Savoy to Clarens. There they picked roses, 'feeling that they might be the posterity of some planted by Julie's hand' and sailed on to Vevey, 'a town more beautiful in its simplicity than any I have ever seen' and where 'Rousseau conceived the design of Julie'. Byron gathered acacia leaves from Gibbon's garden in Lausanne and sent some to Murray. They were both deeply moved by the literary sights that they had seen. Byron wrote to John Murray on 27 June, 'I have traversed all Rousseau's ground — with Heloise before me — & am struck to a degree with the force & accuracy of his descriptions — & the beauty of their reality.'

Though Shelley's reputed good looks, embellished by his biographers into an almost feminine sweetness, may have promoted Byron's interest in him, Byron's homosexual desires were usually reserved for young boys, those whom he could dominate intellectually and almost certainly physically. In his earliest trip through the Turkish Empire he availed himself of the ready supply of boys. When a boy himself, aged ten, Byron was molested by his nurse who nightly climbed into his bed. In his teens he became attached to Lord Grey de Ruthyn, a tenant of his family home, Newstead Abbey. His mother was pleased with the connection between her son and the older aristocrat, but Byron was deeply offended when Grey evidently made sexual overtures. Byron broke off all relations with Grey and hinted darkly to Augusta in a letter of 26 March 1804 of the outrage that he had suffered:

> He was once my *Greatest Friend*, my reasons for ceasing that Friendship are such as I cannot explain, not even to you my Dear Sister . . . but they will ever remain hidden in my own breast. — They are Good ones however, for although I am *violent* I am not *capricious* in my *attachments*. — My mother disapproves of my quarrelling with him, but if she knew the cause (which she never will know,) She would reproach me no more. He Has forfeited all *title to my esteem* . . .

But the situation reversed itself later. He had confessed his love for John Edleston, the Cambridge choirboy, and fell into a depression when he died in 1811, years after their separation. A similar depression was to result from his apparent rejection by his Greek page-boy at Missolonghi in 1824. By contrast, Byron recognized Shelley immediately as his intellectual and social equal — there is not even circumstantial evidence which could point to sexual intimacy.

In addition to a series of dilapidated hotel rooms that reminded Byron of those he had stayed in in Greece five years before, the pair shared an experience that brought them close to death. While they were sailing in the middle of the lake, a squall blew up suddenly and the boat was in danger of capsizing. Neither man was an experienced sailor, despite their mutual fascination with boats, and in the best tradition of the professional mariner, Shelley could not swim a stroke. In a letter to John Murray of 27 June, following the incident, Byron is his usual jaunty self, bragging about his swimming prowess and never for a moment admitting fear:

> Three days ago we were nearly wrecked in a Squall off Meillerie — & driven to shore — I ran no risk being so near the rocks and a good swimmer — but our party were wet — & incommoded a good deal: — the wind was strong enough to blow down some trees as we found at landing.

The way Shelley dealt with the same situation was quite different. He prepared himself to drown quietly and decided not to struggle for life by clinging to his friend. 'My companion, an excellent swimmer, took off his coat,' Shelley wrote to Peacock on 12 July; 'I did the same, and we sat with our arms crossed, every instant expecting to be swamped.' Shelley reflected:

> I felt in this near prospect of death a mixture of sensations, among which terror entered, though but subordinately. My feelings would have been less painful had I been alone; but I know that my companion would have attempted to save me, and I was overcome with humiliation, when I thought that his life might have been risked to preserve mine.

Byron was still impressed by Shelley's calm in 1819. He wrote on 19 May to Murray, 'He answered me with the greatest coolness — that he had no intention of being saved — & that I would have enough to do to save myself, and begged not to trouble me.' Byron must have been somewhat relieved at the noble offer. By contrast to Shelley, he was fiercely attached to the world.

They continued their progress up the lake. Both poets were deeply affected by the castle of Chillon, the watery prison on the lake near Villeneuve that had held prisoners of the Reformation. Shelley described its chill and, in his indictment of tyranny, echoed *The Prisoner of Chillon*, the poem that reflects Byron's own feelings about the dark tower. Shelley wrote:

> These prisons are excavated below the lake; the principal dungeon is supported by seven columns, whose branching capitals support the roof. Close to the very walls, the lake is 800 feet deep; iron rings are fastened to these columns, and on them were engraven a multitude of names, partly those of visitors, and partly doubtless of the prisoners, of whom now no memory remains, and who thus beguiled a solitude which they have long ceased to feel. One date was as ancient as 1670. At the commencement of the Reformation, and indeed long after that period, this dungeon was the receptacle of those who shook, or who denied the system of idolatry, from the effects of which mankind is even now slowly emerging.
>
> Close to this long and lofty dungeon was a narrow cell, and beyond it one larger and far more lofty and dark, supported upon two unornamented arches. Across one of these arches was a beam, now black and rotten, on which prisoners were hung in secret. I never saw a monument more terrible of that cold and inhuman tyranny, which it has been the delight of man to exercise over man.[10]

Byron learned of François Bonnivard (1496–1570) whom Duke Charles III of Savoy had imprisoned in the deepest dungeon of Chillon for four years. The experience and the sense of injustice and inhumanity that characterizes Shelley's prose description of the castle is intensified in Byron's poem, inspired by Bonnivard's story. Borrowing a theme that dominates Shelley's career, Byron shows the necessarily corrupting nature of tyranny in its ultimate destruction of the human spirit.

After suffering persecution, a life in chains, perpetual darkness, cruelty and witnessing the slow death of his three brothers, the prisoner of Chillon is dead within himself:

> At last men came to set me free;
>   I ask'd not why, and reck'd not where;
> It was at length the same to me,
> Fetter'd or fetterless to be,
>   I learn'd to love despair.
> And thus when they appear'd at last,
> And all my bonds aside were cast,
> These heavy walls to me had grown
> A hermitage — and all my own!
> And half I felt as they were come
> To tear me from a second home:
>   . . . .
> My very chains and I grew friends,

> So much a long communion tends
> To make us what we are: — even I
> Regain'd my freedom with a sigh.

Though not as obviously collaborative, the relationship between Byron and Shelley is similar to that of two older poets, Wordsworth and Coleridge. Throughout his life Coleridge harassed Wordsworth to write a

> poem . . . addressed to those, who, in consequence of the complete failure of the French Revolution, have thrown up all hopes of the amelioration of mankind, and are sinking into an almost epicurean selfishness, disguising the same under the soft titles of domestic attachment and contempt for visionary *philosophes* . . . [11]

Shelley, likewise, urged his own friend to apply his genius to some serious purpose and embrace a cause or project worthy of his inherent nobility and depth of character. Shelley also taught Byron to appreciate the formerly abhorred poetry of Wordsworth and, for the duration of that summer, succeeded in instilling in Byron a measure of Wordsworthian hope and its promise of spiritual restoration in nature. Much of *Childe Harold*, Canto III, shares Wordsworth's, not to say Shelley's, worship of the natural world:

LXXV

> Are not the mountains, waves, and skies, a part
> Of me and of my soul, as I of them?
> Is not the love of these deep in my heart
> With a pure passion? should I not contemn
> All objects, if compared with these? and stem
> A tide of suffering, rather than forego
> Such feelings for the hard and worldly phlegm
> Of those whose eyes are only turn'd below,
> Gazing upon the ground, with thoughts which dare not glow?

Despite the empathy they experienced in the summer of 1816, Byron and Shelley's approaches to their art were profoundly different. Shelley was characterized by his contemporaries, both professional critics — those who wrote for influential, widely read literary journals such as *Blackwood's Edinburgh Magazine* and *The Quarterly* — and friends, as possessed of an extraordinary imagination, his poems populated by a uniquely fantastical imagery that at times had meaning only for himself. Thomas Moore remarks on Shelley's 'fancy . . . he had sufficient for a whole generation of poets'. It was 'the medium through which he saw

all things, his facts as well as his theories; and not only the greater part
of his poetry, but the political and philosophical speculations in which he
indulged, were all distilled through the same over-refining and unrealising
alembic.'[12]

During his professional career — a short seven years — Shelley
received important but limited notice for the poems (and two novels)
that he published. Yet, in addition to Leigh Hunt's heroic championing
of his friend in the pages of his own liberal journal *The Examiner*,
the important establishment journal *Blackwood's Magazine* defended
Shelley, at least in the earlier part of his career. Nevertheless, despite
its early stalwart defence, after Shelley published his outrageous play
of murder and incest, *The Cenci*, criticism in *Blackwood's* of its former
darling's flights of fancy was consistently harsh.

Mary, his most loyal critic, could likewise not ignore Shelley's difficult imagery. A criticism runs throughout her commentary and notes
to the collected editions of his poems that she published in 1839, many
years after his death. In contrasting his style with that of Byron, she also
described his influence on the older poet:

> Perhaps during this summer his genius was checked by association with
> another poet whose nature was utterly dissimilar to his own, yet who, in
> the poem that he wrote at that time [*Childe Harold*], gave tokens that
> he shared for a period the more abstract and etherialised inspiration of
> Shelley.[13]

But Moore delineated the contrast between Byron and Shelley most
distinctly in discussing the nature of their friendship:

> The conversation of Mr. Shelley, from the extent of his poetic reading,
> and the strange, mystic speculations into which his system of philosophy
> led him, was of a nature strongly to arrest and interest the attention of
> Lord Byron, and to turn him away from worldly associations and topics
> into more abstract and untrodden ways of thought . . . it would be difficult
> to find two persons more formed to whet each other's faculties by discus-
> sion, as on few points of common interest between them did their opinions
> agree; and that this difference had its root deep in the conformation of their
> respective minds needs but a glance through the rich, glittering labyrinth
> of Mr. Shelley's pages to assure us.
>
> In Lord Byron, the real was never forgotten in the fanciful. However
> Imagination had placed her whole realm at his disposal, he was no less
> a man of this world than a ruler of hers; and, accordingly, through the
> airiest and most subtle creations of his brain still the life-blood of truth
> and reality circulates. With Shelley it was far otherwise . . . [14]

But during the summer of 1816, their contrasting artistic styles and personalities were mutually fascinating. The voyage round the lake had been exhilarating and Byron revelled in the intellectual companionship that intimacy with Shelley provided. The pair sailed home from Ouchy in two days of tranquil weather and arrived back at Diodati on 31 June. The immediate artistic result of their adventure is impressive; Byron wrote *The Prisoner of Chillon* in a matter of days and completed Canto III of *Childe Harold* after his return. Shelley's 'Hymn to Intellectual Beauty', inspired by the reality of Rousseau's landscape, was also completed soon afterwards.

Shelley's poetic masterpiece, *Mont Blanc: Lines Written in the Vale of Chamouni*, was to be inspired by another trip later in that same summer. Mary, Shelley and Claire left William with his nursemaid Elise and set off for Chamonix on 20 July. Byron did not accompany them, probably enjoying another respite from Claire, and instead found new company across the lake at Coppet, the home of Madame de Staël, the novelist and formidable intellectual. In contrast to Byron and Shelley's relaxed, Rousseauesque wanderings on the lake earlier in the summer, the Shelley party progressed along a well-travelled tourist route. They followed the valley of the Arve, steepening into a sharp ravine, from Bonneville to the river's source at the creeping glacier of Montanvert, the Sea of Ice which becomes home to Victor's Monster in Mary's *Frankenstein*. It is also from this point that Shelley looked up to Mont Blanc, its peak shrouded in cloud, and was overwhelmed by the water and ice that surrounded him. He began his poem immediately.

But perhaps the most significant fruit of the Geneva summer was Mary's *Frankenstein*, a project that was to make her famous, and one that also highlighted the beginning of her long and curious relationship with Byron. In the first edition of *Frankenstein* (1818), published anonymously, Shelley had provided a brief preface that mentioned the cold summer of 1816 and a ghost-story competition. He did not mention any names, though he intimated the fame of one of those present. The public at first believed that Shelley had written the terrifying novel himself; if the radicalism it featured did not convince them of the notorious atheist's hand, then the prominent dedication to William Godwin must have confirmed their suspicions. Informed readers would have identified Shelley as the old man's principal disciple. But Byron knew the secret of the novel's authorship and he took some pride in being able to divulge it to Murray and others.

The rapport between Mary and Byron, which had grown as a result of the ghost-story competition and Byron's gentle, humorous badgering, was sufficient to make Claire jealous. Her stepsister had a quiet and very feminine manner. She was fair and delicate with large grey eyes, unlike

Claire, with her coarser manner and appearance. In one of her early letters to Byron, Claire anticipated their camaraderie and at the same time over-compensated for her own jealousy: 'you will, I daresay, fall in love with [Mary]; she is very handsome and very amiable, and you will no doubt be blest in your attachment . . . If it be so, I will redouble my attentions to please her.'[15] To find that Byron and Mary were lovers would have come as no surprise to the English tourists that fed on the imagined morsels from Diodati, but there is no evidence for such a relationship. On the contrary, Mary, despite her admiration for 'Dear Albe' had no delusions about his character. She understood his vanity and disapproved of his promiscuity, despite her own precarious position. In fact, she was intensely moral and certainly the most 'conventional' of the Bohemian group, and presided over it as a kind of mother. She was also appalled by Byron's cruelty. For his part, Byron always found the 'Blues', or aggressively intellectual women, unattractive. The women that he found desirable were usually his social or intellectual inferiors. Mary's confidence in her own talents and intellect (not to mention that she was already spoken for) precluded Byron's sexual interest in her. Indeed, the fact that they were not lovers may have had something to do with the longevity and complexity of their relationship.

The Shelleys returned to England in September and Byron continued his adventures on the Continent. But they were to be brought together again and their intimacy rekindled. And later, after Shelley's death, his widow and the nobleman were to draw closer still.

But what had brought the young people to Geneva in the first place? The story begins with Mary and Percy.

CHAPTER II

MARY AND PERCY

MARY GODWIN AND SHELLEY HAD BEEN LOVERS since the summer of 1814 but their union, by the conventions of their day, was as unlikely as it was romantic. Percy Bysshe Shelley was the grandson of Sir Bysshe Shelley, the first baronet of an old but minor gentry family. He had amassed great wealth for the family by marrying two heiresses in succession and his own son Timothy, Percy's father, had had little trouble winning the Parliamentary seat for Shoreham in Sussex. Like his father, Percy was sent to University College, Oxford, with all the well-tailored clothes and appointments of the heir to a fine fortune. His father and grandfather, staunch Whigs, had every reason to believe that Percy would wholeheartedly embrace his obvious destiny: he would inherit the baronetcy, the family home, Field Place near Horsham in Sussex, and participate quietly in politics, the augmentation of his estate and the administration of his own ancestral corner of England.

But it was clear from an early age that Shelley would not simply slip into his expected role. His years at Eton saw him developing all those eccentric characteristics which in time would lead to a total breakdown of relations between himself and his family. He fiercely refused to fag for the older pupils and wore his light brown hair long, unlike his close-cropped fellows. He indulged in precocious poetry-writing and by the age of seventeen had published two wildly Gothic novels, replete with all the most gruesome conventions of the popular genre: doomed lovers, evil seductions, murders of revenge and jealousy, elixirs of life and the work of the devil. His scientific curiosity saw him setting trees alight with his magnifying glass. But even his two expulsions from Eton could not have prepared his family for the litany of outrages to his class and upbringing that he was to perpetrate by the age of twenty-one.

It is difficult to over-emphasize Shelley's fierce intellectualism. While at Oxford his friend Thomas Jefferson Hogg complained of his 'intolerably shrill, harsh and discordant voice', but marvelled at his unquenchable thirst for knowledge. 'It is no exaggeration to affirm,' he wrote of his friend, 'that out of the twenty-four hours he frequently read sixteen.'[1] Classical verse translation and composition came to him with remarkable ease and, in the few sympathetic obituaries that followed his death, it was not the loss of a great poet that was mourned, but rather that of one of his generation's greatest classicists. Yet he was reading chemistry when he and Hogg met. Shelley's rooms at University College were filled with scientific apparatus, his carpet and furnishings peppered with burn marks and chemical stains.

Hogg described Shelley's enthusiastic demonstration of his expensive equipment and at the same time shaped the prototype for the mad scientist of fiction and film — ironically, despite the accretions of popular culture, most *unlike* Mary's Victor Frankenstein:

> [Shelley] then proceeded with much eagerness and enthusiasm to show me the various instruments, especially the electrical apparatus, turning around the handle very rapidly, so that the fierce, crackling sparks flew forth; and presently, standing upon the stool with glass feet, he begged me to work the machine, until he was filled with the fluid, so that his long wild locks bristled and stood on end. Afterwards he charged a powerful battery of several large jars; labouring with vast energy, and discoursing with increasing vehemence of the marvellous powers of electricity, of thunder and lightning; describing an electrical kite that he had made at home, and projecting another and an enormous one, or rather a combination of many kites, that would draw down from the sky an immense volume of electricity, the whole ammunition of a mighty thunderstorm; and this being directed to some point would there produce the most stupendous results.[2]

If Hogg's description of his friend in some measure sacrifices dry reality for a literary lushness, it none the less highlights an aspect of Shelley's character. The mad scientist was a dedicated scholar, rigorous in his argument in support of his beliefs. But Shelley was also a visionary and enthusiast who, in the heat of the moment, was capable of losing all control.

Shelley's idealism, his complete and total commitment to political reform and radical philosophy was his most remarkable — and vexing — trait. Liberty, Hogg tells us, was the fundamental motivation behind everything that Shelley said or did. And he was well placed to know: Hogg had shared expulsion from Oxford with Shelley in March 1811 for first publishing and then refusing to disavow the pamphlet *The Necessity of Atheism*.

Shelley's political impulses inspired almost all his poetry — certainly the important poems — and most of his actions. *Queen Mab*, written and privately circulated in 1813, spelled out Shelley's fervent radicalism in a comprehensive condemnation of monarchy, government, war, commerce and religion. Its championing of atheism and its corresponding attack on the Old Testament and Christianity outraged its contemporary readers, particularly when a pirated edition of 1821 gave it a wider circulation. It has a power and vehemence shocking even today. Addressing the 'murderer' Moses, Jehovah explains his purpose in Stanza VII:

> From an eternity of idleness
> I, God, awoke; in seven days' toil made earth
> From nothing; rested, and created man:
> I placed him in paradise, and there
> Planted the tree of evil, so that he
> Might eat and perish, and my soul procure
> Wherewith to sate its malice, and to turn,
> Even like a heartless conqueror of the earth,
> All misery to my fame. The race of men
> Chosen to my honour, with impunity
> May sate the lusts I planted in their heart.
> Here I command thee hence to lead them on,
> Until, with harden'd feet, their conquering troops
> Wade on the promised soil through woman's blood,
> And make my name be dreaded through the land.
> Yet ever-burning flame and ceaseless woe
> Shall be the doom of their eternal souls,
> With every soul on this ungrateful earth,
> Virtuous or vicious, weak or strong, — even all
> Shall perish, to fulfil the blind revenge
> (Which you, to men, call justice) of their God.

Shelley was a social reformer, if an unsystematic one, to the very core of his being. He was also deeply charitable and he persisted, throughout his life, in taking the side of the downtrodden and humiliated. Leigh Hunt, who was to become his friend and fervent admirer, related one such incident. At a local ball held in his honour, a young woman was present who had been seduced by one of the sons of the gentry. She was scorned and pointedly ignored by the assembly. With the first dance Shelley, the young squire, was to lead off. He went to the back of the room where the shamed woman sat alone and led her to the floor.

Though his views were to modify in the years to come, Shelley's beliefs as expressed in *Queen Mab* remained fundamentally unchanged throughout his life. And Shelley's first wife, Harriet Westbrook, was the first victim of this idealism. In August 1811 Shelley, himself (at nineteen) still under-age, married the sixteen-year-old Harriet, a friend of his sister. In a kind of rehearsal for his second dramatic exit with Mary three years later, he 'liberated' the girl from the oppression of her boarding school and took her over the border to Edinburgh. There a marriage ceremony, illegal in England, could take place. His father and grandfather, already infuriated by his Oxford antics and his 'conversion' to atheism and radical politics, stopped his allowance.

Though Shelley's urgent sexual attraction to Harriet had precipitated their hasty marriage, their intellectual disparity, despite Harriet's undeniable intelligence and sympathy for his ideals, soon became apparent. If Harriet had allowed herself to be seduced by the idealistic young aristocrat and his passionate talk of love and liberty, she was increasingly bewildered by the development of his vehement radical opinions, a development which corresponded with his diminishing fascination with her. Despite a second marriage ceremony in England to cement the first, Shelley was drawn elsewhere. He left Harriet for long periods to live with the 'sympathetic' and fawning Boinvilles, a mother and daughter who professed themselves wholly committed to his ideals. His radical commitment also made him seek out famous (former) radicals such as William Wordsworth and Robert Southey, but both had forsworn the activism of their youth by the time that Shelley the pilgrim appeared on their Lakeland doorsteps. That same outmoded radical idealism finally brought him, at the age of twenty-one, to William Godwin's door.

Shelley had been surprised to learn from Southey that the once-great Godwin was still alive. He immediately wrote to him from the Lake District on 3 January 1812:

> The name of Godwin has been used to excite in me feelings of reverence and admiration, I have been accustomed to consider him a luminary too dazzling for the darkness that surrounds him, and from the earliest period of my knowledge of his principles I have ardently desired to share on the footing of intimacy that intellect which I have delighted to contemplate in its emanations — Considering then these feelings you will not be surprised at the inconceivable emotions with which I learned your existence and your dwelling. I had enrolled your name on the list of the honorable dead. I had felt regret that the glory of your being had passed from this earth of ours. — It is not so — you still live, and I firmly believe are still planning the welfare of humankind.

Nearly two decades before, Godwin had been one of the most famous literary figures in London. He had enlisted in the Jacobin cause, the philosophical and political movement that had grown up in England in support for the French Revolution. After the combined success of his treatise *Political Justice* (1793) and its companion piece, the novel *Caleb Williams* (1794), Godwin was as feared by the anti-revolutionary government as he was celebrated by radical circles. Since the Terror and the bloody outcome of the Revolution, and during all of Shelley's lifetime, the government and most of the population of England had been fiercely and unequivocally anti-Jacobin and, indeed, anti-French. Godwin's subsequent obscurity in London, where he wrote novels and tried with only marginal success to run a publishing house, was occasionally infiltrated by ardent young men bent on reform in the old Godwinian fashion. Shelley was such a young man, but he sought Godwin out for other reasons as well: for a short time Godwin had been married to the illustrious — and censured — Mary Wollstonecraft.

At the time of their marriage, in 1797, Mary Wollstonecraft, like Godwin, was amongst the most famous literary figures in Europe. She had boldly challenged the conservative Edmund Burke's counter-revolutionary book, *Reflections on the French Revolution* (1790) with her own republican rallying cry, *A Vindication of the Rights of Men*, and she followed it two years later with *A Vindication of the Rights of Woman* (1792). The latter pamphlet, along with her education work *Thoughts on the Education of Daughters* (1787) was to establish Wollstonecraft, in the twentieth century, as the 'mother of feminism'.

Apart from her literary participation in the public, intellectual world of men, Wollstonecraft had led an unconventional life. She ran a school in the 1780s and later lived alone in London, supporting herself by writing. In 1792, after an obsessive infatuation with the (married) painter Henry Fuseli, she moved to Paris. There she became the lover of an American business man, Gilbert Imlay, and their daughter Fanny was born in 1794. After Imlay abandoned her she twice attempted suicide but then addressed herself with determination to earning a living for herself and her daughter.

But she was to find repose with William Godwin, himself a towering figure in the political debate which had surrounded the French Revolution. Four months pregnant by him, she married Godwin in 1797. They maintained separate homes, perhaps in some residual deference to one of *Political Justice*'s most salient principles: its uncompromising condemnation of marriage. Nevertheless, their married life was happy and Wollstonecraft enjoyed the unfamiliar tranquillity that it provided. They were one of the intellectual élite's most prominent couples. But their happiness was to end abruptly. Wollstonecraft died on 10 September 1797, just ten days after the birth of Mary, their only child.

Shelley, 'ardent in the cause of philanthropy and truth'[3] and a keen student of both Godwin and Wollstonecraft, could barely contain his excitement at the prospect of meeting the source of his inspiration. After a respectful correspondence, he hurried to the home of the mentor, to find it severely straitened and somewhat compromised; he had to brave the mayhem of the overflowing house at Skinner Street, near Clerkenwell. The new Mrs Godwin, formerly Mary Jane Clairmont (or Devereux, her marital history and status and that of her children have not been established) could not have been more different from her predecessor.

Indeed, for her whole married life she endured a hopeless comparison by her husband's friends with that illustrious woman of letters. She had a short temper and none of the political or literary accomplishments of her husband's circle. But she was clever. It was said that she won the widower's heart when she called out from her balcony one day, 'Is it possible that I behold the immortal Godwin?'[4]

After ten years of marriage Godwin depended on her and allowed her to run their precarious household as she saw fit. Her own children contributed to the confusion. Mary Jane, a year older than Mary, had artistic pretensions of her own. She was dissatisfied with her name and after much deliberation and experiment came up with the more 'romantic' Claire.[5] Charles, her older brother, was good-natured and likeable and he joined the ranks of other tenuous relations who received countless 'loans' from Shelley. Mrs Godwin's relationship with her stepdaughter, the high-minded and wilful Mary, was always uneasy and not untinged with jealousy. She tolerated the silent, self-effacing Fanny, the fruit of Wollstonecraft's affair with Imlay.

Shelley was struck by the indignities which the great man was suffering. He immediately offered his services and resources in repaying Godwin's considerable debts. But his reasons for attaching himself to the imperious, outdated, political philosopher rapidly changed. At the same time that he discovered disagreement with the old man, Shelley also discovered his sixteen-year-old daughter Mary Wollstonecraft Godwin and his life was changed. He described their meeting to Hogg on 4 October 1814:

> The originality & loveliness of Mary's character was apparent to me from her very motions & tones of voice. The irresi[s]tible wildness & sublimity of her feelings shewed itself in her gestures and her looks — Her smile, how persuasive it was & how pathetic! She is gentle, to be convinced & tender; yet not incapable of ardent imagination & hatred. I do not think that there is an excellence at which human nature can arrive, that she does not indisputably possess, or of which her character does not afford manifest intimations . . . I speedily conceived an ardent passion to possess this inestimable treasure.

Mary's personality was no doubt captivating but so too, according to contemporary reports, were her looks. She had the high, smooth forehead of exceptional intelligence. Her hair was auburn, her eyes large and grey-green, striking in a pale, open face. She was below average height and petite but fashionably plump.

Mary Godwin, whose background contrasted with Percy Shelley's stolid, conservative one, was born to reshape society according to her own principles. She was, unlike Shelley, predestined for fame and a certain degree of notoriety. She had felt the full weight of her own 'responsibility' for her mother's death in giving birth to her and of the expectations focused on her. 'It is not singular,' she wrote, in her 1831 introduction to *Frankenstein*, 'that, as the daughter of two persons of distinguished literary celebrity, I should very early in life have thought of writing.' Shelley was overwhelmed by the beautiful girl's intellectual pedigree and by the evidence that she might well live up to her name. In his dedication to the poem *The Revolt of Islam* (1817) he wrote of her:

> They say that thou wert lovely from thy birth,
> Of glorious parents thou aspiring Child:
> I wonder not — for One then left this earth
> Whose life was like a setting planet mild,
> Which clothed thee in the radiance undefiled
> Of its departing glory; still her fame
> Shines on thee, through the tempests dark and wild
> Which shake these latter days; and thou canst claim
> The shelter, from thy Sire, of an immortal name.

Mary was indeed compelling. Her parents' own romantic story had lent its lustre to her character. She had an active and colourful imagination and Shelley had no difficulty in transforming the ethereal creature he saw hemmed in by the mean rooms of Skinner Street into an oppressed and persecuted genius (persecuted mainly by the likes of the second Mrs Godwin). Mary bewitched the young poet by her devotion to the works of her father and mother, and, most importantly, by her growing commitment to his own ideals and plans. Afternoons were spent in St Pancras churchyard, seated by Wollstonecraft's grave, reading her novels and essays. With Claire acting as go-between for the secret meetings the courtship was swift. Mary was for a time troubled by Shelley's marriage and felt considerable qualms about Harriet but she evidently confessed her love first, as Shelley described in his letter to Hogg:

> I disguised from myself the true nature of affection. I endeavoured also to conceal it from Mary: but without success ... No expressions can convey the remotest conception of the *manner* in which she dispelled my delusions. The sublime & rapturous moment when she confessed herself mine, who had so long been her's in secret cannot be painted to mortal imaginations.

Mary's boldness was also cited by the abandoned Harriet, still unwilling to believe that her husband had strayed because of his dissatisfaction with her. About to give birth to her second child, she despondently wrote to a friend on 20 November 1814:

Your fears are verified. Mr. Shelley has become profligate and sensual . . . Mary was determined to seduce him. She is to blame. She heated his imagination by talking of her mother, and going to her grave with him every day, till at last she told him she was dying in love for him, accompanied with the most violent gestures and vehement expostulations. He thought of me and my sufferings, and begged her to get the better of a passion as degrading to him as to herself . . . He will not be near me. No, he cares not for me now. He never asks after me or sends me word how he is going on. In short the man I once loved is dead. This is a vampire. His character is blasted for ever. Nothing can save him now.[6]

Later, as delighted gossip took flight, the brazen girl was said to have seduced the adulterer — a man whose slim build and habitual stoop did not suggest sexual aggressiveness — on the very grass of her mother's last resting place, a fitting scene for the daughter of an equally brazen woman. Godwin's misguided memoir of his famous wife, published in 1798, had served only to scandalize the public that he had hoped to lead to a better understanding of Wollstonecraft's work. Godwin ingenuously described her love affairs as well as her theories and readers were more interested in the former; the world knew of Fanny Imlay's illegitimacy and that Mary herself had been born only shortly after Wollstonecraft's marriage to Godwin.

But once Mary and Shelley had confessed their mutual love, the pair did not hesitate to act on their desires. Shelley's love for Harriet was a thing of the past and thus, his moral code told him, so too was his commitment. Later, in September, he explained to his wife: 'My attachment to Mary neither could nor should have been overcome: our spirits . . . are united. We met with passion, she has resigned all for me.' After a secret affair of less than six weeks, on 28 July 1814, Mary and Shelley fled together into the summer night and crossed a tempestuous Channel in a delirium of seasickness and excess of passion.

Yet Mary made a great mistake in her daring adventure; she took Claire. Why she did this is unclear, but it is everywhere evident that it was a decision she regretted for the rest of her life. By encouraging Claire's participation in the elopement, Mary helped to create another kind of monster — a three-headed monster — that was to blight her own life. As she fled into the night with the two lovers, Claire became a charter member of Shelley's movable ménage. She was linked to them inextricably until Shelley's death, an intractable obstacle between the lovers. There is certainly circumstantial evidence that Shelley and Claire were lovers and there is no question that their attachment was profound. Byron assumed that Shelley had taken advantage of the willing girl's presence under his roof and he was later to express doubt about the paternity of Allegra (or Alba), his own daughter by Claire. Shelley's devotion to his stepsister-in-law would eventually cause tension between him and Byron. But their future was already sealed; as the sun rose over France, at the end of their rough Channel crossing, Mary and Shelley lost the last chance they had of ousting Claire from their lives.

That evening at their hotel the young people were informed that a fat lady had arrived from England claiming the English gentleman had stolen her daughter. The formidable Mrs Godwin had discovered the girls' note and followed fast on their heels, hoping to save Claire's reputation at the very least. For Mary it was too late and Godwin himself was furious: Shelley had seduced his daughter and ruined her for ever. He was out-raged, ironically, that the pair had seemingly embraced the life-style of his first wife. Determined to stay with the 'criminals', Claire resisted her mother's demands that she should return with her to London, appealing to 'the municipality of Paris, to past slavery, & to future freedom'7 and the thwarted Mrs Godwin gave up and returned to Dover the next day on her own.

But the strange six-week elopement 'honeymoon' that the three took together in France and Switzerland was more an exercise in discomfort than a romantic adventure; the countryside was ravaged by the combined fury of the revolutionary and Napoleonic wars. Shelley, Mary and Claire dragged across Europe, penniless and uncomfortable, appalled by the degradation of the peasantry and altogether disgusted with the French. Their progress across Europe was farcical and Mary recorded their hapless adventures in the journal that she and Shelley kept jointly. Shelley sold his watch and chain in Paris and set about the now familiar task of raising loans for immediate cash. Leaving the city they bought a succession of broken-down mules and donkeys — the first of which, just outside Paris, 'weak & unfit for labour' had to be carried. They hired carts and wagons and were cheated by dishonest drivers. They slept in filthy hotels — 'the dirtiest Scotch Cottage I ever entered,' Mary wrote, 'was exquisitely clean beside' one such hovel. The beds were all 'infinitely detestable'. They ate unpalatable food which they 'could hardly swallow' and sat up in chairs all night, appalled by the greasy sheets in their rooms. Shelley sprained his ankle and monopolized the precious horse that the girls were to share. As Mary noted wearily at the end of August, 'Beds very uncomfortable — Mary groans.'

One night, Claire was successful in invading the lovers' privacy. They let her rest on their bed when, hysterical, she brought tales of rats putting 'their cold paws on her face'. She found similar access to their bed when two months later, after sitting up late trading ghost stories with Shelley, she burst into their room in a frenzied state of terror. She claimed that a pillow on her bed had moved across her room of its own accord. Shelley was infinitely and annoyingly generous on these occasions in Mary's eyes. He automatically believed Claire and recorded in Mary's journal

on 7 October: 'She was positive as to the fact of her self possession &
calmness: her manner convinced me that she was not deceived.' He sat
up by the fire with her for the rest of the night.

Even more disturbing was the way in which the unconventional
nature of their party — two young girls travelling with a man —
seemed to attract undesirable attention. One day a complete stranger
accosted them and offered to even up their numbers by sleeping with
Claire. Mary was growing weary of Claire, weary of the whole enterprise: 'Mary is not well,' she wrote of herself on 22 August, '& all are
tired of wheeled machines — Shelley is in a jocosely horrible mood.'

Dispirited, they finally reached Brunnen on Lake Lucerne on 23 August
and took two miserable rooms in a large, ugly house for six months.
They found the Swiss no more to their liking than the French. After
two days of constant rain and a smoking chimney, England beckoned.
They packed their things for home, with only £28 to see them through
the next few months. The most pleasant part of their entire journey saw
them travelling swiftly down the Rhine to Rotterdam. Though some
beautiful scenery and warm sunshine cheered Mary up, and in Paris
at the beginning of August they had found themselves 'too happy to
sleep', the whole of the trip was a parody of romantic adventure. Three
years later, when they published an account of the voyage, *History of
a Six Weeks' Tour through a Part of France, Switzerland, Germany and
Holland* (1817), the farce and impropriety were discreetly glossed over.
Mary was relieved to be leaving the Continent, but unprepared for the
troubles that awaited them at home.

By 13 September 1814 the three were back in England and immediately addressed themselves to a desperate search for cash. They couldn't
even pay for their passage and persuaded the captain to wait for
his fare. They went to London, calling on Shelley's bankers and
friends in an unsuccessful quest for funds. And then they sought
Harriet, Mary noting self-pityingly, 'Shelley calls on her while poor
Mary & [Claire] are left two long hours in the coach.' The pregnant
Harriet and her daughter Ianthe had taken refuge with her father after
Shelley's abandonment. Not surprisingly Harriet was angry and no
doubt appalled by Shelley's insensitivity, and her agony must have
increased when, as the weeks passed, it was plain from his letters that
Shelley genuinely could not understand her anger. Striving to ease her
pain, she had been spending his money in his absence and Shelley came
away with only £20.

Shelley's financial responsibilities still included his wife and child,
and they were stretched further by Mary and by Claire, who was now
firmly established as a member of his gypsy household. He was also
raising money for Godwin and had, because of Godwin's machinations,
involuntarily taken on many of the old man's debts. In September and

October there was much talk of leaving London and fleeing the ever more pressing creditors. During the last week of October and the first week in November, Shelley was in real danger of being arrested for debt. On his own now, he slunk from boarding house to hotel, venturing cautiously into the sunshine when he might meet Mary at some obscure inn or coffee-house.[8]

This period was in some sense the most desperate and most romantic of their relationship. On Sunday a debtor was immune from arrest, legally beyond the reach of the bailiffs. At midnight on Saturday Shelley slipped into Mary's lodgings and, taking advantage of the relative leniency of the law, the lovers were able to satisfy the passions that had been intensifying all week during their forced separation, fed by their daily exchange of tortured love letters. On 25 October, Mary wrote:

> . . . in the morning I look for you and when I wake I turn to look on you — dearest Shelley you are solitary and uncomfortable why cannot I be with you to cheer you and to press you to my heart oh my love you have no friends why then should you be torn from the only one who has affection for you — But I shall see you tonight and that is the hope that I shall live on through the day — be happy dear Shelley and think of me — why do I say this dearest & only one I know how tenderly you love me and how you repine at this absence from me — when shall we be free from fear of treachery? . . .

Their mutual frustration was great; Shelley's yearning was no less urgent and he wrote two days later:

> Oh my dearest love why are our pleasures so short & so Uninterrupted [sic]? How long is this to last . . . Oh! those redeeming eyes of Mary that they might beam upon me before I sleep! Praise my forbearance oh beloved one that I do not rashly fly to you — & at least secure a *moments* bliss — Wherefore should I delay — do you not long to meet me? All that is exalted & buoyant in my nature urges me towards you — reproaches me with cold delay — laughs at all fear & spurns to dream of prudence!

The strain of this difficult period was starting to tell on Mary. She was already beginning to feel the discomfort of her pregnancy and found their short, furtive meetings exhausting. She apologized for the extravagance of taking a coach home after one such rendezvous. But her passion was unabated. For his part, Shelley had come to depend on Mary physically, emotionally and intellectually. He wrote on 28 October:

> . . . I do not think I am less impatient now than formerly to repossess to entirely engross my own treasured love . . . I could reconcile it to my

own feelings to go to Prison if they would cease to persecute us with interruptions ... My mind without yours is dead & cold as the dark midnight river when the moon is down. It seems as if you alone could shield me from impurity & vice. If I were absent from you long I should shudder with horror at myself. My understanding becomes undisciplined without you.

Shelley elevated Mary above the pedestal of the muse; they were intellectual soul mates; Mary made him feel spiritually complete. But he also missed their sexual intimacy — and sex in general. His desire to 'sport in security with . . . entire & unbroken bliss'9 becomes palpable. On 2 November he wrote:

the remembrance & expectation of such sweet moments as we experienced last night consoles strengthens & redeems me from despondency. *There is eternity in such moments* — they contain the true elixir of immortal life.

This experience, perhaps more than any, impressed the lovers with the strength of their mutual feeling; Mary was to fictionalize it in her novel *Lodore* (1835). It confirmed for both that their relationship was not just sexual, as Harriet and Shelley's had been, but of an altogether higher order; that Shelley had been right to leave his inadequate wife, and that together they would realize their destinies. Shelley's need for Mary Godwin was intellectual as well as emotional. Echoing Godwin and Wollstonecraft, Shelley wrote in a note to *Queen Mab*:

A husband and wife ought to continue so long united as they love each other; any law which should bind them to cohabitation for one moment after the decay of their affection would be a most intolerable tyranny, and the most unworthy of toleration. How odious an usurpation of the right of private judgement should that law be considered which should make the ties of friendship indissoluble, in spite of the caprices, the inconstancy, the fallibility, and the capacity for improvement of the human mind.10

By November Shelley's finances no longer threatened immediate imprisonment and the lovers were reunited in new lodgings. But Mary's idyll did not last long. Claire, who had almost been persuaded to leave the household of the two reprobates by her anxious mother (and, no doubt, by Mary herself), was likewise installed in the lovers' home by the following week.

Shelley evidently welcomed Claire's presence. He was still unceasing in his quest for funds, raising loans and post-obits on the expectation of his inheritance. He borrowed cash from friends and moneylenders and turned over his meagre earnings to Godwin. Almost daily his quest took him far from home and while Mary was nearly incapacitated with pregnancy, Shelley and Claire went out together every day, 'hopping about the town', Mary wrote.[11] They were often gone overnight. Mary read quietly, sometimes for the whole day, and waited patiently for their return.

She was lonely and jealous but she was trying hard to honour one of Shelley's most vexing early principles, that of free love, an extension of his philosophy of marriage: love, physical as well as emotional, should be given and received freely, untrammelled by intrusive law or conventional boundaries. If Mary found Claire's presence in her household troublesome and threatening, Percy revelled in such an unconventional domestic arrangement. During his marriage to Harriet, he had invited the spinster schoolteacher Elizabeth Hitchner to live with them, convinced by his long correspondence with her that she shared his ideals and beliefs. The experiment did not work — Miss Hitchner proved to be intolerable in the flesh and was sent home after three months. During the elopement journey Shelley had written to the abandoned Harriet from Switzerland, inviting her to join him and the Godwin girls in 'some sweet retreat . . . among the mountains'.[12] But Mary subdued her jealousy of Claire and, ever willing at this time in her life, rose to the challenge of Shelley's demonstration of free love.

Having sacrificed his own Oxford career to join his friend in triumphant expulsion, perhaps Thomas Jefferson Hogg believed that Shelley's debt to him was still unpaid. He evidently felt that he was entitled to share all things with his friend (not without the poet's encouragement, of course). Thus, just as he had fallen in love with Shelley's favourite sister, Elizabeth, and had attempted to force his attentions on Harriet and make a triangle out of the Shelleys' marriage, so he continued to dog his friend's connubial arrangements. This time — with Shelley's approval — he set his sights on Mary. Hogg paid court, or rather laid siege, to Mary while Shelley and Claire roamed.

In January 1815, after consultation with Shelley, Hogg declared his love for Mary in a letter. Shelley encouraged Hogg to receive his 'share of [their] common treasure' and Mary was no doubt aware of this. Thus, chiefly to oblige and honour Shelley by putting his beliefs into practice, she accepted Hogg's 'offer'. Though committed to the experiment, Mary none the less felt compelled to love Hogg against her own instinct, and her letters from January to April show her trying hard to work up the required emotion. She was prepared for his first letter, but her response was cautious. On 1 January 1815, she wrote:

> You love me you say — I wish I could return it with the passion you
> deserve — but you are very good to me and tell me that you are quite

happy with the affection which from the bottom of my heart I feel for you . . . But you know Hogg that we have known each other for so short a time I did not think about love — so that I think *that* also will come in time & then we shall be happier I do think than the angels who sing for ever . . . There is a bright prospect before us my dear friend.

Hogg's subsequent visits and attention were undeniably flattering and helped to fill the empty days of a difficult and lonely pregnancy but Mary kept her pressing admirer at arm's length, sending him a lock of her hair as promised but pleading 'phisical causes' when he pressed for a consummation of their 'love'. Her pregnancy, she assured him, was the only thing standing in their way and, for that matter, Shelley was subject to its prohibitions as well. She continued to beg for time, to allow her love for him 'to spring up'.

Mary was not interested in sharing her bed with Hogg and she set about modifying her earlier promises: their love for one another should be manifested in their devotion to Shelley. She wrote on 24 January:

> . . . but our still greater happiness will be in Shelley — I who love him so tenderly & entirely whose life hangs on the beam of his eye and whose whole soul is entirely wrapt up in him — you who have so sincere a friendship for him to make him happy . . . to see his love his tenderness . . . these are joys that fill your heart almost to bursting & draw tears more delicious than the smiles of love from your eyes.

Hogg, ever on the look-out for the sexual main chance, was never to be accepted by either of Shelley's wives.[13]

On 22 February 1815, when she was only seventeen, Mary gave birth prematurely to a baby girl who died a few days later on 6 March. She wrote a pathetic letter to Hogg on the sad day:

> It was perfectly well when I went to bed — I awoke in the night to give it suck it appeared to be *sleeping* so quietly that I could not wake it — it was dead then but we did not find *that* out till morning — from its appearance it evedently died of convulsions . . . I am no longer a mother now.

For several days following the death Mary was ill, in low spirits and constantly thinking of her dead child. 'Whenever I am left to my own thoughts & do not read to divert them they always come back to the same point — that I was a mother & am so no longer,' she wrote in her journal for 13 March. A few nights later she was startled by a remarkable, in some sense prophetic, dream of reanimation that was to remain embedded in her creative imagination:

Dream that my little baby came to life again — that it had only been cold & that we rubbed it by the fire & it lived — I awake and find no baby — I think about the little thing all day . . .

But Mary was resilient and still deeply in love with Shelley. She recovered quickly from what was the first in an avalanche of disappointment and tragedy that would soon come to overwhelm her, leaving her, at twenty-six, 'an aged person'. Hogg continued to visit but over the next few months she drew ever closer to Shelley and Claire's much-anticipated absence added to her pleasure and their intimacy. Some ease in their straitened finances came when Shelley's father finally agreed to an allowance, concerned that he might drive away his son and heir irrevocably (though he refused to acknowledge Mary). Claire was packed off to Lynmouth (Mary celebrated by beginning a new journal) and, alone together for the first time, the lovers enjoyed an early summer tour of Devon and the South Coast.

But Mary did not completely forget the events of the spring. She had anguished over Shelley and Claire's intimacy and had spent nearly every day with Hogg. Though he now drifted from their circle, excluded by Mary's growing animosity towards him and her unassailable love for Shelley, she would harbour the memory of her anxiety about that strange non-affair long after Shelley's death. She had been eager to please her lover, still in the first year of their relationship, and Shelley had taken advantage of her devotion to him. He wanted to test his principle of free love by applying it in practice and he had no qualms about submitting his own beloved Mary to his empirical research. Mary voluntarily participated in the experiment, but it was not until she was older, and the lustre of Shelley's idealism began to tarnish for her, that she recognized his insensitivity. He would have been shocked and surprised to learn that he habitually inconvenienced and upset other people, often those closest to him. He strove hard for consistency in thought and practice yet he caused much heart-break, not least of all, to Mary.

By August 1815 Mary was pregnant again and, after much searching for suitable accommodation, the Shelley household settled into a cottage at Bishopsgate, next to Windsor Great Park. For Mary, life at Bishopsgate was an antidote to the unsettled months that had culminated in the death of her premature baby. Years later, in her futuristic novel *The Last Man*, she drew directly on that experience of domestic tranquillity and the bucolic idyll to furnish her dark fiction with its short episodes of happiness. In that novel Mary's characters live in quiet solitude at Windsor Castle: the quondam heir to the British throne, Adrian Windsor, and his friends Lord Raymond, Lionel Verney and their families. As the plague that is to completely depopulate the world progresses, the survivors retreat into the haven of the Great Park.

The £1,000 allowance from Shelley's father eased the couple's finances. After providing for Harriet and her two children, Claire, her brother Charles and other friends, Mary and Shelley had just enough money to keep their own affairs ticking over and to maintain a carriage, vestige of Shelley's aristocratic upbringing, though Emily Sunstein, author of a recent biography of Mary, has described how the coach was regularly repossessed by its maker. Shelley's republicanism could not obscure his background; he was an aristocrat through and through — one of the reasons that Byron respected him as much as he did — and his careless attitude towards money (his obsession with raising it notwithstanding), also the trappings that he viewed as essential, suggest that he never lost the sense of easy security and the requirement of certain luxuries that characterized his childhood.

At Bishopsgate Mary settled down to study undisturbed. The couple read, together and apart, under the trees or in their respective studies and Mary kept careful lists of all their reading. Like her lover she had a voracious appetite for knowledge and, though she was keen to please Shelley with her learning, she herself had remarkable intellectual curiosity and discipline. As well as the popular novels and narrative poems of the day, Mary read histories, memoirs and classical texts. She read the 'radical' canon diligently, covering the major Jacobin novelists who included, among others, her mother and father, Robert Bage, Charles Brockden Brown and Joanna Baillie. She studied the English poets and the French *philosophes*: Rousseau, Voltaire and Holbach. In 1815 she read Gibbon's *Decline and Fall* as well as his life and letters. Over the following years she learned French, Italian, Latin and Greek.

The happiness of the summer and autumn was darkened only by Godwin's continued ostracism of the couple. He refused to see Shelley or his daughter, or allow them to see Mary's stepsister Fanny, and at the same time expected Shelley's financial help as his due. Wishing to avoid any association in writing with his daughter's seducer, he even went so far as to demand that Shelley's name should not appear on the cheques that he continued to receive from him. But the birth of the couple's son, William, in January 1816, followed by the publication of Shelley's poem *Alastor* in February overcame their sadness at Godwin's cruelty and sealed Windsor in their hearts as a monument to contentment. It is 'the only spot of English ground for which I have any affection', Mary once wrote.[14]

Mary and Shelley's life together was ever characterized by lightning changes of fortune. In April Shelley lost a Chancery suit for immediate access to his inheritance. After the recent death of Shelley's grandfather, Sir Bysshe, in January 1815, his father had inherited the title, but the fate of the family fortune was less straightforward; much of it was entailed. In fact, the complicated details of the Shelley finances, not to mention

Percy's own baroque methods of raising money on the expectation of an inheritance, have exercised literary critic and historian alike. William St. Clair's recent *The Godwins and the Shelleys* (1989) paints a rich picture of the intricate financial ties between Godwin, his uncomfortable disciple and disgruntled father.

With the disappointment of his hopes, Shelley resolved to leave England. His household could live more cheaply on the Continent and his ill-health — Shelley was deemed to be consumptive throughout his adulthood — demanded a better climate. Disheartened by their failure in the courts, but eager to re-experience Switzerland in some style, Shelley, Mary, Claire and the infant William left for Geneva in May 1816.

CHAPTER III

GEORGE GORDON

W HEN LORD BYRON LEFT ENGLAND in the spring of 1816, at the height of a scandal that almost sated the prodigious appetite for gossip that permeated London society, he did not slink off in the night like his ruined friend 'Beau' Brummel. On the contrary, he made a show of his exit, maintaining his heretofore successful and popular act as the hero of his own epics and dramatic verse: Childe Harold, Lara and the Corsair rolled into one flesh.

Byron had agreed to a separation from his wife Annabella, an heiress and self-conscious intellectual whose fascination with mathematics had caused Byron to name her the Princess of Parallelograms. But Byron's agreement was rather a moot point; Lady Byron had left their grand rented home at 13 Piccadilly Terrace[1] in January to return to her parents' home at Seaham, near Durham. Byron proceeded to Dover with his friends and servants, making an ostentatious display of his indifference and defiance, not just to the woman who had slighted him before he could her, but to the band of creditors who had dismantled his home. Before his departure he saw to it that he would travel in a style of almost outrageous grandeur: he had ordered a magnificent coach built to his specifications, an enormous expense at £500. As Thomas Moore wrote:

> Lord Byron travelled in a huge coach, copied from the celebrated one of Napoleon, taken at Genape, with additions. Besides a *lit de repos*, it contained a library, a plate-chest, and every apparatus for dining in it. It was not, however, found sufficiently capacious for his baggage and suite; and he purchased a caleche at Brussels for his servants.

The disgraced noble appeared to be on holiday. But Byron was angry, sad and, though he rarely admitted it, full of remorse for the way that he had treated his wife. He also missed his infant daughter Ada. He wrote from Dover to John Hanson, who looked after his legal and business affairs, and to his adored half-sister Augusta Leigh urging both to send him news of little 'Da' and, as soon as he landed in Belgium, asked his friend John Cam Hobhouse (later Lord Broughton), 'If you hear anything of my little daughter tell it me.' Though he was not to know it at the time, after setting sail for Ostend at the end of that April he was never to see Ada or her mother again.

The drama that was both to animate and plague George Gordon Byron's life began early when, as a six-year-old boy, he unexpectedly became the heir to the title of his great-uncle, the 'Wicked' Lord Byron. In 1798, when only ten years old, George became the sixth Lord Byron. Byron's mother, Catherine Gordon, herself came from an ancient family but her husband, George's father Captain 'Mad Jack' Byron, had soon squandered her inheritance and left her with the dregs of her fortune. After his father's death in 1791, George and his mother lived in severely straitened circumstances. Unlike Percy Shelley's childhood, Byron's was provincial in the extreme, characterized by financial insecurity and the rages and fierce love of his volatile mother.

The status of mother and son as poor relations was dispelled for ever by George's new title. But it was a title without great wealth. Apart from his right to a seat in the Lords on his majority, Byron inherited little more than the dilapidated but remarkably romantic Newstead Abbey near Nottingham, granted to the ancient Byron family by Henry VIII, and a lesser estate at Rochdale in Lancashire. During his school years at Harrow and while at Trinity College, Cambridge, Newstead was let on a long lease and Byron lived with his mother or friends during the holidays. It was at this time that he fell in love with Mary Chaworth, several years his senior, the daughter of a local landowner and Byron's first, traumatic, unrequited passion. He was to claim a lifelong obsession with that boyhood infatuation. Later, after her marriage and her attempts to re-establish an intimacy, Byron seems to have lost his romantic vision of Mary, but he would never relinquish the memory of the devastating hurt that her marriage had wrought on his boyhood. He left Cambridge at the end of 1807, spending more and more time with his rakish friends John Cam Hobhouse, Charles Skinner Matthews and the dandy Scrope Berdmore Davies in dining, drinking and gambling in London.

As soon as he was able, Byron took up residence at Newstead, its ruined twelfth-century cathedral walls at once gloomy and stylish. Once installed, he could indulge his cravings for women and wine with greater efficiency and economy than he could in London. The Abbey's large female staff — the 'Seraglio' — that Byron kept and was to keep for many years was only too obliging. He wrote to Hobhouse on 17 November 1811: 'My Establishment at Newstead improves, I have Lucy, Susan, a very pretty Welsh Girl, & a third of the Nott's breed, whom you never saw, all under age, and very ornamental.' At least one maid at Newstead bore his son.

At Newstead Byron challenged his friends to drink from his famous skull cup, fashioned from the remains of a medieval monk uncovered at the Abbey. Byron described the cup and its manufacture, and the Gothic society that he and his fellows had 'founded':

> I afterwards established at the Abbey a new order. The members consisted of twelve, and I elected myself grand master, or Abbot of the Skull, a grand heraldic title. A set of black gowns, mine distinguished from the rest, was ordered, and from time to time, when a particular hard day was expected, a chapter was held; the *crane* was filled with claret, and, in imitation of the Goths of old, passed about to the gods of the Consistory, whilst many a grim joke was cut at its expense.[2]

Byron also kept a magnificent cellar, a bear and a wolf for his own and his fellows' entertainment, and a page-boy, the beautiful Robert Rushton. If Byron was already striking poses at twenty-one with the luxurious and bizarre accoutrements of his equally unconventional home, he had not yet created the *alter ego* of the criminal aristocrat that was, a few years later, both to inflame and confuse the readers of *Childe Harold's Pilgrimage*, the narrative poem that was to make his fame and fix indelibly his assumed character. But he found notoriety as early as March 1809, when he published his satricial poem *English Bards and Scotch Reviewers*, ridiculing many of the literary greats of his day.

Byron was restless for travel and urgently wanted to leave England. Like the Shelleys who remained in few places for more than a year, Byron was happiest when living the life of a nomad. In July 1809, at the age of twenty-one, he left England, his desperate creditors and the legions of literary men whom he had insulted in his satire, on a two-year voyage that was to take him beyond the familiar routes of the Grand Tour into unexplored parts of the Ottoman Empire. 'I leave England without regret,' he wrote, 'I shall return to it without pleasure.'

He sailed from Falmouth to Lisbon with John Cam Hobhouse, who was to write an account of their journey. From Lisbon they travelled several hundreds of miles on horseback to Seville and Cadiz. Byron's letters are full of excitement, despite his cultivated world-weariness, and he found it difficult to repress his wide-eyed enthusiasm. He found Cadiz 'the prettiest town in Europe', its women more beautiful than the English and indeed more agreeable. He wrote to his mother on 11 August, enclosing the letter in the same packet that contained the enormous lock of hair given him by his amorous landlady: 'If you make a proposal which in England would bring a box on the ear from the weakest of virgins, to a Spanish girl, she thanks you for the honour you intend her, and replies "wait till I am married, & I shall be too happy".'

Byron left Gibraltar at the end of August, taking care to send Robert Rushton home to Newstead — 'you *know boys* are not *safe* amongst the Turks,' he wrote to his mother before sailing. As he later explained much more vividly, 'In England the vices in fashion are whoring & drinking, in Turkey, Sodomy & smoking, we prefer a girl and a bottle, they a pipe and a pathic.'[3] Indeed, Byron was not above sharing the customs of his host country. His adventures in the Ottoman Empire often featured young boys and young men. His letters to Henry Drury, Charles Skinner Matthews, carousing companions from Cambridge and London days, and to Hobhouse after he left Byron to return to England, are full of innuendo and ribaldry, as much in reference to the sensual pleasures of boys as girls. He referred to the 'Hyacinths' of Falmouth and the possibilities offered there. Leslie Marchand, Byron's biographer and editor of his letters and journals, has illuminated his coy references to homosexual dalliance: in several letters Byron refers, in abbreviated code, to a Latin phrase from Petronius' *Satyricon*. Referring to the narrator's relations with a young boy, '*coitum plenum et optabilem*' is translated as 'complete intercourse to one's heart's desire'.[4] Byron wrote to Hobhouse at the end of his long journey, 'Mention to M[atthews], that I have found so many of his antiques[5] on this classical soil, that I am tired of pl & opt Cs, the last thing I could be tired of.'

Yet Byron would not have considered himself homosexual; he was merely indulging in all the sensual possibilities that a young aristocrat of his age would have demanded, and the ease with which he hints of his exploits to several of his friends indicates that he was not unique among them in such matters. He became emotionally attached, too; his relationships with the Cambridge choirboy Edleston and with Rushton did not overstep certain bounds and were therefore tolerated, but Hobhouse was uneasy about Byron's plans to share lodgings with Edleston in London. Notorious homosexuals were often the butt of Byron's jokes. On his way to Falmouth in July he had changed horses at an inn where, he recounted, William Beckford, 'the Great Apostle of Pederasty' had stayed and joked that his known lover, Lord Courtney, had 'travelled the same night on the *same road* only one stage *behind* him'.[6]

From Gibraltar Byron sailed by naval frigate to Malta, stopping in Sardinia and Sicily. He stayed in Malta long enough to establish it as his 'post office' and bank for the ensuing years and to fall in love with the dramatic and celebrated Mrs Constance Spencer Smith. He wrote to his mother on 15 September:

> She has since been shipwrecked, and her life has been from its com-
> mencement so fertile in remarkable incidents, that in romance they
> would appear improbable, She was born at Constantinople, where her
> father Baron Herbert was Austrian Ambassador, married unhappily yet
> has never been impeached in point of character, excited the vengeance of

Buonaparte by a part in a conspiracy, several times risked her life, & is not yet twenty five.

By chance deterred from running off together, Constance and Byron agreed to meet at Malta in a year's time. She accepted his yellow diamond ring in tribute, and the young man sailed for Albania, 'a country rarely visited from the savage character of the natives'. Arriving at Prevesa at the end of September, he found himself the guest of the powerful warlord Ali Pasha, Governor of all Albania, Epirus and most of Macedonia.

The Pasha was impressed by Byron's title and birth, the splendid staff uniform with sabre that he wore for court appearances, and by the young man's great beauty. He was certain that Byron was a man of high birth because of his 'small ears, curling hair, & little white hands', a compliment that Byron took some pride in and repeated in letters. For the three days that he spent with the Pasha, a man of savage reputation, Byron was treated with overwhelming hospitality and wrote again to his mother on 12 November: 'He told me to consider him as a father whilst I was in Turkey, & said he looked on me as his son. — Indeed he treated me like a child, sending me almonds & sugared sherbert, fruit & sweetmeats 20 times a day. — He begged me to visit him often, and at night when he was more at leisure.'

The Pasha also gave Byron a soldier to protect him during his wanderings through the Albanian and Greek provinces. Delighted with the Albanian character ('rigidly honest, & faithful . . . cruel though not treacherous . . . several vices, but no meannesses . . . perhaps the most beautiful race in point of countenance in the world') Byron took another Albanian servant. His suite of attendants, in addition to Hobhouse, was growing quickly.

On his way to Athens at the beginning of December, Byron and his entourage spent a month traversing Aetolia, the Morea and Attica. Settling in Athens for the winter, they lodged in a house with the three Macri daughters, the youngest of whom, twelve-year-old Teresa, received one of Byron's greatest lyrics in tribute: 'Maid of Athens, ere we part,/Give, oh give me back my heart!' The romantic gentleman nearly took Teresa back to England with him, but was dissuaded by her mother's demand for 30,000 piastres.

From Athens Byron crossed the Aegean to Smyrna, visiting Marathon and, further up the coast, the Plains of Troy. Approaching the Dardanelles, he prepared for the single feat that he had anticipated with the greatest eagerness: he would swim the Hellespont from Sestos to Abydos like the mighty lover Leander crossing each night to his Hero. He succeeded on his second attempt and none of his considerable achievements before or since seems to have brought him as much satisfaction. He wrote of the event many times to his mother and friends lest his letters, as so often happened, should be lost on the journey back to England, of almost 3,000 miles.

In fact physical prowess, in pistol shooting, riding, and especially swimming, had great significance for Byron. Lady Blessington, in her memoir of her conversations with the poet at the end of his life, noticed that he fished for compliments on his sporting skill, but also noted with some pleasure (her book was self-importantly meant to dispel the romantic myth) that he was a poor horseman. But Byron's energetic pursuits were not simply the work of vanity. Though the Countess Teresa Guiccioli, Byron's last mistress, claimed, with the help of his boot-maker's testimony, that his celebrated limp was slight and caused by a weakness of the ankle compounded by the fact that one foot was one and a half inches shorter than the other, many of his contemporary biographers believed that he felt stigmatized by it. Indeed, many, and not only his detractors or the sensationalists who flocked to write accounts of his life and death, claimed that the limp was very pronounced, and caused by a severe deformation: a club foot. Whatever version is true, particularly in his youth, Byron frequently demonstrated to himself and others that he was an athlete. He could more than make up for his handicap.

He had trained in boxing, fencing and swimming in London with the prize-fighter 'Gentleman' Jackson and he challenged all comers to swimming races and prided himself on his stamina against great tides or winds. 'If I believed in the transmigration of your Hindoos,' Byron once said to Medwin, 'I should think I had been a *Merman* in some former state of existence, or was going to be turned into one in the next.'[7] His letters are full of his athletic achievements, just as contemporary accounts of his appearance focus on his limp. He revelled in his eventual fame but found that it was not unaccompanied by mental anguish. He had been brought up in obscurity, far from the capital and high society and had to learn very quickly how to comport himself in his new world. But, more disturbingly, he felt his deformity take on ever greater proportions. As his fame grew, his friend Moore noticed, he kept himself more and more from large crowds:

> . . . the true reason, no doubt, of his present reserve, in abstaining from all such miscellaneous haunts, was the sensitiveness, so often referred to, on the subject of his lameness, — a feeling which the curiosity of the public eye, now attracted to his infirmity by his fame, could not fail, he knew, to put rather painfully to the proof.[8]

At the height of his fame Byron was forced to learn quickly how to behave with *élan* in his new milieu, and how to counteract the impression that his awkward gait made on the strangers who besieged him. He believed that his image in repose would no doubt impress more than his figure on the move. Thus he did not dance, despite the vast number of balls he attended; ladies found his striking 'classical' profile, pale skin and aquiline nose compelling enough. Though he was not especially tall — five feet, eight inches — his figure was judged to be fine. He was vain and the radical editor Leigh Hunt would later claim that he dressed and curled his famous dark locks with obsessive care.

Byron planned to stay away from England for as long as possible. His financial situation at home was always uncertain and from his lawyer and agent, John Hanson, he received no information about the sale of his secondary estate at Rochdale. In the single letter from him that reached Byron in two years, Hanson suggested selling Newstead as a way out of his financial distress. Byron would not hear of it, choosing to put off the evil day of his debtors' reckoning. He would travel still further east and, besides, travel and discovery stimulated him more than any other pursuit.

Byron was a great traveller, his sense of aimlessness and his dissatisfaction were assuaged when he could wander without itinerary or direction. Unlike most British travellers of his day he did not patronize those he met; he *enjoyed* foreignness. He was excited by and deeply interested in the unfamiliar and the exotic and tried to learn the many languages that he encountered. The friends and servants that Byron acquired in Albania, Turkey, Greece and later in Italy, remained staunchly loyal. He was not troubled by inconvenience and could say with honesty and a degree of pride that he was just as happy in a shepherd's simple mountain hut as he was in the warlord's lavish palace. Indeed, he finally had to send the loyal Fletcher home, worn out by his complaints against the locals and his thwarted desire for English tea. Byron's views on travel are distinctly modern. He wrote to his mother from Athens in 1811:

> . . . I am so convinced of the advantages of looking at mankind instead of reading about them, and of the bitter effects of staying at home with all the narrow prejudices of an Islander, that I think there should be a law amongst us to set our young men abroad for a term among the few allies our wars have left us . . . Where I see the superiority of England (which by the bye we are a good deal mistaken about in many things) I am pleased, and where I find her inferior I am at least enlightened.

At the same time, Byron worried about his restlessness. All 'I am afraid of,' he wrote, '*is*, that I shall contract a Gipsy-like wandering disposition, which will make home tiresome to me, this I am told is very common with men in the habit of peregrination, and indeed I feel it so.'[9] He could not have been more self-aware; he felt caged as soon as any of the many houses in which he lived over the years began to feel like home. Like Shelley, he had something in him that railed against domestic tranquillity and though he later confessed to having been happy only in Greece, Byron never found a home even there.

By the early summer Byron had reached Constantinople where he spent the next two months, travelling up the Bosporus to the Black Sea. In July he was back in Athens and set out again to wander the Morea. He became the guest of Veli Pasha, son of Ali, a well-known pederast. Like his father he treated Byron with honour, giving him a beautiful horse and urging him to join his retinue for a time. He also presumed intimacy with the English lord, calling him a brave young man and a beautiful boy and making suggestive overtures. Byron was uncomfortable with aggressive older men and wrote to Hobhouse on 16 August 1810:

> He honored me with the appellations of his *friend* and *brother*, and hoped that we should be on good terms not for a few days but for Life. — All this is very well, but he has an awkward manner of throwing his arm round one's waist, and squeezing one's hand in public, which is a high compliment, but very much embarrasses '*ingenuous youth*' ... He asked me if I did not think it very proper that as *young* men (he has a *beard* down to his middle) we should live together, with a variety of other sayings, which made Strane stare, and puzzled me in my replies.

Byron's finances were finally stretched to the limit. He could no longer trust his affairs to Hanson, he had to take charge of them himself; the threat of losing Newstead and all its expensive furniture was too great. He turned his face disconsolately towards England, boarding the *Hydra* in Athens on 11 April 1811, and sharing his journey with the last shipment of Lord Elgin's Parthenon marbles.[10] He had no wish to return and, as he drew closer to Sheerness, he became more depressed. He was now twenty-three, and as he noted to himself in his inimitable jaded manner on 22 May, 'I have outlived all my appetites and most of my vanities aye even the vanity of authorship.' He was also physically drained. A dangerous fever had confined him for several weeks first in Athens and later at Patras and, still weak, it attacked him again in Malta. He was suffering from haemorrhoids and, as he explained to Hobhouse on 15 May, 'I had a number of Greek and Turkish women, and I believe the rest of the English were equally lucky, for we were all *clapped*.' But his letters, as always, remained remarkably high-spirited. 'Dear Hobby,' he wrote from sea, 'you must excuse all this facetiousness which I should not have let loose, if I knew what the Devil to do, but I am so out of Spirits, & hopes, & humour, & pocket, & health, that you must bear with my merriment, my only resource against Calenture.'[11]

By July 1811 Byron was back in England, just days before his mother's death and that of his old Cambridge friend Charles Skinner Matthews. His debts were as pressing as they had been before his journey. Death obsessed him and his depression grew. But in October, the death of choirboy John Edleston was to affect him most profoundly: 'I heard of a death the other day that shocked me more than any of the preceding, of one whom I once loved more than I ever loved a living thing, & one who I believed loved me to the last.'[12]

Leslie Marchand maintains that the love poem 'To Thyrza' was inspired by Edleston and his death:

Ours too the glance none saw beside;
    The smile none else might understand;
The whisper'd thoughts of hearts allied,
    The pressure of the thrilling hand;

The kiss, so guiltless and refined,
    That Love each warmer wish forbore;
Those eyes proclaim'd so pure a mind,
    Even Passion blush'd to plead for more.

The tone, that taught me to rejoice,
    When prone, unlike thee, to repine;
The song, celestial from thy voice,
    But sweet to me from none but thine;

The pledge we wore — I wear it still,
    But where is thine? — Ah! where art thou?
Oft have I borne the weight of ill,
    But never bent beneath till now!

Well hast thou left in life's best bloom
    The cup of woe for me to drain . . .

In fact, Byron composed a number of poems to Thyrza and readers and critics have long speculated on their object. Jerome McGann, the most recent editor of Byron's complete works, has identified a previously unpublished Latin poem of passionate lost love as belonging to the Thyrza group. The first draft manuscript is headed poignantly, 'Edleston Edleston Edleston'.[13]

By the following spring, seven months after the death of his mother, Byron published the first two cantos of *Childe Harold's Pilgrimage*, the poem which largely detailed his adventures of the preceding two years *and* created a character that the world would refuse to regard as fictional; the Childe, in chivalric terms a nobly born youth, was to become interchangeable with his creator. It is difficult to tell from Byron's own records when he had actually worked on this poem of nearly 200 Spenserian stanzas. According to Hobhouse he started *Childe Harold* in Jannina, Ali Pasha's capital in the middle of the Epirus, on the last day of October 1809. When he returned to England he was initially loath to publish what he considered to be somewhat of a jumble of short poems and stanzas. He was finally persuaded by the enthusiasm of Robert Charles Dallas, a fawning and self-important man of letters who claimed distant kinship by marriage to Byron — 'They are not worth troubling you with, but you shall have them all if you like,'[14] he wrote, and made the copyright of the poem over to Dallas as a gift. The older man — over thirty years older than the twenty-four-year-old Byron — acted eagerly on the poet's behalf. Despite Dallas' efforts the poem was turned down by several publishers, scared off by its provocative stand on matters of religion and politics. But John Murray was brave enough and shrewd enough to take the risk. The first edition of 500 copies sold out within three days and, in his own words, Byron 'awoke one morning and found myself famous'. Whereas *English Bards and Scotch Reviewers*, after many editions, had earned him more ill-will than celebrity, *Childe Harold* brought him to the attention of the height of London society, to the very circle of the Prince Regent, to whom he was presented at a party in June.

Byron's fame launched him into a new world. Suddenly, he was deluged by a torrent of adulation. He received tributes from smitten young ladies every day. He was engaged everywhere, the prize of Lady Jersey and of the hostesses of Holland House and Melbourne House, the great social and political centres of the capital city. In 'place of the desert which London had been to him but a few weeks before', wrote Thomas Moore, 'he now not only saw the whole splendid interior of High Life thrown open to receive him, but found himself, among its illustrious crowds, the most distinguished object.'[15]

Lady Melbourne, over thirty years his senior, was to become Byron's confidante. She was an imposing figure, an influential political hostess and a woman of considerable experience who had had a number of lovers (including the Prince of Wales it was whispered) and Byron grew to have more respect and affection for her than for any other woman he was to know. She adopted a strange role in her relationship with the young star; she was party to Byron's affair with her daughter-in-law Lady Caroline Lamb and was in some sense an accessory to the cuckolding of her own son, William. After the affair ended Lady Melbourne suggested that her niece, Anne Isabella Milbanke, known as Annabella, would make a suitable bride for Byron and she even conveyed Byron's first (rejected) proposal of marriage to the girl.

But Byron's affair with Lady Caroline Lamb, though it lasted no more than three months, remains his most celebrated. Byron was fascinated by Caroline from the moment he met her, or rather heard of her, and she had been eager to make the acquaintance of the brilliant poet — 'mad, bad and dangerous to know', as she noted in her journal. But many young ladies had fallen in love with the romantic figure of the Childe and besieged the poet at any public appearance. At one such gathering Caroline deliberately *avoided* an introduction to Byron, surrounded as he was at the time by a swarm of admirers. Her move, if calculated to intrigue him, was a resounding success: *he* now sought *her* acquaintance. Their affair was indiscreet, though Caroline was not new to such intrigue — she had already had one lover during her seven-year marriage. She sent Byron messages and notes by her page and Byron's friends, the ever-pragmatic Hobhouse in particular, grew concerned for his reputation. The lovers quarrelled often and sometimes in public; she offered him all her jewels, came to him disguised as one of her own pages, and often waited for him outside balls and parties to which she was not invited. Caroline knew no control: 'your heart — my poor Caro, what a little volcano! that pours *lava* through your veins,' Byron marvelled.[16] He was enslaved by his passion: 'I have always thought you the cleverest most agreeable, absurd, amiable, perplexing, dangerous fascinating little being that lives now or ought to have lived 2000 years ago . . . ' he wrote. Caroline's eccentricity and unpredictability were as exciting as they were dangerous. She was not a noted beauty, she was too boyish and slim for the age and she was anything but placid or demure. But with her pointed chin and doll-like eyes — a gamine face — she was acknowledged to be fatally attractive and Byron succumbed.

But by the end of July 1812, Byron had already begun to grow weary of Caro's instability. Indeed, her attention-getting antics were becoming decidedly distasteful to him. She finally outraged society irrevocably when, dispensing with the sham of secrecy altogether, she made a public scene more egregious than any of her former exploits. There are various accounts of Caroline's shame including those printed in newspapers at the time: almost a year after their break-up the former lovers were present at the same ball and, in answer to a series of sarcastic remarks by Byron, Lady Caroline produced a knife or shard of glass and in a loud whisper threatened Byron with it. Passing her swiftly, he did not hear her threat and only learned the following day that, in hysterics, she had cut her own hand causing a considerable flow of blood. Byron violently denied all knowledge of the particulars of the event and his responsibility for her actions. He wrote to Lady Melbourne on 6 July 1813:

> I know not what to say or do — I am quite unaware of what I did to displease — & useless regret is all I can feel on the subject — Can she be in her senses? — yet — I would rather think myself to blame — than that she were so silly without cause. — I really remained at Ly.

> H's till 5 totally ignorant of all that passed — nor do I know where this
> cursed scarification took place — nor when — I mean the room — &
> the hour.

Caroline contradicted Byron's story but she was nevertheless aware
of the magnitude of her impropriety. She later wrote of the incident,
'I never held my head up after — never could. It was in all the papers
and not truly put.'[17]

Long before this incident Byron had been thoroughly disgusted by
Caroline's behaviour. His cultivated unconventionality was no match
for her more authentic brand, the dizzying extremes of aristocratic
eccentricity were more than his provincial upbringing could accommodate. Yet Caroline refused to fade quietly into the background like
his former conquests. He would have to adopt a more ruthless means
of convincing her that he no longer loved her.

In the autumn of 1812 Byron took steps to marry. He had been
interested in Lady Melbourne's niece, the serious, intelligent heiress
Annabella Milbanke, when he first met her in the spring. He had even
admired some of her poetry. Now rid of Caroline, he was free to reflect
on his prospects and on his needs. He was still hard up for money and
in August began proceedings to sell his beloved Newstead. The initial
sale fell through (Byron thought he would be collecting £140,000
in September) but Newstead would not be taken off his hands until
1817.[18] He had still not relinquished his patrician reluctance to accept
money for his poetry — the work of a gentleman must remain exclusively amateur, he as yet ostentatiously maintained. But now he needed
financial security and for all his bravado and carefully nurtured persona
of the lone wolf, he also needed the security of a wife and family. He was
willing to barter his coronet for a fortune, as he often joked. Annabella,
with the expectation of her own personal fortune, fitted the bill. Through
Lady Melbourne's agency he proposed to her in October 1812 and was
promptly rejected. Somewhat relieved — Byron never really resolved his
ambiguity about marriage — he set about enjoying all the pleasures that
fame and deferred fortune could afford him.

Love and adventure beckoned. He began a comfortable liaison
with the forty-year-old Lady Oxford, whose liberal views on politics
and love had given her a bevy of children by several different fathers.
Her company and congenial home were a relief from the pyrotechnics of
Caroline, and Byron was particularly delighted by her beautiful children.
She also introduced him to the Princess of Wales, and Byron paid many
visits to the royal home in January and February of 1813.

The affair with Lady Oxford ended quietly in June when she left
England with her husband, and Byron turned his attention to others.
Lady Melbourne was again party to his attempts at cuckolding, this

time in the case of his old friend Webster, whose wife Lady Frances, though confessing her love, would not yield her person to Byron. Byron moved on, furious when later he heard that she had succumbed to the Duke of Wellington. He spent more time in London in the company of his carousing friends Moore, Rogers and the dramatist Charles Colman — 'My head aches with the vintage of various cellars,' he wrote, 'and my brains are muddled as their dregs.' He visited the editor Leigh Hunt in prison and spent much time with Sheridan, appalled and fascinated by the playwright's profligacy and poverty, and not infrequently conveyed Sheridan home when he himself was only slightly less drunk than the famous dramatist. He met the formidable Madame de Staël, woman of letters, whose home on Lake Geneva he was to frequent in 1816. It was about this time that Byron, by now the most famous poet of the day, received a copy of *Queen Mab* from Shelley. Shelley no doubt introduced himself with the missive, and Byron may have been aware of the two novels he had published while at Oxford, but Shelley had carefully removed his name from the small edition of the poem that he had had printed for private circulation. We do not know what Byron thought of the poem or if he knew who Shelley was at this time.

But by the summer of 1813 Byron was deeply involved in a love affair that would have consequences far outstripping any of his other liaisons. The only woman he could ever love,[19] he discovered, was none other than his half-sister, the Honourable Augusta Byron Leigh, five years his senior. Byron and Augusta shared the same father, Captain John Byron, known as 'Mad Jack', who had exceeded his own notoriously disreputable father in drinking, gambling and womanizing by the age of twenty-two. But he was also handsome, charming and, after some years in France, polished in the ways of polite society. Augusta's mother, Lady Carmarthen, left her husband to elope with the dashing guardsman; she secured a divorce from her husband and married Captain Byron. She died shortly after Augusta's birth in 1774. Having worked his way through his widow's fortune, Mad Jack wasted no time in finding another heiress to sustain him, battening on the unsuspecting Catherine Gordon in 1785.

Both Byron and Augusta knew what it was to be parentless, short of money, and subject to a precarious existence at the whims of relatives. Augusta was raised by her grandmother Lady Holderness and then by other relatives and friends. They did not meet until Byron went to Harrow, but carried on an intermittent correspondence for many years. As his affair with Lady Oxford ended, Byron met Augusta again, by this time the mother of many children. She was gentle, indulgent and silly, a great contrast to Byron's strident mother, the only other family he had known. They fell in love almost immediately, as mysterious to one another as new lovers, but equally close and comfortable as the near relations that they were. Augusta seemed untroubled by the question- able morality of her affair and became her brother's lover, apparently after little resistance or with few forebodings. Byron, by contrast, was well aware of their transgression and initially was racked both by desire and by the determination to subdue his illicit impulse. It was under the influence of this passionate indecision that he wrote *The Corsair*, in December and January 1813–14. This Oriental tale consolidated his fame, exemplifying the current vogue for things exotic and Eastern, and 10,000 copies were sold on its first day of publication. Augusta's influence it seems was not entirely detrimental.

Byron and Augusta snatched time together at Augusta's home, Six Mile Bottom near Newmarket, and at Newstead. They exchanged golden brooches engraved with the letter 'X', the poet's symbol for Augusta. On Byron's twenty-sixth birthday they were snow-bound at the old Abbey, enjoying a full cellar and well-heated rooms. Augusta's pregnancy was the perfect excuse; they could not possibly think of leaving until the weather and the roads improved. Colonel George Leigh, Augusta's first cousin and husband, did not suspect, or simply turned a blind eye to the situation. He was a man of fashion and at race tracks around the country ran recklessly through far more money than he had and Byron was a willing and regular benefactor. Later, Augusta, who remained perpetually short of cash (though she had been Lady-in-Waiting to the Queen) would regularly beg money from the publisher John Murray by virtue of his professional relationship with her brother.

Throughout the summer Byron planned to take Augusta — 'Goose' as he affectionately called her — abroad with him but the practical prob- lems posed by her numerous offspring seem to have put paid to the idea. They both knew that they should separate, and Augusta encouraged her half-brother to marry. Augusta seemed incapable of jealousy, or indeed of any complicated emotion. She took her affair with her half-brother as a matter of course, a natural extension of their filial affection. Gentle and decidedly free from any literary pretension, she was the epitome of the unchallenging and compliant woman.

And even as Byron sought his half-sister's arms he was again involved in a correspondence with Miss Milbanke, which she initiated, and he could not help but respond to her curious, compelling letters. That summer Byron was sowing the seeds of his own destruction. The first nail in his coffin was incest. The second was his disastrous and bewildering marriage.

In September 1814 Byron proposed again, captivated by the lively intelligence that seemed to him to shine from Annabella's carefully considered letters. This time he was eagerly accepted. He was delighted and wrote on 18 September 1814:

Your letter has given me new existence — it was unexpected — I need not say welcome — but *that* is a poor word to express my present feelings — and yet equal to any other — for express them adequately I cannot. — I have ever regarded you as one of the first of human beings — not merely from my own observation but that of others — as one whom it was as difficult *not* to love — as scarcely possible to deserve; — I know your worth — & revere your virtues as I love yourself and if every proof in my power of my full sense of what is due to you will contribute to *your* happiness — I shall have secured my own.

But as the negotiations for the marriage settlement dragged slowly on, the prospective bridegroom had time to reflect on his impending marriage. He wrote to Annabella constantly, anticipating his moral reformation under her guidance. Like Shelley, he imagined in his mate a purity and superiority of spirit that would redeem and protect his own, compromised and degraded soul. As the weeks passed, he grew less sure about his future happiness and more convinced that Augusta would remain his only love. He delayed his visit to Seaham, Annabella's home near Durham, and hesitated in London. When he finally set off he stopped at Augusta's home and at Newstead. At last, in November, he and Annabella met. After two years of acquaintance and weeks of mutual anticipation they could barely communicate. Byron found Annabella uncommonly reticent, and she was disturbed by his moodiness. The marriage was almost called off but, perversely, Byron was even more determined to see it through. Annabella managed to persuade him to return to London and during that separation it must have become clear to both that to proceed would be disastrous. At Six Mile Bottom for Christmas, Byron is said to have written his fiancée a decisive letter breaking off the engagement, but was prevented by Augusta from sending it.

As he drew near Seaham on 30 December, accompanied by the ever-faithful Hobhouse, Byron was dreading the wedding ceremony, to which, he announced to his surprised and disillusioned in-laws, no guests would be invited. The ceremony took place in the drawing-room on the morning of 2 January 1815. There was no wedding breakfast or reception and the strained couple, after the congratulations of the small family group, climbed into their carriage for the day-long journey to their honeymoon at Halnaby in Yorkshire.

Byron's relations with his new wife soured remarkably soon, in the carriage on the way to the honeymoon in fact. But again, different parties record different versions of the events. There is no doubt that the atmosphere inside the carriage, after the 'ordeal' of the wedding ceremony, was painfully tense. Byron broke into one of his wild Albanian songs and then, according to Lady Byron's biographer, drawing liberally on Annabella's own recorded memories of the journey, he became savage. 'It *must* come to a separation!,' he reputedly said, 'You should have married me when I first proposed.' The fierce cold outside and Byron's words conspired to freeze the already reserved young woman's heart. According to her, her husband continued: 'She might have saved him once; now it was too late. Enough for him that she was his wife for him to hate her — now; when he first offered himself, she had it all in her power. Now she would find that she had married a devil.'[20]

Such threats — she would pay for his honourable refusal to break off the engagement — interspersed with reassurances that he was making fun, blighted the bridal journey and wedding night. After supper that night he asked if she would be sleeping with him, as he hated to share his bed with a woman, but she could if she chose.[21] One young woman was as good as the next, he reputedly said, and that night, as they lay within the red curtains of the bed hangings, he imagined himself in hell with Proserpine his consort. Annabella's pride as a good judge of character was severely tested in the first hours of intimacy with her husband.

Byron, naturally, told another version of events. He never denied his moodiness, but maintained that Annabella could never tell when he was joking. He denied the rumours of the bridal coach ride:

> ... I was surprised at the arrangements for the journey, and somewhat out of humour to find a lady's-maid stuck between me and my bride.[22] It was rather too early to assume the husband; so I was forced to submit, but it was not with a very good grace. Put yourself in a similar situation, and tell me if I had not some reason to be in sulks. I have been accused of saying, on getting into the carriage, that I had married Lady Byron out of spite, and because she had refused me twice. Though I was for a moment vexed at her prudery, or whatever you may choose to call it, if I had made so uncavalier, not to say brutal a speech, I am convinced Lady Byron would instantly have left the carriage ... [23]

Strangely, the honeymoon was not unmitigated misery and Byron realized, as he came out of his black moods, that he could enjoy his wife's company. They found nicknames for each other: she was Bell, or Pippin, her face round like an apple, and he her Duck. He continued to write in his usual flippant manner to Lady Melbourne and the letters from the 'Moon' are charming, they show him tentatively happy but embarrassed to admit it. 'You would think we had been married these 50 years,' he wrote, 'Bell is fast asleep on a corner of the Sopha, and I am keeping myself awake with this epistle.' But the letters also show a certain cynicism, as if Byron viewed his contentment with suspicion, unbecoming to a man who had, after all, forsworn in his most famous verse any possibility of happiness. After six days of marriage he wrote to Lady Melbourne on 7 January:

> Bell & I go on extremely well so far without any other company than our own selves as yet — I got a wife and a cold on the same day — but have got rid of the last pretty speedily — I don't dislike this place — it is just the spot for a Moon — there is my only want a *library* — and thus I can always amuse myself — even if alone — I have great hopes this match will turn out well — I have found nothing as yet that I could wish changed for the better — but Time does wonders — so I won't be too hasty in my happiness.

What the letters do not reveal, but is expressed in their later recollections, is Byron's uncontrollable irritability and Annabella's corresponding lack of understanding. A visit to Augusta's after the honeymoon, where Annabella began to suspect something illicit between her sister-in-law and her husband, was the final act in their wedding farce. Byron and Augusta sat up together long after his wife had gone to bed and it was alleged that he made unkind comparisons between the two women with details that necessarily implied intimacy with both. Nothing short of a miracle could possibly save such an obviously doomed marriage.

Annabella could be annoyingly and naïvely self-righteous, but Byron seemed determined to hurt her from the very beginning. His cruelty towards his wife — a woman that he was unquestionably eager to marry — remains one of the inexplicable mysteries surrounding his life. He seems to have found his behaviour just as mysterious himself. Was it possible, determined as he was to maintain a romantic vision of his own alienation and 'criminality' (who did Harold think he was, seeking domestic love?) that he had to drive his beloved away? In looks Annabella was unremarkable but she was more intelligent than any of the other young women he knew. Indeed, she was studious and, like Mary Shelley, widely read in classical and 'serious' literature which they discussed together. She loved his poetry and could comment intelligently on it. She was not, as some biographers have imagined, particularly cold. Indeed, Byron remarked on her considerable passion to Lady Melbourne. But she was very inexperienced, self-conscious, serious and uncommonly attached to her dignity. Perhaps she also lacked some imagination in regard to her husband. She mistook his worldliness for maturity and could not appreciate that his fantasies about himself were still rich and vigorous. She was much too 'perfect' for the complicated man that she had married and her simplicity and innocence inflamed Byron's own guilt about marrying her. He recollected to Thomas Medwin:

> You ask if Lady Byron were ever in love with me — I have answered that

question already! — No! I was the fashion when first she came out: I had the character of being a great rake, and was a great dandy — both of which young ladies like. She married me from vanity, and the hope of reforming and fixing me. She was a spoiled child, and naturally of a jealous disposition; and this was now increased by the infernal machinations of those in her confidence — She thought her knowledge of mankind infallible — She had the habit of drawing people's characters after she had seen them once or twice. She wrote pages and pages about my character, but it was as unlike as possible — She was governed by what she called fixed rules and principles, squared mathematically.[24]

The year that their marriage lasted proved that they were ill-matched and Byron had been as active as ever in the diversions that London and his rakish friends could offer. He was frequently drunk, and often violent. His interest in the theatre culminated in affairs with actresses from the Drury Lane Theatre where he had been appointed a place on the management sub-committee, helping to select scripts. He neglected his new wife and rarely took her out. He was many months behind in his rent on their imposing house. She despised the friends that he brought home. Soon after the birth of their only daughter, Ada, in December 1815, Annabella left her husband for ever on 15 January.

It was not long after this that Claire Clairmont, jealous of her stepsister's poet lover, Shelley, took steps to secure her own. She set her sights on the loftiest possible conquest. At seventeen, she pursued Byron with a single-minded purpose which, if subsequently ruinous to her reputation and prospects, none the less testified to her courageous unconventionality. Her boisterous flouting of society's expectations had much in common with the behaviour of her stepfather's first wife. In fact Wollstonecraft's own daughter, Mary, had adopted a rather more stately conduct. Mary worshipped her mother's memory but her tumultuous sexual history disturbed her. Claire, on the other hand, embraced the Wollstonecraftian headlong pursuit of the desired. Her first frank letter of seduction, signed 'E. Trefusis' (presumably calling on the name of the poetess Ella Trefusis, sister of Lord Clinton who had been the recent cause of some well-publicized duels)[25] reached Byron in the early spring of 1816:

If you condescend to answer the following question you will at least be rewarded by the gratitude I shall feel. If a woman, whose reputation has yet remained unstained, if without either guardian or husband to control she should throw herself upon your mercy, if with a beating heart she should confess the love she has borne you many years, if she should secure to you secrecy and safety, if she should return your kindness with fond affection and unbounded devotion, could you betray her, or would you be silent as the grave?[26]

A second letter followed, requesting a meeting that same evening, to which Byron consented.[27] Claire would never have elicited a response from the poet had she not been William Godwin's 'daughter'. The once-famous radical philosopher was now decidedly out of fashion, but he was still held in high esteem by literary liberals and idealists. Byron — the Childe — was besieged with love letters and anonymous missives from stricken young ladies, all captivated by the Childe's dark romantic adventures as well as by Byron's already legendary beauty. Thick dark curls worn unconventionally long fell over his high forehead. His dark eyes and deeply curved lips — lascivious almost — were becoming familiar as more and more editions of *Childe Harold* were printed and engravings of Byron's portrait were circulated. Few women seem to have been disenchanted by reports of, or the sight of, his uneven, some said limping, gait. Claire knew that she must appropriate some glamour to attract his attention. She herself, though not a great beauty, was often described as 'handsome'. After their first meeting, Byron was tempted more by her extreme youth and eagerness than her looks. Claire proposed a plan for consummating their union:

> Have you any objection to the following plan? On Thursday Evening we may go out of town together by some stage or mail about the distance of ten or twelve miles. There we shall be free and unknown; we can return early the following morning. I have arranged everything here so that the slightest suspicion may not be excited. Pray do so with your people.[28]

Byron obliged her beating heart with his readiness to take advantage of any situation. Perhaps in an attempt to dissuade her from following him, Byron had insisted that they could meet in Geneva only if she were suitably accompanied. Now she needed the protection of her sister's own dubiously respectable household. But to travel with the Shelleys was additional insurance for Claire; she knew that Byron would be drawn by the younger poet. Such bait might ensure his attention upon their arrival in Geneva. She had doggedly written to him all that spring, planning their assignation — or so she believed it to be — in secret from Percy and Mary. She planned to call herself 'Madame Clairville'. 'I chose to be married,' she wrote to Byron, 'because I am so, and the Madames have their full liberty abroad.'[29] Claire's monumental self-delusion that Byron felt any love for her is difficult to credit, even when one remembers her considerable youth. Her talent for self-dramatization, and indeed for fantasy, was nowhere more exercised than in the campaign she mounted for Byron's attention.

When Byron set out in artificially high spirits for Dover at the end of April and crossed the English Channel, 'kicking the dust of England from his feet' and vomiting on passage only once ('As a veteran I stomached the sea pretty well — till a damned "Merchant of Bruges" capsized his breakfast close by me — & made me sick by contagion'[30]) he crossed it for the last time. Byron talked of England for the next eight years, unaware that he would never return nor see his wife and child again. He always planned to come back and cherished the hope that he would be reunited with his family until the very day of his death. He was a cynical man, but, for all that, he knew that he could only regain his place in society, with Annabella and Ada, by expiating his sin in some great act of heroism or sacrifice. He cast about for such a project for many years until the sound of a suitable trumpet called him to Greece, to a hideously mismanaged and misrepresented war.

But in May 1816 Byron still smarted from being hurled out of the door of English high-life.[31] His considerable debts must have pained him too. He had left Piccadilly Terrace particularly early in the morning on 23 May to avoid the bailiffs, who indeed seized everything just after he left. He trundled over the Alps in his overweighted coach, breaking down all along the way, to arrive in Geneva at a hotel full of the same English society that he had fled. At the Hotel d'Angleterre was Percy Bysshe Shelley. Perhaps it was an immediate pleasure to Byron to meet the eccentric revolutionary for the first time, but he also recognized that this pleasure was to be somewhat tarnished — Shelley was of course accompanied by the troublesome Claire, only three months from her seduction of Byron and nearly as tenacious in her demands for his attention as the tedious Lady Caroline.

CHAPTER IV

THE ENCHANTMENT
ENDS

O N THE SHORES OF LAKE GENEVA IN 1816 the young writers felt free. They had abandoned England and could almost imagine that the confines of that society, which they flouted but could never completely ignore, had magically melted away and released them. The Shelleys' enthusiasm for their new life was unqualified, but Byron was rather more circumspect; he was *not* free, like his companions, to return to England if he so desired. It would take some time for the stories of his cruelty to Lady Byron and the whispers about his relationship with Augusta Leigh to die down.

But for that summer Mary, Shelley, Claire and Byron were buoyed up on the wave of their own imaginations and a shared craving for a romantic world shaped by those imaginings. And they had borne fruit. Byron's ghost story competition had inspired Mary to invent a story that would become the best-known product of English Romantic Literature. Byron had teased and cajoled her in the days following the soirée that had hatched the competition. He greeted her each morning, 'Have you thought of a story?', until, with her famous dream, she awoke with the vision of her tale in her mind:

> When I placed my head on my pillow, I did not sleep, nor could I be said to think. My imagination, unbidden, possessed and guided me, gifting the successive images that arose in my mind with a vividness far beyond the usual bounds of reverie. I saw — with shut eyes, but acute mental vision, — I saw the pale student of unhallowed arts kneeling beside the thing he had put together. I saw the hideous phantasm of a man stretched out, and then, on the working of some powerful engine, show signs of life, and stir with an uneasy, half vital motion.[1]

From that moment her project was clear. She was determined to mould her vision into a novel and with Shelley's encouragement her narrative began to take shape. From the middle of August and throughout the autumn and winter she recorded 'write' or 'work' in her journal almost every day.

But their continental holiday had to end, the party was broken up. Byron, whose meat and drink for so long had been the London high-life, was craving the gossip and bustle of his days in London. Seeing off his friends of the summer, not without some relief, he begged the loyal Hobhouse and the always amusing Scrope Davies to come to his aid in exile and beguile him into an atmosphere of the old days.

Shelley meanwhile was summoned home to deal with the vexed question of his father's estate. After the disappointment of the spring when it seemed that Shelley's inheritance would be withheld indefinitely, the troublesome prospect of yet more litigation ended the enchanted summer with the call of reality. The Shelley household left Geneva on the morning of 29 August 1816. Taking passage from Le Havre on 7 September, dispirited and ill, they arrived in Portsmouth the following afternoon. Mary, Claire, William and the nursemaid Elise went directly to Bath the following day to find lodgings. Claire's pregnancy had to be kept from the Godwins for as long as possible and they hoped that the anonymity of a provincial town would minimize gossip before the baby's expected birth in January. Shelley went to London to deliver the other fruits of Byron's summer; *The Prisoner of Chillon* and Canto III of *Childe Harold's Pilgrimage* were ready for John Murray to publish. In his exile Byron had not forgotten his public, nor had Murray forgotten the unprecedented sales of Cantos I and II and the earlier Oriental tales, *Lara* and *The Giaour*. But Mary and Shelley might well have prolonged their summer idyll; the months ahead brought tragedy, sorrow and disappointment.

Ensconced in fashionable Bath, Mary bought a piano for the miserable Claire, who still continued to send out a stream of pleading love letters to an unresponsive Byron:

> ... I would do anything, suffer any pains or degradation so that I might be so very happy as to receive a letter from you ... I do not like to be the object of pity, and nothing makes me so angry as when Mary and Shelley tell me not to expect to hear from you. They seem to know how little you care for me, and their hateful remarks are the most cruel of all. How proud I should be of a letter to disappoint their impertinent conjectures.[2]

For his part, Byron was determined to avoid all communication and contact with Claire. He had never loved her and her pathetic letters did not move him. He would resolutely avoid her hereafter and his rancour would grow.

Shelley, meanwhile, was immediately besieged with angry demands for money from Godwin, who nevertheless still refused to see him. He was also depressed on another account. His poem *Alastor* had been coolly received by the critics. They found its images obscure and too highly wrought and failed to see that Shelley was subtly criticizing one of William Wordsworth's poetic ideals. The older poet glorified the artist as a 'solitary', one wilfully removed from the world. Shelley believed that this self-isolation was not only counter-productive but almost immoral, and the difficult narrative of *Alastor* attempted to communicate this, apparently unsuccessfully. His secret envy of Byron's easy critical and popular success must have grown during the summer and he could not help feeling keenly the sharp jabs of the reviewers. Indeed, his glorious friend was not far from his mind — he was full of ideas for Byron's career (he had apparently already suggested an epic on the French Revolution) and for the direction that his great poetic gift should take. Shelley offered effusive praise and a lecture. He wrote from London on 29 September:

> You contemplate objects that elevate, inspire, tranquillise. You communicate the feelings, which arise out of that contemplation, to mankind; perhaps to the men of distant ages ... I do not know how great an intellectual compass you are destined to fill. I only know that your powers are astonishingly great, and that they ought to be exerted to their full.
>
> It is not that I counsel you to aspire to fame. The motive to your labours ought to be more pure, and simple. You ought to desire no more than to express your own thoughts; to address yourself to the sympathy of those who might think with you ... I would not that you should immediately apply yourself to the composition of an Epic Poem; or to whatever other work you should collect all your being to consummate. I would not that the natural train of your progress should be interrupted; or any step of it anticipated. I delight in much of what you have already done. I hope for much more, in the same careless spirit of ardent sentiment. I hope for no more than that you should, from some moment when the clearness of your own mind makes evident to you the 'truth of things', feel that you are chosen out from all other men to some greater enterprise of thought; and that all your studies should, from that moment, tend towards that enterprise alone: that your affections, that all worldly hopes this world may have left you, should link themselves to this design.

We do not know if Byron felt the younger and demonstrably less successful poet's earnest advice to be presumptuous. Perhaps he was flattered by Shelley's worship of his talent and its implication of the younger man's inferiority (not that Shelley was sincere in this self-deprecation). Shelley wrote again on 17 January 1817: 'I often talk, and oftener think, of you; and that, though I have not seen you for six months, I still feel the burden of my own insignificance and impotence ... '

Whether Shelley really believed Byron to be the better poet is also unknown but, from the time that their friendship was first formed, Shelley felt compelled to try to influence Byron for a specific purpose: that of pursuing a noble project to exercise his poetic, emotional and spiritual talent. Shelley wanted Byron to realize his obvious potential and believed that through his own persistent urging, the deed would be accomplished. Though Shelley did not believe Byron's work to be trivial, he believed that it could be more ambitious in its political scope. He may also have felt that, unlike his own poetry, Byron's responded directly to public taste and did not reflect Byron's political or philosophical ideals; perhaps the intellectual rigour that he found in the nobleman's character was not sufficiently reflected in the poetry.

Despite the all-pervading tension that reigned in her temporary home, Mary managed to work with speed and dedication on *Frankenstein*. She had formidable powers of concentration and could work most productively within the maelstrom of emotions and responsibilities that beset her. She was solely responsible for the management of the household, for Claire and for William. She was still reading extensively; it is difficult to see how she fitted the writing of her novel into her busy day.

Shelley and Mary's return to England was met with a series of tragedies. On 10 October 1816, Fanny Imlay, the neglected stepdaughter of Godwin and half-sister to Mary, was found dead at an inn in Swansea. An empty bottle of laudanum stood on the table by her body, near the gold watch sent by Shelley and Mary from Geneva. Only days before, her unsuspecting family had believed that she was on her way to Dublin, resigned to an obscure and tedious life with her dead mother's sisters. Then, too late for them to effect a rescue, she had sent word to Mary and Shelley of her desperate intentions. Their sense of powerlessness was devastating. Meanwhile, Godwin's behaviour, when he learned of the death, was remarkably cold-blooded. Fear of scandal had damaged his humanity; he could not forget the uproar that had met his publication of Mary Wollstonecraft's memoirs, wherein he had so candidly described his dead wife's love affairs. Her illegitimate daughter must not be identified and the whole tale dragged through Grub Street once more. 'Go not to Swansea,' he wrote to Mary, 'disturb not the silent dead; do nothing to destroy the obscurity she so much desired that now rests upon the event.' On Godwin's instruction, Fanny was buried anonymously by the parish.

The Godwins and Shelleys felt guilty, and realized in retrospect that they had recognized Fanny's depression and done nothing about it. After the departure of Mary and Claire from the confines of Skinner Street, Fanny had been left a lonely and lost inmate. Her innocent discontent when she regarded her own miserable position, especially when exciting letters from Geneva, painting scenes of Paris, Mont Blanc and

Plate 1 Mary Godwin Shelley in middle age; the only formal portrait taken from life.

Plate 2   William Godwin in 1802. Mary Shelley's father and author of Enquiry Concerning Political Justice.

Plate 3   Mary Wollstonecraft Godwin. Mary Shelley's mother and author of A Vindication of the Rights of Woman.

Plate 4 Percy Bysshe Shelley, in Rome, 1819. By an amateur painter, Amelia Curran, a friend of the Shelleys, this is the only portrait of Shelley taken from life.

Plate 5 George Gordon, 6th Baron Byron, aged about 25, at the height of his new fame following the publication of Childe Harold's Pilgrimage.

Plate 6 Lady Caroline Lamb, dressed as a page-boy. This miniature was given to John Murray, Byron's publisher, by Caroline herself.

Plate 7 Newstead Abbey, Nottinghamshire.

Plate 8 Augusta Leigh, Byron's half-sister and sometimes lover.

the glamorous Lord Byron reached her, served to deepen her depression. Mary could not have been aware of the torment that her letters caused her sister. She wrote on 17 May 1816:

> You know that we have just escaped from the gloom of winter and of London; and coming to this delightful spot during this divine weather, I feel as happy as a new-fledged bird, and hardly care what twig I fly to, so that I may try my new-found wings. A more experienced bird may be more difficult in its choice of a bower; but, in my present temper of mind, the budding flowers, the fresh grass of spring, and the happy creatures about me that live and enjoy these pleasures, are quite enough to afford me exquisite delight, even though clouds should shut out Mont Blanc from my sight.

Fanny may even have been in love with Shelley, as Godwin and his wife were quick to claim. But she had been neglected, taken for granted, in the drama and bustle of the lives that must have seemed so much more important than her own. The sentiments of her pathetic suicide note were all too true:

> I have long determined that the best thing I could do was to put an end to the existence of a being whose birth was unfortunate, and whose life has only been a series of pain to those persons who have hurt their health in endeavouring to promote her welfare. Perhaps to hear of my death will give pain, but you will soon have the blessing of forgetting that such a creature ever existed . . . [3]

But Mary bought her family mourning clothes. Fanny's death left Mary and Shelley bereft. Fanny had been their ally during the trying months of penury in London that followed their elopement and she had risked Godwin's rage by continuing to see them and bring them news. She was Mary's link with their dead mother, and she may even have had a dim memory of the woman who had given them birth. Shelley's lines on the tragedy expressed their collective sadness and guilt:

> Her voice did not quiver as we parted,
>   Yet knew I not that heart was broken
> From which it came, and I departed
>   Heeding not the word then spoken.
> Misery — O Misery,
> This world is all too wide for thee.

Mary pressed on with *Frankenstein* throughout the autumn and early winter and began to think of having another child. 'Tell me shall you be happy to have another little squaller?' she wrote to her husband on 5 December. She moved the now obviously pregnant Claire and Elise into separate lodgings, all too aware of the rumours that had conjured up the so-called League of Incest between the Godwin sisters and Byron and Shelley at the notorious Villa Diodati. People could easily assume that the expected child was Shelley's. Then the second tragedy, which held a guilty blessing for Mary and Shelley, struck in December. The body of the abandoned Harriet Shelley, heavily pregnant, was found in the Serpentine in Hyde Park, another evident suicide.

Since Shelley had abandoned her before the birth of their second child, Harriet had been living at her father's house. She left there in the summer of 1816, staying in various lodgings, and evidently took a lover, an army officer, who in turn left her to return to his post sometime in the autumn. Shelley, perhaps in an effort to assuage his own guilt and to substantiate the groundless claims that she had been unfaithful to him before his own affair with Mary, maintained that Harriet had become a common prostitute. From 9 November her parents reported her missing — she had removed herself secretly to new lodgings to prevent their detection of her condition — and a month later, on 10 December, her body was recovered from the lake. An inquest was held on 'Harriet Smith' and another anonymous burial was charged to the expense of the parish. A veil was firmly drawn by the Westbrooks over the circumstances of their daughter's death, never to be lifted, even during the following months in their legal struggle to keep her orphaned children from Percy's custody.

Harriet's tale was an embarrassment to her family, but it was to be even more embarrassing to Shelley's offspring and to the industry of veneration that they erected and maintained in his memory. Harriet's fall and destruction were almost certainly due to her husband's attachment to Mary and to Mary's acceptance of a married man. But something of a conspiracy to blacken Harriet's name was initiated by the Godwins immediately after her death in their efforts to secure Shelley's marriage to Mary. Such rumours were later reinforced and 'confirmed' in the 1880s by Jane, Mary's daughter-in-law and keeper of the poet's sacred flame. The 'official' memoir of Mary and Shelley's relationship and marriage was carefully manipulated to deny responsibility for Harriet's death. Mark Twain must have been among the first to challenge the accepted doctrine of Harriet's unworthiness and to detect the unmistakable whiff of defamation. His essay of 1891 'In Defense of Harriet Shelley' argues, with humour and vitriol, her side of the seamy tale and attempts to vindicate her memory. He wrote:

> How any man in his right mind could bring himself to defile the grave of a shamefully abused and defenseless girl with these baseless fabrications, this manufactured filth, is inconceivable ... The charge

insinuated by these odious slanders is one of the most difficult of all offenses to prove; it is also one which no man has a right to mention even in a whisper about any woman, living or dead, unless he knows it to be true . . .

Against Harriet Shelley's good name there is not one scrap of tarnishing evidence, and not even a scrap of evil gossip, that comes from a source that entitles it to hearing.[4]

It could hardly be denied that Harriet's death was convenient. Later in the same month, Mary and Shelley were married, to Godwin's undisguised joy: his daughter was redeemed and Shelley's anticipated wealth was officially at his finger-tips. A 'marriage takes place on the 29th,'[5] Mary wrote coyly in her journal. Everyone involved was satisfied, although Shelley was somewhat bewildered to have embraced for a second time an institution that he had consistently abjured. The most enthusiastic reporter of the news was Godwin, whose delight in the marriage had completely overcome his commitment to his early doctrines of Political Justice:

> my daughter is between nineteen and twenty. The piece of news I have to tell, however, is that I went to church with this tall girl some little time ago to be married. Her husband is the eldest son of Sir Timothy Shelley, of Field Place, in the county of Sussex, Baronet. So that, according to the vulgar ideas of the world, she is well married, and I have great hopes the young man will make her a good husband. You will wonder, I daresay, how a girl without a penny of fortune should meet with so good a match. But such are the ups and downs of this world.[6]

Mary was also unable to maintain a dignified silence. In a letter to Byron of 13 January 1817 she added:

> Another incident has also occurred which will surprise you, perhaps; It is a little piece of egotism in me to mention it — but it allows me to sign myself — in assuring you of my esteem & sincere friendship
>
> Mary W. Shelley

There was to be some more momentary relief from the onslaught of misery. On 12 January Claire gave birth to Byron's daughter and Mary notified the poet. Claire named her daughter Alba but, like her mother, the little girl was to be known by a variety of names. Byron preferred Allegra, and so she was generally called. Mary and Shelley expected Byron to provide for his daughter, as they had discussed at the end of the summer, and to suggest the conditions of his custody. Even Claire agreed that Allegra would benefit from an aristocratic upbringing. But the reluctant father was no happier with the idea of his illegitimate family than he had been with Claire on her own. He felt uneasy about the affair and accepted that he must sooner or later acknowledge the child, but he was in no hurry to do so; Claire had grown even more abhorrent to him. His receipt of the news of the birth was delayed but he wrote to Augusta in May 1817 of his mixed feelings:

> I am a little puzzled how to dispose of this new production (which is two or three months old though I did not receive the accounts till Rome), but shall probably send for it & place it in a Venetian convent — to become a good Catholic — & (it may be) a *Nun* — being a character somewhat wanted in our family. — They tell me it is very pretty — with blue eyes & dark hair — & although I never was attached nor pretended attachment to the mother — still in case of the eternal war & alienation which I forsee about my legitimate daughter — Ada — it may be well to have something to repose a hope upon — I must love something in my old age — & probably circumstances will render this poor little creature a greater (& perhaps my only) comfort than any offspring from that misguided & artificial woman — who bears & disgraces my name.

But in the new year all thoughts of Claire's disappointment and Byron's whereabouts were forgotten. The Westbrooks, Harriet's parents, filed a suit in Chancery to win custody of their grandchildren, Ianthe and Charles Shelley. This took their father by surprise and, as Shelley fought for his children, Mary stood firmly by him, pleased to welcome his children into her home. She left Claire, William and Allegra in Bath and joined Shelley in London; a greater fear than the loss of Harriet's son and daughter beset her — her own child could be taken away in a further action if she and Shelley were deemed unfit parents. 'It is possible that the interference exercised by Chancery in the instance of my two other children might be attempted to be extended to William,' Shelley wrote to Byron on 9 July, hoping to encourage him to respond with his plans for his own daughter.

Mary was suitably shaken, both for Shelley's welfare and for William, though they had resolved to flee the country with him if any further legal action was taken. Meanwhile she did all she could to support her husband, proclaiming her love for the older children and her willingness to let them supersede William in seniority — he would be helped third at table. She stayed at Skinner Street and also with Percy at the Vale of Health in Hampstead, the home of Leigh and Marianne Hunt, new friends who would support the Shelleys through this crisis and remain their friends for life.

Leigh Hunt was editor of the liberal weekly newspaper *The Examiner*. He championed political reform and the radical writing of Shelley, John

Keats, William Hazlitt and indeed the whole of the 'Cockney School' (which included his own poetry) in the pages of his liberal journal. In 1812 he and his brother John had been sentenced to two years in jail for 'libelling' the Prince Regent. Byron had visited the 'martyr to freedom' frequently during his prison sentence in 1813 and described his character in words that he would later recant again and again:

> Hunt is an extraordinary character, and not exactly of the present age. He reminds me more of the Pym and Hampden times — much talent, great independence of spirit, and an austere, yet not repulsive aspect. If he goes on *qualis ab incepto*, I know few men who will deserve more praise or obtain it . . . he is a man worth knowing; and though, for his own sake, I wish him out of prison, I like to study character in such situations. He has been unshaken, and will continue so. I don't think him deeply versed in life; — he is the bigot of virtue (not religion), and enamoured of the beauty of that 'empty name', as the last breath of Brutus pronounced, and every day proves it. He is, perhaps, a little opinionated, as all men who are the *centre of circles*, wide or narrow — the Sir Oracles, in whose name two or three are gathered together — must be, and as even Johnson was; but, withal, a valuable man, and less vain than success and even the consciousness of preferring 'the right to the expedient' might excuse.[7]

Byron's praise illustrates the celebrity that Hunt acquired by enduring a harsh prison sentence; he was, for the time, the darling of the liberals and he had many visitors in his jail cell. He was released in 1815 and earned Byron's gratitude for taking his side on the separation from Lady Byron. But once Hunt had fallen from the heights that his unjust incarceration had raised him to, he lost his lustre for the famous poet. His character was changed in Byron's eyes: he always needed money; he was a lower-class hack writer and presumptuous poetaster. When Byron attempted to return Hunt's early kindness years later in Italy, he regretted his efforts even as he proffered his hand. They parted enemies and Hunt revenged himself in 1828 when he published *Lord Byron and Some of His Contemporaries*, taking advantage of their former intimacy to savage the poet's character.

As Byron grew less enamoured of Hunt, the Shelleys became still more attached to him. His large family was to become an important part of the Shelleys' lives in Italy and Hunt remained the sole, steadfast defender of Shelley's poetry. He and Marianne buoyed up the young couple during the trying weeks of Shelley's Chancery suit, taking them to the theatre and opera and introducing them to Hazlitt and Keats. For a time they even provided a home for Allegra, hoping to quell rumours that she was Shelley's child. Mary did not forget the Hunts' kindness on that occasion and others and for the rest of her life did all she could to repay it. She often nursed Marianne through her numerous pregnancies and the inevitable illnesses that went with them — Mary never could persuade her to loosen her stays in the last months — and grew attached to the Hunts' children. She pleaded on Leigh's behalf when he fell out with Byron, arranged loans for him, and lent him money of her own when she had it. Hunt never demurred when offered money, especially the annuity that Mary presented him with after Shelley's death, even though she herself was short of funds. Both Mary and Byron were often vexed by the speed with which Hunt and Marianne went through the money that they lent — the family consumed almost all of Mary's savings. But they remained friends.

Shelley prepared his own statement of defence in the Chancery hearings and refused to listen to his advisers, his lawyer and Godwin among them, who recommended that he should simply deny, or excuse as the naïve ideas of a young man, his principled (and compromised) stand against marriage and the Church. Instead, he played into the hands of his opponents, reiterating his radical beliefs. The Lord Chancellor, Lord Eldon, announced his decision on 27 March 1817. The blasphemies of *Queen Mab*, coupled with Shelley's abandonment of Harriet and his unlawful domestication with Miss Godwin, lost him his case — he was declared an unfit parent. Charles, three, and Ianthe, five, were placed with a clergyman, both to receive a conventional education. However, Shelley was somewhat mollified: the chidren would not be allowed to reside with the Westbrooks either — Shelley saw Harriet's sister Eliza as the evil genius who had poisoned the naturally forgiving Harriet's mind against him and whose spite had prompted the Chancery proceedings in the first place. Worse still, he claimed that 'the beastly viper' had driven her own sister to suicide in order exclusively to secure her inheritance. Shelley was granted visiting privileges, but — another example of his inexplicable, periodic hard-heartedness — he chose never to see his oldest son and daughter again.

When the case was all over, Shelley needed to recover in peace from his loss. Characteristically, the injustice of the court's decision cut deeply, but his sorrow at losing his and Harriet's children seems to have been less painful. In March his household settled into Albion House in Marlow, near the home of the writer Thomas Love Peacock. The house was large and well furnished; it had to be. To save money the Hunts, their four children and Marianne Hunt's sister Bessy (whose relationship to Hunt was not unlike Claire's to Shelley and helped to compound the allegations of the Shelleys' League of Incest) left their home in Hampstead and moved into Albion House for two months, joining the 'political as well as poetical' company there.

Unfortunately Claire returned to Shelley's protection as well and somewhat tarnished Mary's sparkling idyll; 'give me a garden & *absentia*

Clariae and I will thank my love for many favours,' she had written to Shelley in December 1816. But the compensation was Allegra. 'She is very beautiful, and though her frame is of somewhat a delicate texture, enjoys excellent health,' Shelley wrote to the absent father in April 1817. 'Her eyes are the most intelligent I ever saw in so young an infant. Her hair is black, her eyes deeply blue, and her mouth exquisitely shaped.' The little girl became a favourite — Mary and Shelley adored her and they were sure that her father must feel the same when they finally met. Passed off as the child of a London friend residing in the country for her health, Allegra delighted the household. The home was a happy one, further swelled by Mary's second child, Clara, born in September. The Shelleys were now fully reconciled with Godwin and the former oppression of his rage and resentment was lifted. Claire, meanwhile, had 'resumed her maiden character'. If Godwin fully understood her situation he did not mention it, but accepted her child. (The fact that Claire was not his daughter may well have spared him any real anxiety about her reputation.)

During the summer, while drifting on the river in his boat, or lying under the trees, Shelley composed. He always carried a book and pencil, writing most readily out of doors. He had grown more quiet and contemplative, Mary recalled. The 'wild dream' that he 'possessed the power of operating an immediate change in the minds of men and the state of society' had faded somewhat, 'sorrow and adversity had struck home; but he struggled with despondency as he did with physical pain'. He was ill during 1817, but he was productive, writing *Laon and Cythna*, later recast as *The Revolt of Islam*.

The Revolt of Islam is in some respect a development of the same themes that Shelley had presented so vehemently in *Queen Mab*. Not surprisingly its hero is a 'youth nourished in dreams of liberty, some of whose reactions are in direct opposition to the opinions of the world; but who is animated throughout by an ardent love of virtue, and a resolution to confer the boons of political and intellectual freedom on his fellow creatures'. So Mary described the not unfamiliar character of Laon, neglecting to mention in her editor's note to the poem that the woman Shelley had originally created as a mate for his hero, 'full of enthusiasm for the same objects', was also his sister. The idea of incest was always to fascinate Shelley's circle and at the same time it was alleged to be one of its most outrageous crimes. He would later write, 'Incest is like many other *incorrect* things a very poetical circumstance.'[8] But Shelley defused a potentially explosive situation in this case. In the revised edition of *The Revolt* the couple were no longer brother and sister but became instead childhood friends (a transformation that was also to take place between the 1818 and 1830 editions of *Frankenstein*, where Elizabeth becomes a foundling instead of Victor Frankenstein's cousin). Again the poem was dedicated to Mary and to her illustrious heritage, but the long dedication also indicates how lonely Mary must have been during the periods of Shelley's greatest creativity, when the composition of an important work caused his physical and emotional withdrawal from her and from their children. He would return to her at the conclusion of an ambitious project as if from a long journey:

So now my summer-task is ended, Mary,
  And I return to thee, mine own heart's home;
As to his Queen some victor Knight of Faëry,
  Earning bright spoils for her enchanted dome;
  Nor thou disdain that, ere my fame become
A star among the stars of mortal night
  (If it indeed may cleave its natal gloom),
Its doubtful promise thus I would unite
With thy beloved name, thou child of love and light.

II

The toil which stole from thee so many an hour
  Is ended — and the fruit is at thy feet.
No longer where the woods to frame a bower
  With interlaced branches mix and meet,
  Or where, with sound like many voices sweet,
Waterfalls leap among wild islands green
  Which framed for my lone boat a lone retreat
Of moss-grown trees and weeds, shall I be seen:
But beside thee, where still my heart has ever been.

Mary was coming to the conclusion of her own artistic toils. On 14 May 1817, she was able to write 'Finis' triumphantly in her journal. *Frankenstein* was now complete and with Shelley's help she would find a publisher and see it through the press. She went up to London. She would not be discouraged when Murray refused her novel, or when Ollier, Shelley's publisher, likewise returned it. Lackington Allen & Co., who finally accepted *Frankenstein* in August, showed far greater vision than the others. Shelley wrote the short preface, and, as a woman, Mary withheld her name from the title page. A first print run of 500 copies was negotiated and Shelley managed to secure one third of the profits of the first edition for his wife. He did so on the grounds that the novel would certainly fail to sell out its first run. But Lackington proved to be as shrewd as Murray had once been in his acceptance of *Childe Harold: Frankenstein* was an instant success and it has never been out of print.

And it was not long before the 'Author of *Frankenstein*' was known to be a woman — an outrage in itself — and a remarkably young one at that. The book was widely and favourably reviewed, most prominently by Walter Scott[9] in the pages of *Blackwood's*, and it made Mary a celebrity. It helped the book's notoriety, too, when it was learned that young Mary Godwin was a beautiful, very demure woman, in startling contrast to the horrific story that she told.

But it was not until 1831 that Mary finally came forward publicly to claim her offspring in print in the new introduction that she wrote for the *Standard Novels* edition of *Frankenstein*. She provided a detailed background to the circumstances of its creation, elaborating on the series of conversations at the Villa Diodati that carried on long into the night. She described the literary competition that Byron had instigated, his subsequent encouragement of her project, and a collection of German ghost stories that they had read together. Byron himself wrote a fragment called 'The Vampyre', the beginnings of a tale of a young man and his association with an enigmatic aristocrat. Polidori took up the same theme, more or less continuing and concluding Byron's effort, and published his story, with some confusion about its authorship, in the *New Monthly Magazine* in 1819.

Mary was aware when she wrote the new introduction in 1831, seven years after Byron's death, that the public was still eager for information about the poet and she could offer an intimate memoir. She wrote:

> In the summer of 1816, we visited Switzerland and became the neighbours of Lord Byron. At first we spent our pleasant hours on the lake, or wandering on its shores; and Lord Byron, who was writing the third canto of Childe Harold, was the only one among us who put his thoughts upon paper. These, as he brought them successively to us, clothed in all the light and harmony of poetry, seemed to stamp as divine the glories of heaven and earth, whose influences we partook with him.
>
> But it proved a wet, ungenial summer, and incessant rain often confined us for days to the house.

Though the new introduction also provides some insight into Mary's own childhood influences and her vital creative imagination, she intended her creation to ride the back of the monster that the burgeoning Byron industry had become. The introduction continues:

> 'We will each write a ghost story,' said Lord Byron; and his proposition was acceded to. There were four of us. The noble author began a tale, a fragment of which he printed at the end of his poem of Mazeppa. Shelley, more apt to embody ideas and sentiments in the radiance of brilliant imagery ... commenced one founded on the experiences of his early life. Poor Polidori had some terrible idea about a skull-headed lady, who

was so punished for peeping through a key-hole — what to see I forget — something very shocking and wrong of course — I busied myself *to think of a story*, — a story to rival those which had excited us to this task. One which would speak to the mysterious fears of our nature, and awaken thrilling horror — one to make the reader dread to look round, to curdle the blood, and quicken the beatings of the heart . . . Many and long were the conversations between Lord Byron and Shelley, to which I was a devout but nearly silent listener.

The new preface hinges largely on Byron's presence and the Shelleys' friendship with him. Though Mary explains, 'My husband . . . was, from the first, very anxious that I should prove myself worthy of my parentage, and enrol myself on the page of fame. He was forever inciting me to obtain literary reputation . . . ' Byron, nevertheless, was the catalyst that ultimately stirred Mary's imagination into print; he was particularly solicitous about her progress in the days following their memorable soirée and refused to allow her to relinquish the challenge like the others. Byron encouraged her; 'You and I . . . will publish ours together.'[10] He was entrusted with the secret of Mary's authorship and later, when revealing it to Murray, wrote on 15 May 1819: 'methinks it is a wonderful work for a Girl of nineteen — *not* nineteen indeed — at that time.'

Thus in the summer of 1817 Byron was not far from Mary's thoughts. *Frankenstein* was complete and she had just reread Canto III of *Childe Harold's Pilgrimage*, the poem of their enchanted summer. Murray had been delighted with the manuscript that Shelley had brought to him in the autumn, and he was still happier with the poem's subsequent success. Caroline Lamb, still clinging to her lost poet and cultivating a proxy friendship with his publisher instead, had more apposite words to say about Byron and his latest production:

Be not dazzled by his success — be not thrown into wild delight because his genius has shown forth — misfortune and rage have occasioned this, and whenever he may speak of *himself* Lord Byron will succeed. Self is the sole inspirer of his genius — he cannot, like Homer, Dante, Virgil, Milton, Dryden, Spenser, Gray, Goldsmith, Tasso, write on other subjects well; but what he feels he can describe extravagantly well, and therefore I never did doubt he would write again as at first.[11]

Lofty company indeed, but Caroline's comment is not without insight. It points to the egocentricity of what was to become known as the Romantic movement and illustrates the newness of the concept at the time. Using oneself or a fictional character based on one's own experience as the focus of an artistic work was a largely unknown phenomenon in published poetry, and society was still coming to terms with it. William Wordsworth produced three separate versions of his monumental auto-biographical poem, *The Prelude*, changing and expanding it throughout his long life. But Wordsworth was concerned about potential accusations of self-centredness and egotism and the poem was not published until after his death in 1850. In his later years, Byron tried to disavow his Harold persona and to claim that he and the Childe were *not* one and the same. One of his most devoted defenders, Teresa Guiccioli, writing her memoir of the poet long after his death, championed his case: 'Lord Byron shone at a period when a school called Romantic was in the progress of formation. That school wanted a type by which to mould its heroes, as a planet requires a sun to give it light. It took Byron as that type, and adorned him with all the qualities which pleased its fancy; but the time has more than arrived when it is necessary that truth should reveal him in his true light.'[12]

If Caroline was cool about Byron's latest additions to Harold's adventures, Mary was deeply affected. In Canto III Harold finds some solace in nature, upon Leman, the lake of Geneva. His lines recalled their quiet evening boat trips, cherished in Mary's memory:

LXXXV

Clear, placid Leman! thy contrasted lake,
With the wild world I dwelt in, is a thing
Which warns me, with its stillness, to forsake
Earth's troubled waters for a purer spring.
This quiet sail is as a noiseless wing
To waft me from distraction; once I loved
Torn ocean's roar, but thy soft murmuring
Sounds sweet as if a Sister's voice reproved,
That I with stern delights should e'er have been so moved.

LXXXVI

It is the hush of night, and all between
Thy margin and the mountains, dusk, yet clear,
Mellow'd and mingling, yet distinctly seen,
Save darken'd Jura, whose capt heights appear
Precipitously steep; and drawing near,
There breathes a living fragrance from the shore,
Of flowers yet fresh with childhood; on the ear
Drops the light drip of the suspended oar,
Or chirps the grasshopper one good-night carol more.

Mary responded to the poignancy of the lines. She wrote in her journal on the evening of 28 May:

> I am melancholy with reading the 3rd Canto of Childe Harold. Do you not remember, Shelley when you first read it to me? One evening after returning from Diodati. It was in our little room at Chapuis — the lake was before us and the mighty Jura. That time is past and this will also pass when I may weep to read these words and again moralize on the flight of time.
>
> Dear Lake! I shall ever love thee. How a powerful mind can sanctify past scenes and recollections — His is a powerful mind, one that fills me with melancholy yet mixed with pleasure as is always the case when intellectual energy is displayed. I think of our excursions on the lake. How we saw him when he came down to us or welcomed our arrival with a goodhumoured smile — How very vividly does each verse of his poem recall some scene of this kind to my memory — This time will soon also be a recollection — We may see him again & again — enjoy his society but the time will also arrive when that which is now an anticipation will be only in the memory — death will at length come and in the last moment all will be a dream.

Mary's melancholy was not uncharacteristic, nor was her elegiac strain over-dramatic. The summer of 1816 was probably the happiest time of her life and she was already looking back to it, from the distance of less than a year, with longing and regret. She was nineteen. On this night, at her father's home, triumphant with the conclusion of her first novel, six months pregnant, she was chilled by the certain notion that her happiness would not last and that her contentment, even now, was suspended by a delicate thread.

There was still no response from Italy to the news of Allegra's birth. Perhaps John Murray, Byron's publisher, could supply some word of the errant father. Shelley, meanwhile, wrote repeatedly throughout the summer to his recalcitrant friend, imploring him to state his plans for Allegra. Her presence in their household was a growing embarrassment: 'We are exposed to what remarks her existence is calculated to excite. At least a period approaches when it will be impossible to temporize with our servants or our visitors. There are two very respectable young ladies in this town, who would undertake the charge of her, if you consent to this arrangement.'

Byron responded at last. He would like his child brought or sent to Italy but would have nothing to do with Claire. Immediately, Shelley thought of Pisa, of Rome and Florence. His own health was at its lowest ebb; the mild climate would ease his physical suffering, which his doctors believed to be the onset of consumption, and in addition the liberal climate would soothe his politicized soul. He turned his mind to an idealized exile and Mary caught his enthusiasm, her only concern Godwin's distress at the anticipation of their departure.

The autumn, their last months in England, must have been frantic, especially for Mary, who had given birth to Clara in September. Shelley was again arranging loans both for himself and Godwin and was absent in London much of the time. The seven Hunts came back and then left without tipping the housemaid, so Mary had to arrange for a suitable gift herself: a stout dress of sturdy fabric. She was left in Marlow to arrange for the proper closing down of Albion House — she had learned her lesson when they hurried from Bishopsgate in 1816 and forfeited much of their property. Still nursing, she provided meals for the daily visits of Peacock and Hogg. She also had to see *Frankenstein* safely into print and received the first proofs of her novel shortly after Clara's birth. Soon after, the *History of a Six Weeks' Tour through a Part of France, Switzerland, Germany and Holland* was published anonymously. The travelogue made up of the joint journal and letters relating to the elopement journey and the summer of 1816 received favourable reviews and its success added to Mary's laurels when she was discovered to be the author of *Frankenstein*. Mary had worked on it in the last weeks of her pregnancy and was delighted to see it in print. She was not so fortunate with *Frankenstein*. She did not have the pleasure of seeing her first novel in the bookshops. On the day of its publication, 11 March, she and her family left London for Italy. Only on her return to England in 1823, when her husband could not share her joy, would she discover just what a success *Frankenstein* had become.

Shelley and Mary were elated to be leaving England for the Continent again, pleased to be abandoning Albion House which, at the conclusion of the summer, had proved to be so damp that all their books were mildewed. They left with high hopes of freedom, of inexpensive luxury, of the leisure to write, of a reunion with Byron. This time they would not be deterred from their goal or waylaid in the icy beauty of the Alps. They made for the warm south at last.

CHAPTER V

VENICE

A FEW DAYS BEFORE THE SHELLEYS' DEPARTURE from Lake Geneva in August 1816, Byron welcomed John Cam Hobhouse and Scrope Davies, friend of Beau Brummel and a distinguished member of the dandy set, to Diodati. He was overjoyed to see his old friends — they had been young bucks together, men of fashion. The visit recalled his happiest days of Levantine travel with Hobhouse, the abandon of the Newstead house parties, and the glorious days of carefree libertinism in London, when a dinner party might begin at nine, course following course until one in the morning, when the cloth was cleared for the serious business of drinking.

Scrope and Hobhouse arrived on 26 August, missing by just a week the notorious Matthew 'Monk' Lewis. He had written *The Monk*, an outrageous novel of lustful priests, mad nuns, black magic and rape, which had caused a sensation when it appeared in 1796, when its author was only nineteen years old. Mary, Shelley and Claire had still been at the villa while Lewis was there and felt the *frisson* of his company as he entertained the sensation-seeking group with his collection of German ghost stories.

Hobhouse and Byron set out for Chamonix and Mont Blanc. They did not follow the well-trodden trail of the Shelleys' venture there earlier in the summer but took a rougher route. They climbed some of the lesser peaks, challenging Byron's fitness to the utmost. He was, he confessed to Augusta, not as strong as he had been. He was deeply impressed by the wild scenery, it breathed a kind of savagery — 'Avalanches falling every five minutes nearly — as if God was pelting the Devil down from Heaven with snow balls ... we looked down ... upon a boiling sea of cloud — dashing against the crags on which we stood,' he wrote to Augusta in September. It struck him as profoundly as it had Mary and Shelley and, like the lovers, he would draw on his experience in his poetry. In *Manfred*, the eponymous hero, a necromancer tortured by the memory of his lost beloved (his sister, we are not surprised to learn), lives in a dark castle on an Alpine crag.

Byron was high-spirited, excited by the physical effort of each long day's travel, by the deep snow, lightning and high-plunging cataracts. He threw snowballs at Hobhouse, laughed when they tumbled and slid down a bank of snow at a summit peak and was delighted to find that the 'boatmen' who rowed them the length of Lake Brientz to Interlaken were three pretty young women. And he missed Augusta, for whom he kept a journal of the trip:

> In the evening four Swiss Peasant Girls of Oberhasli came & sang the airs of their country — two of the voices beautiful — the tunes also — they sing too that *Tyrolese air* & song which you love — Augusta — because I love it — & I love because you love it — they are still singing — Dearest — you do not know how I should have liked this — were you with me — the airs are so wild & original & at the same time of great sweetness.

'May your sleep be soft and your dreams of me,' he signed off hopefully on 28 September.

Byron stayed at some of the same hotels that the Shelley party had visited earlier in the summer and he took the opportunity to amend their singular entries in the hotel registers. Considering his friend's already wounded reputation, he crossed out the Greek word 'atheist' that Shelley had written next to his name and observed wryly that Mary and Claire had joined in, indicating the party's destination as '*l'enfer*' (hell). But Byron was not just trying to protect his friends. He disapproved of Shelley's atheism and, in particular, his determination to proclaim it at every opportunity.

A fortnight later Byron and Hobhouse were back at Diodati and Scrope was on his way home, loaded with presents for Byron's nieces and for Ada. The poet sent agates, polished stones, a crystal necklace and a granite ball, 'seals & all kinds of fooleries' from the rocks of Mont Blanc. He still felt keenly the break-up of his own family and sought a substitute in that of his sister. He wrote to Augusta in September, expressing the sadness which invariably followed, or perhaps lay behind his high spirits:

> she — or rather the Separation — has broken my heart — I feel as if an Elephant had trodden on it — I am convinced I shall never get over it — but I try — I breathe lead. — While the storm lasted & you were all pressing and comforting me with condemnation in Piccadilly — it was bad enough — & violent enough — but it is worse now. — I have neither strength nor spirits — nor inclination to carry me through anything which will clear my brain or lighten my heart.

His travels with Hobhouse at his side again had been a great success, the weather had been favourable, the scenery beautiful but Byron was still tormented:

in all this — the recollections of bitterness — & more especially of recent & more home desolation — which must accompany me through life — have preyed upon me here — and neither the music of the Shepherd — the crashing of the Avalanche — nor the torrent — the mountain — the Glacier — the Forest — nor the Cloud — have for one moment lightened the weight upon my heart — nor enabled me to lose my own wretched identity in the majesty & the power and the Glory — around — above — & beneath me.

Yet Byron stirred himself and administered his proven antidote to ennui, anxiety and sadness. He set off again, indulging his taste for exotic travel.

He had been disappointed by the tameness of the Low Countries as he had made his way towards Geneva in the spring, though the field of Waterloo, where he collected relics of the battle, had impressed and moved him. The roads of northern Europe were too flat, the scenery too familiar from a thousand travelogues, and the renowned Dutch master paintings risible. He had written to Hobhouse on 1 May 1816:

as for Rubens — and his superb 'tableaux' — he seems to me (who by the way know nothing of the matter) the most glaring — flaring — staring — harlotry impostor that ever passed a trick upon the senses of mankind — it is not nature — it is not art . . . I never saw such an assemblage of florid night-mares as his canvas contains — his portraits seemed clothed in pulpit cushions.

The grey landscape of northern Europe held no magic for Byron — he had been seduced early by the attractions of a bright and sunny climate. He would no longer deny himself, he would take up residence in the sun. Byron like Keats lifted to his lips the brimming 'beaker full of the warm South'. With Hobhouse he left for Italy in October.

Travelling at a leisurely pace they went first to Milan, Verona (where Byron chipped some fragments of granite from the picturesquely decaying reputed 'tomb of Juliet' to send to his daughter and nieces) and then set off for their ultimate destination, Venice.

They arrived in November. In December Hobhouse left to tour the country with his brother and sister and Byron wasted no time in taking on a new mistress — he was in love again by the time Murray published the third canto of *Childe Harold*, for which he had paid £2,000. Byron gave a minute description of his newest heroine to Moore on 17 November:

Marianna . . . is in her appearance altogether like an antelope. She has the large, black, oriental eyes, with that peculiar expression in them which is

seen rarely among *Europeans* — even the Italians — and which many of
the Turkish women give themselves by tinging the eyelid, — an art not
known out of that country, I believe. This expression she has *naturally*,
— and something more than this. In short, I cannot describe the effect
of this kind of eye, — at least upon me. Her features are regular, and
rather aquiline — mouth small — skin clear and soft, with a kind of
hectic colour — forehead remarkably good: her hair is of the dark gloss,
curl, and colour of Lady J[ersey's]: her figure is light and pretty, and she
is a famous songstress ... her natural voice (in conversation, I mean) is
very sweet; and the naïveté of the Venetian dialect is always pleasing in
the mouth of a woman.

Marianna's spirit was not unlike Caroline's, but she could not have
been more different from the other demure English ladies that Byron
had hitherto known and loved. In the new year, 1817, he told Thomas
Moore a comical story of his new lover:

Venice is in the *estro* of her carnival, and I have been up these last two
nights at the ridotto and the opera, and all that kind of thing. Now for
an adventure. A few days ago a gondolier brought me a billet without
a subscription, intimating a wish on the part of the writer to meet me
either in gondola or at the island of San Lazaro, or at a third rendezvous, indicated in the note ... so, for all response, I said that neither
of the three places suited me; but that I would either be at home at ten
at night *alone*, or at the ridotto at midnight, where the writer might meet
me masked. At ten o'clock I was at home and alone (Marianna was gone
with her husband to a conversazione), when the door of my apartment
opened, and in walked a well-looking and (for an Italian) *bionda* girl of
about nineteen, who informed me that she was married to the brother of
my *amorosa*, and wished to have some conversation with me. I made a
decent reply, and we had some talk in Italian and Romaic (her mother
being a Greek of Corfu), when lo! in a very few minutes, in marches,
to my very great astonishment, Marianna S[egati], *in propria persona*,
and after making polite courtesy to her sister-in-law and to me, without
a single word seizes her said sister-in-law by the hair, and bestows upon
her some sixteen slaps, which would have made your ear ache only to hear
their echo. I need not describe the screaming which ensued. The luckless
visitor took flight. I seized Marianna, who, after several vain efforts to
get away in pursuit of the enemy, fairly went into fits in my arms; and,
in spite of reasoning, eau de Cologne, vinegar, half a pint of water, and
God knows what other waters beside, continued so till past midnight.

The absurdity of the scene was compounded still further when Marianna's husband entered and seeing his fainting wife upon the sofa and

the room in confusion, was outraged. Italians are not jealous, Byron explained, but the moment was still awkward: 'he must have known that I made love to Marianna, yet I believe he was not, till that evening, aware of the extent to which it had gone. It is very well known that almost all the married women have a lover; but it is usual to keep up the forms, as in other nations.'

The husband was appeased and the shameless sister-in-law told her story to all who would listen; none were scandalized and all were heartily amused. Byron began to learn the customs of the city and to settle into his new home. 'A woman is virtuous (according to the code),' he explained, 'who limits herself to her husband and one lover; those who have two, three or more; are a little *wild*'. Marianna kept him interested for well over a year, despite her deceitfulness. When a jeweller offered him a set of diamonds which he had only shortly before presented to his beloved, he was unable to resist a fine jest; he bought back the jewels and coolly returned them to his mistress.

In fact, Venice delighted him — its women kissed 'better than those of any other nation'. His box for the season at the excellent Venice opera was a good deal cheaper than that he had had in London — £14 instead of the enormous price of £400.[1] One could easily afford to see and be seen and join the card games and suppers held in the elegant boxes during the performance. Venice suited Byron completely. He wrote to Moore in November 1816, 'It is my intention to remain at Venice during the winter, probably, as it has always been (next to the East) the greenest island of my imagination . . . It has not disappointed me; though its evident decay would, perhaps, have that effect upon others. But I have been familiar with ruins too long to dislike desolation.' The decadence of Venice, quite naturally, also appealed to Monk Lewis, who came to visit Byron in July 1917. 'Apollo's Sexton', as Byron had dubbed him in *English Bards and Scotch Reviewers*, counted the city as 'one of his enthusiasms'.

Yet Byron was somewhat troubled on a number of matters. He was concerned that soft, uncontentious living did not offer him any challenges. His mind would suffer from lack of stimulation. Thus, having conquered and subdued the Italian tongue, and ever determined to place himself in difficulty both physical and intellectual, he decided to study the exceptionally difficult Armenian language. 'I found that my mind wanted something craggy to break upon,' he wrote to Moore in December 1816, and 'I have chosen, to torture me into attention.' He crossed the lagoon each day to study with the monks at the Armenian monastery on the island of San Lazzaro. For all his commitment to pleasure, Byron was remarkably disciplined and there were very few nights when a long evening of drinking, dining and flirting were not followed by many hours of composition well into the morning. His habit of rising after one in the afternoon was thus not unjustifiable. One of his most famous poems was written after just such a late night: in June 1814 Byron went to a ball and there he saw his widowed cousin, Mrs Wilmot, in mourning, wearing a black spangled dress. He had been deeply moved by her sadness and beauty and when he arrived home that night he called for brandy. By the following day he had written 'She Walks in Beauty, Like the Night'.

To increase his anxiety, in the autumn of 1816 Byron had heard that Annabella was planning to travel, and to take Ada with her. He was alarmed at the news and shared his concern with Augusta, the go-between for himself and his wife. He was concerned that his only legitimate heir should be exposed to the dangers of the volatile world outside of England at such a young age. Let 'it be *immediately settled & understood that in no case is my daughter to leave the country,*' he wrote to Hanson. He would take legal action if necessary. But Byron knew that his own rights were uncertain — did he have any power in England, and did it still extend to his daughter? His threat really amounted to a bluff; perhaps he was testing his influence. Would his wife's family consider his wishes at all? By the following spring it became clear that he would have to fight for Ada — the Milbankes were preparing Chancery proceedings to obtain full rights over his daughter. Like Shelley, he would struggle and fail to be a father to his offspring — she would be lost to him for ever. He sent Ada a portrait of himself, but, so it has been rumoured, this was kept from her until her twenty-first birthday.

In November 1816 Byron had still desired a reunion with Annabella, but now she was his sworn enemy, he cursed the woman who gave his daughter birth. He concluded the third canto of *Childe Harold's Pilgrimage* with all the sadness of thwarted fatherhood:

CXV

My daughter! with thy name this song begun;
My daughter! with thy name thus much shall end;
I see thee not, I hear thee not, but none
Can be so wrapt in thee . . .

CXVII

Yet, though dull Hate as duty should be taught,
I know that thou wilt love me; though my name
Should be shut from thee, as a spell still fraught
With desolation, and a broken claim:
Though the grave closed between us, — 'twere the same,
I know that thou wilt love me; though to drain
My blood from out thy being were an aim,

And an attainment, — all would be in vain, —
Still thou would'st love me, still that more than life retain.

CXVIII

The child of love, though born in bitterness,
And nurtured in convulsion. Of thy sire
These were the elements, and thine no less.
As yet such are around thee, but thy fire
Shall be more temper'd, and thy hope far higher.
Sweet be thy cradled slumbers! O'er the sea
And from the mountains where I now respire,
Fain would I waft such blessing upon thee,
As, with a sigh, I deem thou might'st have been to me.

Gossip from London still worried Byron. He was distressed to hear that Shelley's wife had drowned herself: 'do you mean his *wife* — or his Mistress?' he asked with concern in a letter to his old friend Douglas Kinnaird on 20 January 1820. 'Mary Godwin? — I hope not the last — I am very sorry to hear of anything which can plague poor Shelley.' He did not hear about Harriet's death from Shelley himself until the beginning of February. In fact, Byron's correspondents were a lifeline. From Murray he received news of the literary world and the valuable supplies that he could not buy in Italy; he frequently requested such preparations as red tooth powder, magnesia and soda powders. Something of a hypochondriac, Byron required medicines for stomach and bowel complaints and headache. From Murray, Augusta (swiftly falling prey to the domineering Annabella's righteous plans for her moral redemption), from his old friend Douglas Kinnaird, and the delightful Thomas Moore he could also judge the standing of his reputation. Shelley too wrote to discuss Byron's new poetry and to report on rumours that he was leaving again for Greece and Asia.

At the beginning of 1817 Byron still hoped to weather the scandal of the separation and return to London, if not to his wife. He was distressed to learn of Caroline Lamb's novel *Glenarvon*, a thinly disguised fictionalization of their affair, with himself cast as the ruthless and evil protagonist, giving further credence to the stories of his cruelty to Annabella. The novel was a popular success — even Mary read it soon after her return to England in September 1816 — and Byron's hopes that his devilish reputation would be forgotten were dashed. His wrongs to the unfortunate Caroline were heaped upon the crimes already committed against his pitiful wife — Byron had to remain in exile, and since he was forced to make his life in a foreign land, he would throw off all the bonds that his English life had wrapped around him. If the rumours of the goings-on at the Villa Diodati in 1816 were largely false, those that were generated by Byron's conduct in Venice were almost certainly grounded in fact. The excesses of his life there were censured even by his most loyal and sympathetic biographers; even Thomas Moore was unable to suppress his moral outrage.

If the rumours were to be believed, he purchased the under-age daughters of the poor and brought them back to his palazzo. Moore was certainly aware — and disgusted — that in his quest for feminine beauty, Byron gradually rejected the company of the high-born and turned to the 'lower orders,' consorting with the dregs of Venetian society.

'Venice & I agree very well,' Byron wrote to Kinnaird on 20 January, 'in the mornings I study Armenian — & in the evenings I go out sometimes — & indulge in coition always — The Carnival is begun.' While in cramped lodgings in Bath, on 12 January, Claire Clairmont was giving birth to Byron's daughter, her father, like all the inhabitants of Venice, abandoned himself completely to the pursuit of pleasure before the onset of Lent. It was during the Carnival, in the first weeks of the new year, that music, masques, operas, parades, mummeries, parties and routs carried on long into the night. Assignations with mysterious ladies in gondolas, balconies above the canals or islands in the lagoon were the order of the day. It would seem that all the endless dinners, bottles of claret, 'white brandy' and champagne that London could offer, the famous street-walkers that haunted her alleys and the actresses that graced the stage of Drury Lane, Covent Garden and the beds of the dissipated aristocracy, were no match for the carnal riches of the Venice Carnival. Celebration coloured Byron's verse:

I

'Tis known, at least it should be, that throughout
    All countries of the Catholic persuasion,
Some weeks before Shrove Tuesday comes about,
    The people take their fill of recreation,
And buy repentance, ere they grow devout,
    However high their rank, or low their station,
With fiddling, feasting, dancing, drinking, masking,
And other things which may be had for asking.

II

The moment night with dusky mantle covers
    The skies (and the more duskily the better),
The time less liked by husbands than by lovers
    Begins, and prudery flings aside her fetter;
And gaiety on restless tiptoe hovers,

Giggling with all the gallants who beset her:
And there are songs and quavers, roaring, humming,
Guitars, and every other sort of strumming.

III

And there are dresses splendid, but fantastical,
   Masks of all times and nations, Turks and Jews,
And harlequins and clowns, with feats gymnastical,
   Greeks, Romans, Yankee-doodles, and Hindoos;
All kinds of dress, except the ecclesiastical . . .

(from *Beppo, A Venetian Story*)

After his first Carnival, his intensive training in the casinos, coffee-houses and clubs of London notwithstanding, Byron was again laid up with a serious fever. Spent by his excesses, with the cold light of day shining grimly on the lees of revelry, Byron was inspired to write one of his most famous short lyrics to the ever-appreciative Thomas Moore:

So, we'll go no more a roving
   So late into the night,
Though the heart be still as loving,
   And the moon be still as bright.

For the sword outwears its sheath,
   And the soul wears out the breast,
And the heart must pause to breathe,
   And love itself have rest.

Though the night was made for loving,
   And the day returns too soon,
Yet we'll go no more a roving
   By the light of the moon.

In April 1817, plump and hearty again, Byron set off on a long-awaited visit to Rome and a reunion with Hobhouse. He passed hurriedly through Florence on the way and bumped into Lord and Lady Jersey whose early interest in the young poet had been sustained through the separation scandal — they seemed pleased to see him. He made a lightning tour of the famous galleries and gave vent to some characteristic art criticisms: 'I also went to the Medici Chapel — fine frippery in great slabs of various expensive stones — to commemorate fifty rotten & forgotten carcases — it is unfinished and will remain so.'[2] He dispatched another completed poem to Murray, *The Lament of Tasso*, and proceeded on his way. Passing through the Apennines, he nearly lost his recently acquired savage mongrel dog, Mutz, to an even more aggressive mountain pig.

He arrived in Rome and sent Murray yet more poetry. More productive than ever, he had completed the third act of his drama *Manfred*. He had also by this time relinquished his costly notion of the gentleman poet who would receive no payment for his effusions. He was negotiating vigorously for the purchase of copyright with Murray and earning large sums from his generous publisher — 'I won't take less than three hundred g[uinea]s for anything,' he wrote on 5 May. Italy was cheap, but he was spending lavishly.

In Rome he also found time to indulge in his famous literary pastime, the savaging of the Poet Laureate. Byron saw Robert Southey as his greatest ideological enemy and an abysmal poet who spun endless deadening verses. He reviled the old man as a traitor to his youth: he had once shared radical views with the young Coleridge, in the 1790s. 'Ballad-monger Southey', as Byron attacked him in *English Bards and Scotch Reviewers*, had become, like Wordsworth, an inveterate Tory royalist. But his worst offence, in Byron's eyes, was to be a hypocrite. Byron had learned from his usual London sources that one of Southey's early radical plays had come back to haunt him in the shape of a pirated edition. Southey had been embarrassed and Byron took great pleasure from that knowledge:

> Southey's Wat Tyler is rather awkward — but the Goddess Nemesis has done well ... I hate all intolerance — but most the intolerance of Apostacy — & the wretched vehemence with which a miserable creature who has contradicted himself — lies to his own heart — & endeavours to establish his sincerity by proving himself a rascal — *not* for changing his opinions — but for persecuting those who are of less malleable matter — it is no disgrace to Mr Southey to have written Wat Tyler — & afterwards to have written his birthday or Victory Odes (I speak only of their *politics*) but it is something for which I have no words for this man to have endeavoured to bring to the stake (for such he would do) men who think as he thought & for no reason but because they think so still, when he has found it convenient to think otherwise.[3]

Byron may well have had Percy Shelley in mind as the antithesis of Southey. Never wavering in his commitment to republicanism and liberal reform, Shelley was ever as firm, as Southey was, in Byron's view, slippery. But Byron had a still greater reason for hating the Poet Laureate; he believed, incorrectly, that Southey was the perpetrator of one of the most damaging rumours about him and the Shelleys:

> The Son of a Bitch on his return from Switzerland two years ago —

said that Shelley and I 'had formed a League of Incest and practised our precepts &c.' — he lied like a rascal -— for they *were not Sisters* — *one* being Godwin's daughter by Mary Wollstonecraft — and the other the daughter of the Present Mrs G[odwin] by a *former* husband . . . He lied in another sense — for there was no promiscuous intercourse — my commerce being limited to the carnal knowledge of the Miss C[lairmont] — I had nothing to do with the offspring of Mary Wollstonecraft — which Mary was a former Love of Southey's — which might have taught him to respect the fame of her daughter.[4]

That Southey had been in love with Wollstonecraft (they were friends at one time) was pure speculation on Byron's part, further ammunition in his battle to expose the Laureate's hypocrisy. But he was as much incensed by the injustice done to Mary's (and Shelley's) reputation as to his own.

And the Shelley party must have come to Byron's mind with still greater force at this time. While in Rome he finally received word of Allegra's birth, almost four months after the event. He was not sure what to do about her, but he had accepted that she was his daughter and he felt some responsibility. It is interesting, in light of the fact that Byron may have fathered at least one other child — a boy — with a servant at Newstead, that he should have been so concerned for Allegra. Why, when he had shown no interest in this illegitimate offspring, did Allegra, whose mother he clearly hated, win his respect and recognition? In the letter to Augusta quoted earlier, he maintained that Allegra might compensate him for the legitimate daughter that he was certain to lose, that she would be someone to love him in his old age. But more than that, perhaps it was her association with Shelley, Mary and with William Godwin[5] that made Allegra an important person for Byron. With the exception of her mother, he respected and admired her family. He did not wish to be diminished in their eyes.

Rome, Byron claimed rather unconvincingly, excited him as much as Athens and Constantinople had. The city whose image was to burn so brightly for Mary and Shelley was not lost on their compatriot; but where they were fascinated, he was interested. He remarked on no special feeling when the city came into view across the plain. He did not think of it as his spiritual home as Mary and Shelley did and he would pay it only one more short visit. What he found noteworthy in the city was the public execution of three robbers. Witnessing the guillotine in action, Byron, and no doubt the other spectators, could only have been reminded of the excesses of the French Revolution, whose own machine of destruction had only recently ceased churning. Peering through his opera glasses he had a fine view of the proceedings and described them in detail, as so many witnesses of the Terror had before him:

> the ceremony — including the *masqued* priests — the half-naked executioners — the bandaged criminals — the black Christ & his banner — the scaffold — the soldiery — the slow procession — & the quick rattle and heavy fall of the axe — the splash of the blood — & the ghastliness of the exposed heads — is altogether more impressive than the vulgar and ungentlemanly dirty 'new drop' & dog-like agony of infliction upon the sufferers of the English sentence. Two of these men — behaved calmly enough — but the first of the three — died with great terror and reluctance — which was very horrible — he would not lie down — then his neck was too large for the aperture — and the priest was obliged to drown his exclamations by still louder exhortations — the head was off before the eye could trace the blow — but from an attempt to draw back the head — notwithstanding it was held forward by the hair — the first head was cut off close to the ears — the other two were taken off more cleanly ... the pain seems little — & yet very striking to the spectator — & the preparation to the criminal — is very striking and chilling.[6]

Byron spent less than a month in Rome before he hurried back to Marianna, his beloved Venice and his accustomed revelry.

In June Byron moved to the Villa Foscarini on the Brenta river at La Mira on the mainland, which he had taken for the summer to avoid the notoriously bad air of the hottest months in the city. He was delighted to receive extracts from Thomas Moore's latest, and to that date greatest, success, *Lalla Rookh*, a volume of four 'Oriental' narrative poems as told to the eponymous princess by her storyteller as she travels to meet her betrothed. Byron never tired of Moore, he wrote to him assiduously (even when letters in return were rare), and he was, generally speaking, pleased by Moore's fame. Ironically, the two had initially met as enemies. Byron attacked Moore in *English Bards and Scotch Reviewers* and accepted his challenge to a duel of honour with eagerness. But apologies quickly followed on both sides and the pair became friends. Byron admired the songs of Moore's ever-growing *Irish Melodies,* and his satirical, highly amusing *The Fudge Family in Paris.* He received some of Byron's finest and most spirited letters and light verse in tribute. Celebrating his pleasure in *Lalla Rookh* Byron wrote:

> My boat is on the shore,
>   And my bark is on the sea;
> But, before I go, Tom Moore,
>   Here's a double health to thee!

Here's a sigh to those who love me,
　　And a smile to those who hate;
And, whatever sky's above me,
　　Here's a heart for every fate.

Though the ocean roar around me,
　　Yet it still shall bear me on;
Though a desert should surround me,
　　It hath springs that may be won.

Were't the last drop in the well,
　　As I gasp'd upon the brink,
Ere my fainting spirit fell,
　　'Tis to thee that I would drink.

With that water, as this wine,
　　The libation I would pour
Should be — peace with thine and mine,
　　And a health to thee, Tom Moore.

If Byron occasionally expressed his disapproval of the easy popularity of both the man and his verses, Moore, in turn, was ever loyal and devoted. Later, in his biography of Byron, he attempted to redress all the wrongs that his friend's reputation had suffered.

Meanwhile, Venice was inspiring Byron to heights more lofty than those of pleasure. At the Villa Foscarini, with Marianna in residence and Hobhouse and Monk Lewis visiting, Byron mulled over his Venetian experience. In September 1817 he made a 'discovery' which was to change his poetic style completely and secure his place among the greatest poets of the language. John Hookam Frere, comic poet, distinguished editor and adviser to John Murray, had just published a mock-epic in the guise of 'William and Robert Whistlecraft' and the poem was brought to Byron by English friends. Frere's witty epic was an imitation of a Renaissance Italian colloquial style, well adapted for conversational tone, extended digression, satire and bathos. Searching for a means of reflecting the comedy, exoticism and absurdity of Venice — necessarily different from that employed in *Childe Harold* — Byron found the relaxed and idiosyncratic form that he needed. It represented a breakthrough that was eventually to result in *Don Juan*; Italy produced Byron's immortal voice. Moore later shrewdly commented: 'graceful and powerful as were his flights while society had still hold of him, it was not till let loose from the leash that he rose to the true region of his strength.'[7]

Byron began work on *Beppo, A Venetian Story*, a comic illustration of the Italian custom of the *cavaliere servente*, or urbane 'escort' of the married woman. In that poem Laura, the heroine, has bid goodbye to her husband, a merchant sailor and, finding herself alone at night and afraid of house-breakers, ' . . . thought it prudent to connect her / With a vice-husband, *chiefly* to *protect her*'. She chooses, according to custom, a refined nobleman to act as her companion:

XXXI

And then he was a Count, and then he knew
   Music, and dancing, fiddling, French and Tuscan;
The last not easy, be it known to you,
   For few Italians speak the right Etruscan.
He was a critic upon operas, too,
   And knew all niceties of sock and buskin;
And no Venetian audience could endure a
Song, scene, or air, when he cried 'seccatura!'

XL

But 'Cavalier Servente' is the phrase
   Used in politest circles to express
This supernumerary slave, who stays
   Close to the lady as a part of dress,
Her word the only law which he obeys.
   His is no sinecure, as you may guess;
Coach, servants, gondola, he goes to call,
And carries fan and tippet, gloves and shawl.

Beppo was finished by the end of October and Byron found, to his amusement, that he was *himself* a *cavaliere servente*, in thrall to his own married Venetian lady. What is more, her husband, on weekend visits to his own mistress, came to visit his wife in the home of her lover. And it was not long before Byron acquired an additional attachment. In August he met Margarita Cogni, the wife of a baker, 'with large black eyes, a face like Faustina's, and the figure of a Juno — tall and energetic as a Pythoness', as he described her to Moore in September. Byron was partial to this kind of 'fine animal', who, like Medea, had passion enough to murder if crossed. They had met during one of Byron and Hobhouse's rides along the Brenta river: amongst the peasants with whom she was strolling in the evening, Margarita, tall and beautiful, struck Byron immediately. She was poor, illiterate and married but he immediately proposed a rendezvous. Very soon, La Fornarina, as Byron called her (she was married to a baker), even more unpredictable, aggressive and ill-educated than his first mistress, began to supplant

Marianna Segati in his desires. He was almost certainly in love with her, proud of her authentic Venetian manner, of the fact that she could not read, and that her peasant clothes so became her majestic figure. She was lithe and strong, unlike the women who had had children and grown 'relaxed and doughy and *flumpity* in a short time after breeding'. One night, as he returned to his palazzo from a near fatal storm at sea, she was on the steps of his door

> with her great black eyes flashing through her tears and the long dark hair which was streaming drenched with rain over her brows & breast; — she was perfectly exposed to the storm — and the wind blowing her hair & dress about her tall thin figure — and the lightning flashing round her — with the waves falling at her feet — made her look like Medea alighted from her chariot — or the Sibyl of the tempest that was rolling around her.[8]

He had never before described his women in such minute physical detail. La Fornarina was Byron's heroine, a savage goddess, the vision of a dream, the perfect antithesis of his sheltered, intellectual and un-demonstrative wife. He could barely tear himself away. For 'two years — in the course of which I had — more women than I can count or recount — she was the only one who preserved over me an ascendency,' he wrote to Murray in August 1819. But she was 'wild as a witch — and fierce as a demon' and like Lady Caroline Lamb, years before, her dangerous glamour became too threatening. Besides, she came to deny her natural charm by casting aside her quaint peasant garments and demanding expensive gowns. She learned to read and Byron's dream was shattered. She was bodily removed from his home where, ironically, she had served so efficiently as housekeeper. Byron ignored her threats of violence and never met her again. The poet's alarming ability to follow the most intense passion and love with indifference, or even hatred, was a resonating characteristic of his restless unhappiness.

In December 1817 he learned that a buyer had finally been found for Newstead. After years of trying to dispose of the property that in his youth he swore he would never part with, Byron was overjoyed at the news that Hanson, his agent, sent. He immediately issued instructions that all his debts — estimated by Byron himself at over £12,500 — should be paid off as soon as possible. He looked forward, finally, to having the funds to back up the extravagant life-style that he had been precariously enjoying for so long. With perhaps some demonstration of nostalgia, he expressed pleasure that the buyer, Major Thomas Wildman, was 'a man of honour' and a school friend from Harrow. He paid £94,500 for Newstead (Byron would have been happy with £80,000) and over the years renovated it extensively.

And Byron was reminded of the absurd Dr Polidori again. The presumptuous doctor had sent Murray an abysmal play, hoping that he could share a publisher with his former employer. Murray was not interested and asked Byron to formulate a polite rejection. He obliged:

> Dear Doctor, I have read your play
> Which is a good one in its way, —
> Purges the eyes and moves the bowels,
> And drenches handkerchiefs like towels
> With tears, that, in a flux of grief,
> Afford hysterical relief
> To shatter'd nerves and quicken'd pulses,
> Which your catastrophe convulses . . .

Not long after the shadow of Polidori returned, Shelley evoked the spirit of the Geneva summer for Byron again, in a letter from Milan in April 1818. He and Mary had visited Lake Como: they would take a house on the shore for the summer. Would he spend a few weeks with them? Shelley hoped to rekindle the spirit of their idyllic summer, when the great poet seemed to be his philosophical pupil, and to attempt, once again, to reclaim his soul and his talent from what he had since learned was Byron's degrading, dissipated life in Venice. 'Our mode of life is uniform, and such as you remember it at Geneva, and the situation which I imagine we have chose . . . is solitary, and surrounded by scenery of astonishing grandeur, with the lake at our feet.' But where Claire was, Byron would not go, no matter how drawn he was to his friend.

In fact, Byron was not to be waylaid by new loves or affections of the past. He was delighted with the results of the new style he had developed in *Beppo*. He got the fourth and final canto of *Childe Harold* out of the way and dispatched *Beppo* to Murray. The following summer, firmly dedicated to his new satirical voice, he began work on *Don Juan*, the poem that was to represent his break from the past, become his masterpiece and occupy him for the rest of his life.

CHAPTER VI

REUNION: *JULIAN AND MADDALO*

I T WAS BYRON'S LIFE IN VENICE, even more than his days of rakish excess in London with his fashionable young friends, that set the seal on his reputation as a womanizing and profligate devotee of sensation. In preparation for his new project (*Don Juan*), Byron signed a three-year lease in May 1818 for one of the most magnificent palaces on the Grand Canal, the Palazzo Mocenigo. To Thomas Moore the old building looked damp, dark and uncomfortable and he longed for the comforts of his hotel. But Byron filled his home with footmen, maidservants, gondoliers, an illiterate secretary and a querulous menagerie: savage dogs, monkeys and peacocks, in keeping with the exotic beasts of Newstead. Moore was filled with horror at his friend's life-style:

> Highly censurable, in point of morality and decorum, as was his course of life while under the roof of [Marianna Segati], it was (with pain I am forced to confess) venial in comparison with the strange, headlong career of licence to which, when weaned from that connection,[1] he so unrestrainedly and, it may be added, defyingly abandoned himself.[2]

Byron's behaviour in Venice had already become legendary and English tourists sought him out as a noted curiosity of the city. Gondoliers, as they transported visitors across the lagoon, embroidered tales of the 'English Milord's' extravagant debauchery. Tourists lay in wait for his gondola as it approached its landing place on the Lido and studied him minutely with their viewing glasses, fascinated and disgusted. Ostensibly in quest of paintings, some boldly entered the Palazzo Mocenigo and, bribing his servants, pushed their way into the monster's bedroom. The same grapevine that had thrown its tendrils round the Villa Diodati in 1816 sent dark tales of Byron's prodigious profligacy and dissoluteness back to England.

Mary, Shelley and Claire trembled for the welfare of their darling Allegra, delivered to her father in May 1818. They were still further shaken when the rumours were confirmed. When Shelley and Claire arrived in Venice to see the little girl the Hoppners, the British consul in Venice and his Swiss wife who were friends of Byron, told them of his 'daring career of libertinism',[3] details of which had already been offered by the boatman who had brought them from the mainland the day before. 'The account which they gave of Albe unfortunately corresponds too justly with what we have heard,' wrote Shelley to Mary in Bagni di Lucca on 24 August 1818. Byron himself confirmed it, as witnessed by the delineation of his life-style to a former partner in debauchery. He wrote from the Palazzo Mocenigo a few months after Allegra's arrival:

> Venice is not an expensive residence . . . it has theatres — society — and profligacy rather more than enough — I keep four horses on one of the Islands where there is a beach of some miles along the Adriatic . . . I have my Gondola — about fourteen servants including the nurse . . . in the two years I have been at Venice — I have spent about *five* thousand pounds — & I needed not have spent one *third* of this — had it not been that I have a passion for women which is expensive in its variety every where but less so in Venice than in other cities. — You may suppose that in *two years* — with a large establishment — horses — houses — box at the opera — Gondola — journeys — women — and Charity — (for I have not laid out all upon my pleasures — but have bought occasionally a shillings-worth of Salvation) — villas in the country — another carriage & horses — books bought — in short every thing I wanted — & *more* than I ought to have wanted — that the sum of five thousand pounds sterling is no great deal — particularly when I tell you that more than half was laid out on the Sex — to be sure I had plenty for the money — that's certain — I think at least two hundred of one sort or another — perhaps more — for I have not lately kept the recount.[4]

Byron, however, did not complain of venereal disease as he had on his way back from Constantinople and Athens in 1811. Like other sophisticated men of fashion he used condoms. As William St. Clair has pointed out in *The Godwins and the Shelleys*, the thin animal membrane that Byron acquired at considerable expense could protect his lovers from pregnancy just as it could protect him from disease. If Byron's prodigious claims for his promiscuity in Venice are to be believed, then the rare commodity that he imported from England was impressively successful on both counts. He was not troubled by venereal disease or by unwanted children again.

None the less, he was suddenly responsible for a child, an intrusion, no doubt, into his world of instant self-gratification. But he was determined, at least initially, to make up for the loss of his legitimate daughter with Allegra. His early separation from Ada had caused him great pain over the years and he pumped friends for information about her development. He was overjoyed to learn (no doubt to the pique of

Lady Byron) that she was like him in many ways. And Allegra was welcome on her own account; Byron had a strong sentimental attraction to children in general. Indeed, in attempting to rehabilitate his reputation after his death, Moore, in his biography of the poet, emphasized this engaging trait.

Byron was also the father of another child. In his youth he wrote a short poem, 'To My Son', in tribute to an offspring of the Newstead seraglio:

> Oh, 'twill be sweet in thee to trace,
> Ere age has wrinkled o'er my face,
> Ere half my glass of life is run,
> At once a brother and a son;
> And all my wane of years employ
> In justice done to thee, my Boy!
>
> Although so young thy heedless sire,
> Youth will not damp parental fire;
> And, wert thou still less dear to me,
> While Helen's form revives in thee,
> The breast which beat to former joy,
> Will ne'er desert its pledge, my Boy![5]

Byron did not desert his pledge. He probably left the boy and his mother a small legacy, but he had no contact with his son, who in any case probably did not survive childhood.

Lady Oxford's eleven-year-old daughter, Lady Jane, inspired some unashamedly romantic verse, such as 'To Ianthe', a poem which first appeared in the seventh edition of Cantos I and II of *Childe Harold*. Byron's lines celebrate not just the purity and beauty of youth, but the tender love of a nurturing mother, one in stark contrast to Byron's own violent parent:

> Ah! may'st thou ever be what thou art,
> Nor unbeseem the promise of thy spring,
> As fair in form, as warm yet pure in heart,
> Love's image upon earth without his wing,
> And guileless beyond Hope's imagining!
> And surely she who now so fondly rears
> Thy youth, in thee, thus hourly brightening,
> Beholds the rainbow of her future years,
> Before whose heavenly hues all sorrow disappears.

'To Ianthe' highlights Byron's sentimental attraction to children, both male and female, though in keeping with his custom of shocking guests, he once claimed to have attempted a seduction of the little girl.

Byron's appreciation of childhood innocence was not unrelated to his sexual interest in young boys. In Greece he took Eustathios Georgiou, with the 'ambrosial curls hanging down his amiable back' into his retinue, tolerated the imperious boy's tantrums and even the parasol he carried to protect his face from the sun. Their parting, Byron related to Hobhouse in July 1810, 'was vastly pathetic, as many kisses as would have sufficed for a boarding school, and embraces enough to have ruined the character of a county in England'. The Thyrza poems for the young John Edleston also call to mind the last poem that Byron ever wrote, 'On This Day I Complete My Thirty-Sixth Year', in which he mourned his inability to evoke love in the young Greek boy who had become his page.

But Claire Clairmont, whose insights into Byron's character are often astute, offered another reason (apart from the Hellenic) for Byron's attention to children. She wrote to him after his ill-treatment of her:

> let a person depend on you, let them be utterly weak and defenceless, having no protector but yourself, and you infallibly grow fond of that person. How kind you are to children! how good-tempered and considerate towards your servants, how accommodating even to your dogs! And all this because you are sole master and lord; because there is no disputing your power, you become merciful and just. But let someone more on a par with yourself enter the room, you begin to suspect and be cautious, and are very often cruel.[6]

Since their arrival in Milan in April the Shelleys had been visiting Pisa and Leghorn (Livorno) and in June had settled at the Casa Bertini at Bagni di Lucca, about twenty kilometres north of Lucca, in June. Shelley was suffering from a creative block and had turned temporarily to translating classical texts. He was excited about his work on Plato's *Symposium*, revealing as it did, he believed, the authentic customs and manners of the ancient Greeks. Though he was still bothered by a sharp pain in his side, he enjoyed the tranquillity of their new southern life after the demands of London. In the evening he and Mary rode together and during the day, after reading in the hot sun, he bathed in a favourite pool in the chestnut forest, clambering about its rocks and waterfalls. Their pleasure was increased by news from England that *Frankenstein* had been well received by the critics.

But Claire was agitating to see her daughter and in August Shelley took the anxious mother to Venice to see how Allegra was settling into her new and still more eccentric home and to find out if Byron could be softened in regard to the child's mother — at the very least he must let her have access to her daughter. In the event, Shelley concealed the fact that Claire was with him and managed to arrange for mother and daughter to meet in the country while he and Byron were occupied in Venice.

Shelley did not meet his old friend again with unqualified pleasure. He had been shocked by the harsh terms that Byron had set Claire: her separation from Allegra was to be permanent. Shelley did not yet realize the full force of Byron's hatred for Claire, and even urged that the parents might meet together with their child. He tried to emphasize the inhumanity of Byron's plan in a letter of 22 April 1818, explaining that to separate mother and child was unnatural and that the child would 'grow up either in ignorance, or in contempt of one of its parents', a fate that Lady Byron had evidently already planned for Ada. And Shelley was disgusted by Byron's excessive promiscuity.

But when he arrived at Mocenigo on 23 August he was soon as enchanted as ever by his old friend. They seemed to take up where the summer of 1816 had ended and on that first day they rode together on Byron's horses along the sea shore of the Lido, falling immediately into deep conversation:

> Our conversation consisted in histories of his wounded feelings, & questions as to my affairs, & great professions of friendship & regard for me. He said if he had been in England at the time of the Chancery affair, he would have moved Heaven & Earth to have prevented such a decision.[7]

By the end of the week-long visit the two had easily resumed the intimacy of two years before. Shelley was seduced, dazzled and exhilarated by their intellectual union.

The day on the Lido inspired one of Shelley's most interesting poems; it commemorates his friendship with Byron and delineates the differences in their approaches to their art and to life. It also captures Shelley's frustration at Byron's refusal to realize what Shelley saw as his great potential. Soon after the visit Shelley began *Julian and Maddalo, a Conversation*. In his preface to the poem he explained its two contrasting personalities with great care:

> Count Maddalo is a Venetian nobleman of ancient family and of great fortune, who, without mixing much in the society of his countrymen, resides chiefly at his magnificent palace in that city. He is a person of the most consummate genius; and capable, if he would direct his energies to such an end, of becoming the redeemer of his degraded country. But it is his weakness to be proud: he derives, from a comparison of his

own extraordinary mind with the dwarfish intellects that surround him, an intense apprehension of the nothingness of human life. His passions and his powers are incomparably greater than those of other men, and, instead of the latter having been employed in curbing the former, they have mutually lent each other strength. His ambition preys upon itself, for want of objects which it can consider worthy of exertion. I say that Maddalo is proud, because I can find no other word to express the concentered and impatient feelings which consume him; but it is his own hopes and affections only that he seems to trample, for in social life no human being can be more gentle, patient, and unassuming than Maddalo. He is cheerful, frank, and witty. His more serious conversation is a sort of intoxication; men are held by it as by a spell. He has travelled much; and there is an inexpressible charm in his relation of his adventures in different countries.

Julian is an Englishman of good family, passionately attached to those philosophical notions which assert the power of man over his own mind, and the immense improvements of which, by the extinction of certain moral superstitions, human society may yet be susceptible. Without concealing the evil in the world, he is for ever speculating how good may be made superior. He is a complete infidel, and a scoffer at all things reputed holy; and Maddalo takes a wicked pleasure in drawing out his taunts against religion . . . Julian is rather serious.

Shelley's extraordinary, terse evaluation of himself and Byron sheds considerable light on the quality, tone and subject of their long conversations. For all their philosophical differences, the two poets were instinctive soul-mates, their disagreements seem only to have fired their friendship. Their challenge to one another was unique, neither had another friend or colleague with whom he was equally engaged, though Shelley's extraordinarily intense friendship with Hogg at Oxford was a kind of template for such a relationship. Even Godwin's great mind did not rivet Shelley's attention so completely. Byron's wit and humour was undisputed, and he was always pleased to perform for visitors and correspondents, but Shelley's company could also stimulate serious discussion and elicit unselfconscious opinions on the nature of poetry and art that are rarely seen in Byron's letters. Shelley appreciated Byron's charm, but he also saw through this social posing. He expected great things from the poet and refused to be deflected by his superficially brilliant manner. He demanded that Byron should realize the potential of his great gifts in some fashion and never ceased to urge him — to badger him indeed — to make use of his powers. Shelley's conviction that Byron was destined for universal greatness had not wavered since 1816.

Shelley's aristocratic nature appealed to Byron; Lady Blessington in her memoir of conversations with the famous poet noted, 'I never met any one with so decided a taste for aristocracy.' But Byron was gratified to find Shelley's venerable pedigree — a family almost as ancient as his own — matched and even surpassed by tremendous intelligence and sensitivity. And he valued Shelley for the stalwart faith that he placed in his (Byron's) capacity as a poet and as a man. The frustrated ambition that Shelley identified in Byron's character found a balm in Shelley's sympathy for that profound anxiety. Shelley *understood* the older poet's tortured personality and Byron, in his inimitable way, could tease out with 'wicked pleasure' the complexities of his friend. Their conversations, in Shelley's memory, were lit by the flame of a romantic fire that intensified and vivified the experience into poetry:

I rode one evening with Count Maddalo
Upon the bank of sand which breaks the flow
Of Adria towards Venice: a bare strand
Of hillocks, heaped from ever-shifting sand . . .
Where 'twas our wont to ride while day went down.
This ride was my delight. I love all waste
And solitary places; where we taste
The pleasure of believing what we see
Is boundless, as we wish our souls to be:
And such was this wide ocean, and this shore
More barren than its billows: and yet more
Than all, with a remembered friend I love
To ride as I then rode; — for the winds drove
The living spray along the sunny air
Into our faces; the blue heavens were bare,
Stripped to their depths by the awakening north;
And, from the waves, sound like delight broke forth
Harmonizing with solitude, and sent
Into our hearts aërial merriment.

So, as we rode, we talked; and the swift thought,
Winging itself with laughter, lingered not,
But flew from brain to brain; — such glee was ours,
Charged with light memories of remembered hours,
None slow enough for sadness . . .
Our talk grew somewhat serious, as may be
Talk interrupted with such raillery
As mocks itself, because it cannot scorn
The thoughts it would extinguish: — 'twas forlorn,
Yet pleasing, such as once, so poets tell,
The devils held within the dales of hell,

Concerning God, freewill and destiny.
Of all that Earth has been, or yet may be;
All that vain men imagine or believe,
Or hope can paint, or suffering can achieve,
We descanted; and I (for ever still
Is it not wise to make the best of ill?)
Argued against despondency; but pride
Made my companion take the darker side.
The sense that he was greater than his kind
Had struck, methinks, his eagle spirit blind
By gazing on its own exceeding light.[8]

Shelley's style in the poem is adapted to reflect the natural tones of conversation. It is without his usual flamboyant imagery and remains one of his most successful (and indeed, accessible) long poems. Byron's presence here directly influenced Shelley's style, just as Shelley had affected his friend's poetry during that summer in Geneva.

But before Shelley completed *Julian and Maddalo*, tragedy struck his family and again it was Claire who was its catalyst. Mary did not complain when Claire dragged her husband off to Venice to see Allegra, and she waited patiently for word of the resolution of her troublesome stepsister's problems. Shelley did not reveal to Byron that Claire had accompanied him to Venice, telling him instead that she and Mary were awaiting instructions in Padua. When Byron appeared to be on the verge of discovering the deceit, and the fact that Claire was already with her daughter in the country, Shelley had to send for Mary immediately in order to safeguard the complicated ruse. She was to move house again, on her own, and take charge of the children. But this time Mary's own baby Clara was ill and a dash across the country during its hottest months was risky. Shelley was insistent and for Claire's sake his instructions forbade any delay. The journey took four days and little Clara, weakened by a new attack of dysentery and fever, grew emaciated. By the time Shelley met his wife and daughter in Padua, there was little hope. Yet he insisted on a race of nearly thirty miles to Venice, in search of a better doctor, and on 24 September 1818, the year-old Clara died in her mother's arms at a Venetian inn, waiting for a doctor who did not come. Had she not been moved from Bagni di Lucca she might have lived. In his attempt to do good for others Shelley was wilfully blind, he ignored his greatest responsibilities and he betrayed Mary, whom he loved most.

Mary was still a very young woman — just twenty-one — and she eventually recovered from Clara's death, but she would never forget its circumstances. Her love for her husband was still strong, but some of his lustre had faded, he was diminished in her eyes. She would no longer be reticent in her criticism of both his poetry and his character and she began to show some sympathy with the complaints of his critics: his work was inaccessible, too highly charged with the imagery of his difficult philosophies rather than with the power of personal experience and emotion. The received wisdom found that his visionary poems lacked a human dimension and she herself, in her edition of Shelley's poetry of 1839, would largely agree with this evaluation.

Mary fell into the first of the depressions that were to shadow her life, and baffle her husband. She could not recover from Clara's death with the swiftness and optimism that had helped to heal the wounds of the loss of her premature baby nearly four years before. She clung to the three-year-old William more tightly than ever and began to nurture a quiet resentment of Shelley. This death, added to all those that had preceded it, brought with it the foreshadow of doom. Mary's prescience — evoked first in her melancholy musings on Canto III of *Childe Harold* — was vindicated. Sorrow had embedded itself in her spirit and when tragedy after tragedy assaulted her in the course of the next three years, she seemed to be waiting for it.

The Shelleys spent a month in Venice weathering an initial scare over William's health. Mary visited Byron where she encountered the formidable Fornarina. Perhaps thinking it best to protect her from the tigress-like defences of Margarita, who saw every woman as a threat, Byron subsequently called on Mary at her hotel on the Grand Canal, near the Palazzo Mocenigo. During those weeks Byron gave her his memoirs to read, those that would later be so rashly destroyed by his anxious friends after the poet's death. The author of *Frankenstein* had earned Byron's literary respect (Shelley had sent a copy of the novel to Byron in April) and he gave her the memoirs for her professional opinion on their worthiness — might they be published? Mary thought they were very fine and indeed, years later, when the notoriety surrounding the destruction of the memoirs was at its height, she claimed that there had been little to cause scandal. Byron himself pointed out that they constituted a memoir, and not 'confessions' when he sent a section of them later in the year for the approval of Lady Byron. While she was in Venice Mary also copied out his long poem *Mazeppa*, a powerful narrative piece retelling the fable of the Cossack tied to a wild horse. She read the first canto of *Don Juan*, a poem that she first judged depraved, but quickly came to recognize as a masterpiece. She would encourage Byron to continue to work on the poem when all his other friends and advisers urged him to stop.

For the next few weeks, with Claire safely installed at Padua with the children, Mary and Shelley relished their reunion with Albe. As at Diodati, Shelley stayed up late into the night talking with Byron at Mocenigo while Mary waited in the hotel near by. They rode together on the Lido and shared more ghost stories. Mary enjoyed the sights but disliked Venice; there were no walks in the watery city and the stench of the canals at low tide gave her a headache. The sight of the 'zucche' or gourds that were sold everywhere made her sick and she found the citizens 'some of the worst specimens of Italian'.[9] For himself, Shelley was disgusted with Venice's degradation as a 'slave' to the 'Austrian yoke ... I had no conception of the excess to which avarice, cowardice, superstition, ignorance, passionless lust, & all the inexpressible brutalities which degrade human nature could be carried, until I lived a few days among the Venetians,' he wrote to Peacock on 8 October.

In fact, Venice was *not* the favoured haunt of the English tourist; this in itself was the main reason for Byron's residence there. In this respect the Shelleys were more conventional than their friend, who was, much to their surprise, thriving in the city: 'Mary & myself — saw Lord Byron and really we hardly knew him — he is changed into the liveliest, & happiest looking man I ever met.'[10] In the poem that he wrote in the little summer-house in the garden at Este in the autumn, *Lines Written Among the Euganean Hills*, Shelley celebrated (and much romanticized) Byron's life in Venice. He addressed the city, in thrall to the occupying forces of the Austrian Empire:

> ... a tempest-cleaving swan
> Of the songs of Albion,
> Driven from his ancestral streams,
> By the might of evil dreams,
> Found a nest in thee; and Ocean
> Welcomed him with such emotion
> That its joy grew his, and sprung
> From his lips like music flung
> O'er a mighty thunder-fit,
> Chastening terror ...

But again their reunion was for a limited time only. At the end of October Shelley went to fetch Allegra from Claire and with much regret returned her to her father's care, her future still unresolved. The Shelley entourage left Venice and travelled in a leisurely fashion south, their ultimate destination Naples, a requisite stop on any Grand Tour.

Soon after the Shelleys' departure, John Hanson arrived at the Palazzo Mocenigo, suffering profoundly from his excessive xenophobia, and carrying the papers relating to the sale of Newstead. He had hoped that Byron would meet him half-way in Geneva, but his client would not be moved from Venice. Byron was enraged that Hanson had neglected to bring magnesia, tooth powder and his books (apparently well over a cart-load had been ordered). He would take his revenge by terrifying the timid attorney:

> five men died of the Plague the other day — in the Lazaretto — I shall take him to ride at the Lido — he hath a reverend care & fear of his health — I will show him the Lazaretto which is not far off ... I will tell him of the five men — I will tell him of my contact with [Dr.] Aglietti in whose presence they died — & who came into my Box at the ... Opera the same evening — & shook hands with me; — I will tell him all this — and as he is a hypochondriac — perhaps it may kill him.[11]

Over the summer Byron had been struggling with the violent Margarita who had run away from her husband and taken up residence at Mocenigo. She ruled over his home and servants like a jealous warlord. He was also hard at work upon *Don Juan*. He had finished the first canto by the middle of September and he announced the birth of his new poem — with considerably more pride and delight than he had notified his friends of Allegra's nativity — to Moore on 19 September: '[it] is meant to be a little quietly facetious upon every thing. But I doubt whether it is not — at least, as far as it has yet gone — too free for these very modest days. However, I shall try the experiment, anonymously, and if it don't take, it will be discontinued.'

He also took the opportunity once again to attack the Poet Laureate. 'It is dedicated to S[outhey] in good, simple, savage verse, upon the [Laureate's] politics, and the way he got them.'[12] *Don Juan* was to grow over the next five years, its wide-ranging, all-encompassing shape dictated apparently by the whims of its digressing, chatty, world-weary narrator. But it remained steadfastly vigilant in its opposition to cant, hypocrisy and foolish politics, beginning with an attack on Wordsworth and Southey for degrading English poetry from the divine heights of Pope and Dryden, and for acting as political traitors, betraying their own youthful ideals. Readers were outraged. *Blackwood's Edinburgh Magazine* of August 1819 praised the poem's and Byron's undiminished genius, but found its transgressions insupportable. Others could find no merit at all. The career of the hapless Juan, victim of every amorous lady who came his way, was an assault on high society and on public morals. Furthermore, the anti-war cantos, VI and VII, launched an effective attack on monarchy and political policy.

Byron came round from his now familiar carnival excesses in 1819 to be met by the happy news that the money from Newstead had been paid. For ten days he had not been in bed before eight in the morning and he had acquired his usual post-carnival illness, this time a stomach complaint. But his new wealth eased the pain and he now addressed himself to making money from his writing with even greater assiduity. He was negotiating with Murray for the copyright to the first two cantos of *Don Juan*. 'Tell Hobhouse that "Don Juan" must be published,' he wrote to Kinnaird on 22 February. The 'loss of the copyright would break my heart ... my "regard for my fee" is the ruling passion and I must have it.' In order to sell the copyright he reluctantly agreed to remove the dedication to Southey. Eventually he was urged to desist from the project entirely by friends who believed it would damage his reputation still further. But the *Don* was not to be resisted; to satisfy his worried friends he would publish the two cantos anonymously, but he would proceed.

Meanwhile, the Shelleys had already reached Rome. If Byron's enthusiasm for the Eternal City had been satisfied in a matter of days, the Shelleys crossed the Compagna di Roma, a broad plain, empty and windswept like the beach where Shelley rode with Byron, and felt as if they had somehow come home. They spent a week on this first visit in November 1818, packing in a staggering amount of sight-seeing. In a single day they went to Monte Cavallo (the Piazza Quirinale), the Baths of Diocletian, Santa Maria dei Angeli, Santa Maria Maggiore, the 'Sept Salle delle Terme di Tito' and, as on every day of their stay, to the Coliseum and the Forum. In the evenings they read, composed and wrote letters. After an urgent request to Peacock for English pencils, they were on their way to Naples.

After they traversed the desolate Pontine marshes, with their dual threat of miasmic fevers and bloodthirsty bandits, the Shelleys arrived in the south. Mary began to recover from Clara's death, soothed by the legendary beauty of Naples. Shelley took rooms for them on the fashionable main boulevard in full view of the spectacular Bay, in the shadow of Vesuvius. They visited the celebrated Greek and Roman ruins, finding themselves in the classical world that had coloured and vitalized their education: Pompeii, Heculaneum, the temples at Paestum, the Bay of Baiae with its sunken Roman villas[13] where Virgil wrote the *Georgics* and where they delighted in the memory of his presence. The mouth of the underworld at Lake Avernus, its associated Elysian fields at Solfuratura, and the cave of the Cumean Sibyl all figure in Mary's introduction to her ambitious futuristic novel *The Last Man* (1826).

But in Naples they faced a new scandal, one that would not simply disappear with the conclusion of the incident. A child, a girl, born in December 1818, was evidently adopted by Shelley in order to aid an anonymous Englishwoman or, perhaps, to console Mary for the loss of Clara. He adopted the child in Naples, placing her with foster parents without Mary's initial knowledge, but with the assistance of their Swiss nursemaid Elise and her soon-to-be-husband Paolo Foggi, another servant in the Shelley household. The child died in 1820 and the mystery of her birth and parentage was never revealed, but Paolo and Elise later turned on their masters, using their knowledge of the Shelley family to spread rumours, among them the notion that the child was Shelley's but not Mary's. Further rumour over the years has elaborated on the contributions of the Foggis to add that Claire was the child's mother, and Shelley scholars, to this day, speculate on the actual facts of the 'Neapolitan charge', as the mystery-child has become known.

In March 1819, attached as they had become to Naples, the Shelleys set off to return to Rome. On the day of their arrival they hurried to view the Coliseum — their favourite building. They would take up residence in Rome for three months, passing their days in energetic sight-seeing, walking and reading. Mary, Shelley and little William had their portraits painted. Mary was once again busy and happy. But Rome was to bring the Shelleys the greatest grief they would know as a couple. On 25 May, Mary recorded in her journal, 'William is not well.' The little boy had become ill with an attack of worms. The condition was treated and he recovered quickly, his mother recording his improvement on the 28th. Still, the doctors urged the Shelleys to take him from the stifling city before it grew any hotter. But William was already too weak to move. In the evening of 2 June, he became ill again and developed a high fever. On the 5th the fever still raged and Mary began to see that her child would not recover. The fever could not be brought down. Finally, on 7 June three-year-old William died, victim of the malaria that so haunted all visitors to the south of Italy. He was buried in the Protestant cemetery in Rome, in the shade of the magnificent pyramidical tomb of Cestius. The Shelleys fled the city on the 10th, Mary paralysed by a grief from which she would never completely recover. Her journal ended abruptly. When she was finally able to write a letter, it was to a friend in Rome, the same who had painted William's portrait less than a month before. She had accepted responsibility for erecting William's headstone:

> Let us hear . . . if you please — anything you may have done about the tomb — near which I shall lie one day & care not — for my own sake — how soon — I shall never recover that blow — I feel it more now than at Rome — the thought never leaves me for a single moment — Everything on earth has lost its interest for me.[14]

Shelley too was devastated by the child's death, 'his heart . . . was full of burning love for his offspring',[15] for his 'Will Mouse'. He composed a poem in his despair, stricken by his loss, but also by Mary's inability to cope:

> My lost William, thou in whom
>   Some bright spirit lived, and did
> That decaying robe consume
>   Which its lustre faintly hid,
> Here its ashes find a tomb,
>   But beneath this pyramid
> Thou art not — if a thing divine
> Like thee can die, thy funeral shrine
> Is thy mother's grief and mine.
>
> Where art thou, my gentle child?
>   Let me think thy spirit feeds,
> With its life intense and mild,
> The love of living leaves and weeds,
> Among these tombs and ruins wild; —
>   Let me think that through low seeds
> Of the sweet flowers and sunny grass,
> Into their hues and scents may pass,
> A portion — [16]

Mary's third child had been wrested from her grasp and she would be cheated out of her resting place by his side. Even Shelley was denied reunion with his little son after death: when he too was buried at the Protestant cemetery in Rome, William's grave was opened to place him with his father. The tomb contained the remains of an adult and the toddler's body was never found.

All the happiness that Mary had grabbed with both hands as she fled into the night with Shelley in 1814 was being called to account. William had become such a focus of her life — his budding personality had featured prominently in her letters and journal — that his loss seemed even more unbearable than Clara's. Mary fell into deep and impenetrable depression; her grief crippled her so that she withdrew even further from her husband. She would not recover quickly, and not before she had seized on a literary project of immense, emotion-obliterating ambition. They moved back to Livorno and Mary began a new journal on 4 August:

> I begin my journal on Shelley's birthday — We have now lived five years together & if all the events of five years were blotted out I might

be happy — but to have won & then cruelly have lost the associations of four years is not an accident to which the human mind can bend without much suffering.

Mary was not yet twenty-three. She had lost an infant and two children. Two suicides weighed heavily on her. A shadow that was never completely to lift settled over her heart.

While the Shelleys suffered the most intense grief, Byron was basking in the pastime which, above all others, anaesthetized his anxieties. At the beginning of April 1819 he fell in love with the woman who was to become his longest — and last — attachment. He had first met the nineteen-year-old Countess Teresa Guiccioli the year before, a few days after her marriage to a wealthy and much older Ravennese aristocrat, the Count Alessandro Guiccioli. At that meeting Teresa was not yet ready to acquire a *cavaliere servente* or lover-escort. But this time it took only days for Byron to realize the depth of his passion. On 6 April he wrote to Hobhouse:

> She is pretty — but has no tact — answers aloud — when she should whisper — talks of age to old ladies who want to pass for young — and this blessed night horrified a correct company at the Benzona's — by calling out to me 'Mio Byron' in an audible key during a dead Silence of pause in the other prattlers, who stared & whispered [to] their respective Serventi. — One of her preliminaries is that I must never leave Italy; — I have no desire to leave it — but I should not like to be frittered down into a regular Cicisbeo.[17] — What shall I do! I am in love — and tired of promiscuous concubinage — & have now an opportunity of settling for life.

Following their meeting at the conversazione, the couple, who would soon be lovers, met the next day in Byron's gondola and in the succeeding days, with the connivance of Teresa's maid, they met more intimately, probably going to Byron's summer villa at La Mira — where Marianna had formerly held sway — for the consummation of their love. Teresa was happy, in love for the first time, and Byron was only slightly anxious about the increasingly public nature of his new affair. Besides, it had been some time since he had had a great lady as a mistress (Teresa, daughter of Count Gamba of Ravenna, was a countess in her own right) and he had to conduct proceedings in a fashion to which he had grown unaccustomed. But just as he succumbed to the narcotic of the affair, on 13 April, Teresa was called away from Venice. The Count was to visit one of his country residences, and then to return home to Ravenna. He must be accompanied by his young wife.

Byron missed her deeply — he had no choice but to follow. Leaving Venice on 1 June, he stopped at Bologna and, using the key to her apartments there, which she had left for him, he wandered in her rooms and garden, reading her books and inscribing them with love letters. He arrived in Ravenna on 10 June. Throughout the summer, as his place at Teresa's side grew to be accepted, her husband, a worldly, manipulative man who had been married twice before, began to withdraw, leaving the field to Byron as *cavaliere servente*. He, of course, maintained the rules of such an arrangement by acknowledging his wife's lover as nothing more than a close friend to them both and never allowing Byron to appear as a permanent member of his household. He evidently recognized that the Englishman could be of some use, particularly as a source of funds, but the lovers came to transgress even the very liberal code of love accepted in Italian society. After one of her many illnesses, Byron brought his mistress back to Venice *without* her husband to be attended by its greatest doctor. Persuaded to go to the country for Teresa's health, the couple could not believe their luck: it was prescribed that the Countess should reside, under Byron's protection, at La Mira. The remainder of the summer and the early autumn was perhaps the most tranquil and gratifying period of Byron's life. Almost overnight he had renounced the promiscuous life that he had taken such pride in and perhaps for the first time began to experience domestic tranquillity with a lover. He finally felt what it was to be a husband and, as he drew closer to Teresa's accepting father and brother, the Counts Ruggero and Peitro, what it meant to be a member of a family.

Despite his intensifying family cares and his own ill health, Shelley's thoughts were still often with Byron. He had not yet succeeded in turning the great man's heart and mind satisfactorily to a suitable occupation and the failure rankled. Despite the discussions of *Julian and Maddalo* and the optimism that Shelley had felt after their time together in Venice, the poet was still, in Shelley's view, degrading himself and his talents. Shelley did not yet know of Teresa's benign influence and after another reading of *Childe Harold*'s fourth and last canto, with all its bitterness and cynicism, Shelley wrote to Peacock in December 1818:

> The spirit in which it is written is, if insane, the most wicked & mischievous insanity that ever was given forth. It is a kind of obstinate & selfwilled folly in which he hardens himself. I remonstrated with him in vain on the tone of mind from which such a view of things alone arises. For its real root is very different from its apparent one, & nothing can be less sublime than the true source of these expressions of contempt & desperation. The fact is, that first, the Italian women are perhaps the most contemptible of all who exist under the moon; the most ignorant the most disgusting, the most bigotted, the most filthy. Countesses smell so of garlick

that an ordinary Englishman cannot approach them. Well, L[ord] B[yron] is familiar with the lowest sort of these women, the people his gondolieri pick up in the streets. He allows fathers & mothers to bargain with him for their daughters, & though this is common in Italy, yet for an Englishman to encourage such sickening vice is a melancholy thing. He associates with wretches who seem almost to have lost the gait & phisiognomy of man, & who do not scruple to avow practices which are not only not named but I believe seldom even conceived in England. He says he disapproves, but he endures. He is not yet Italian & is heartily & deeply discontented with himself, & contemplating in the distorted mirror of his own thoughts, the nature & destiny of man, what can he behold but objects of contempt & despair?

Shelley's attack on Byron was indeed strident, perhaps provoked in part by Byron's appalling treatment of Claire and Allegra,[18] and almost certainly by his hatred of the institution of prostitution, subject of one of his extended notes to *Queen Mab*. But Shelley was equally disturbed by his own inability to influence the poet for good, as he had done, if only temporarily, at Geneva and had attempted a second time, whilst riding on the Venice Lido. Once again Shelley's altruistic plans had come to nothing and shown only how ineffectual he could be. Yet he must try again to save the great poet's soul. They would meet again, after Byron's 'insanity' at Venice had subsided and his life, with Teresa, became more stable. Shelley would have one last opportunity to encourage his friend to live up to his potential.

CHAPTER VII

PISA

F ROM AUGUST 1819 UNTIL MAY 1822 the Shelleys moved house ten times around the area of Livorno, Pisa and Florence. They were constantly on the move, fleeing the most intense heat. From 1820 they strayed no further in their various choice of homes than the environs of Pisa and the coast at Livorno.

Byron also moved. In December 1819 he left Venice to follow his mistress and her husband to their home in Ravenna, and later to follow her and her family, first to Florence and then to Pisa, where he was reunited with the Shelleys. Moving house for Byron was a more complicated business than it was for Mary and Percy. He needed his comforts about him and he was loath to dispose of the acquisitions that he had made during his long stay in Venice. Thomas Medwin, a second cousin of Shelley and member of the circle at Pisa, described the great man's travelling equipage in the autumn of 1821: ' . . . seven servants, five carriages, nine horses, a monkey, a bull-dog and a mastiff, two cats, three pea-fowls and some hens . . . formed part of his livestock; and all his books, consisting of a very large library of modern works, (for he bought all the best that came out,) together with a vast quantity of furniture . . . '[1]

After the blissful summer at La Mira, Byron and Teresa had moved back to Venice and the Palazzo Mocenigo, where Teresa nursed her lover through a severe illness, strengthening his attachment to her. By contrast, throughout the remainder of the summer and autumn, Mary Shelley, who was living at Livorno, could find no relief from her devastating depression. She wrote a remarkable, disturbing novella during this period. An attempt no doubt to exorcise her relentless grief, it exposes a profound spiritual disorder. *Mathilda* (unpublished until 1951) is the story of a daughter's incestuous love for her father, the reciprocation of that emotion, the father's death, the daughter's self-imposed exile, and her potentially redemptive relationship with an ascetic poet that also ends in death. Of all the doom-laden works that Mary ever wrote *Mathilda* is certainly the most personal, painful and raw. It was also her contribution to the theme of incest that so fascinated her husband and Byron.

At the same time that Byron was beginning to find stability with

Teresa Guiccioli, Shelley was feeling emotionally abandoned by Mary. Her depression crippled her instinctive compassion and dulled her taste for life and for Shelley. He grew ever lonelier and concealed his thoughts in a secret notebook which she discovered after his death:

I

The world is dreary,
  And I am weary
Of wandering on without thee, Mary;
  A joy was erewhile
  In thy voice and thy smile,
And 'tis gone, when I should be gone too, Mary.

II

My dearest Mary, wherefore hast thou gone,
And left me in this dreary world alone!
Thy form is here indeed — a lovely one —
But thou art fled, gone down the dreary road,
That leads to Sorrow's most obscure abode;
Thou sittest on the hearth of pale despair,
  Where
For thine own sake I cannot follow thee.[2]

Mary was pregnant and Shelley awaited the birth of another child with desperation, barely allowing himself to hope that it would restore her spirits. Though Godwin's loss of a lawsuit regarding back rent on the Skinner Street house resulted in an enormous demand on Shelley's tightly stretched resources, the couple were overjoyed at the birth of a son, Percy Florence, born in his namesake city on November 1819, after an uncomplicated, two-hour labour. Mary wrapped the infant in flannel petticoats and waited for the consignment of baby clothes promised by the Hunts.

Almost immediately, she plunged into her dark novel of the Italian Renaissance, *Valperga, or the Life and Adventures of Castruccio, Prince of Lucca*, whose central character, fiercely ambitious but emotionally complex, owes so much to Mary's observation of Byron's personality. Shelley, meanwhile, though still suffering from the old pain in his side that defied diagnosis or treatment, was working on one of his most important prose pieces, *A Philosophical View of Reform*, a political pamphlet intended to be 'an instructive and readable book, appealing from the passions to the reason of men',[3] and arranging with great excitement for the publication of *Prometheus Unbound*, which he considered to be his best work.

Shelley revelled in the spirit of revolution that he believed inhabited the relatively liberal Tuscany, the only Italian state that offered some relief from the oppression of the Austrians or the Papal authorities. In *A Philosophical View of Reform* he offered his optimistic views on the recent currents of liberalism and reform focused, as he saw it, in Italy. In fact, he was also stimulated by the sense that the whole of Europe was in a positive ferment and that the repressive Castlereagh regime in England was softening and growing more lenient towards liberal sentiment now that the panic over Napoleon and the French had subsided there. The bloodless deposition of Ferdinand VII of Spain in January, celebrated by Shelley in 'Ode to Liberty', was further encouragement to his hopes; so too was the uprising by the citizens of Naples in which they revolted against a repressive regime and demanded a constitution. Mary was also swept up in her husband's enthusiasm and the cautious renewal of her pleasure in life was further encouraged by the departure of Claire for Florence in October 1820.

At the beginning of November 1819 Teresa's husband Count Guiccioli came to Venice to reclaim his wife. At Byron's insistence, she returned with her spouse to Ravenna and for a short time the poet enjoyed his stoic self-denial. But his uncharacteristic restraint was not to last. He wrote to her from Venice on 10 December:

> You have always been (since we met) *the only object of my thoughts*. I believed that the best course, both for your peace and for that of your family, was for me to leave, and to go *very far away*, to remain near and *not* approach you, would have been impossible for me. But you have decided that I am to return to Ravenna. I shall return — and do — and be — what you wish. I cannot say more — Since your departure — I have not gone out of the house — and scarcely out of my room — nor shall I go out unless it be — to come to you or to leave Italy . . .

Initially resolved to return to England with Allegra, he abruptly changed his mind. Instead, he closed up Mocenigo with great haste, selling gondola, bed, silver coffee pots and sugar basins, tables, chairs, dogs, monkeys and a fox and, summoned by Teresa's anxious father, hurried to the home of his ailing mistress. He arrived in Ravenna on 24 December with his little daughter and her 'whole treasure of toys'. In the new year he settled comfortably into the upper-floor apartments of the Palazzo Guiccioli in Ravenna and into his role as *cavaliere servente* to Teresa. He was happy, but slightly embarrassed by his awkward new identity — he had not yet learned how to fold a lady's shawl or to recognize his mistress's from among the others in the cloak room. He wrote to Murray on 21 February 1820, explaining his subservient role:

> Their system has it's rules — and it's fitnesses — and decorums — so
> as to be reduced to a kind of discipline — or game at hearts — which
> admits few deviations unless you wish to lose it. — They are extremely
> tenacious — and jealous as furies — not permitting their Lovers even to
> marry if they can help it — and keeping them always close to them in
> public as in private whenever they can. — In short they transfer marriage
> to adultery — and strike the *not* out of that commandment. — The reason
> is that they marry for their parents and love for themselves. — They exact
> fidelity from a lover as a debt of honour — while they pay the husband
> as a tradesman . . . You hear a person's character — male or female —
> canvassed — not as depending on their conduct to their husbands or wives
> — but to their mistress or lover.

In fact, Byron was so at home in Italian society that a return to
England was increasingly difficult for him to envisage. When Moore saw
him in the summer of 1819 he was struck by his foreign appearance, his
long hair, whiskers and an Italian style of dress. London, Byron decided,
would be as strange to him as Peking.

Moreover, things at home had changed. Hobhouse was standing for
Parliament, but only after serving a few months in Newgate Prison for
his pamphlet which, read superficially, appeared to be an incitement to
violent revolution. Byron was unsympathetic towards his loyal friend and
had even stopped writing to him for a time, disgusted by his disaffection
from the aristocratic Whigs and his subsequent association with the hard
core of radical reform and its ungentlemanly proponents, Henry 'Orator'
Hunt and William Cobbett.

Byron had also received word of Scrope Davies's ruin. Overcome by
gambling debts, the brightest spark of the years of London libertinism
had fled his creditors and, like the equally compromised Beau Brummel,
whose inimitable style of dress had been adopted by the Prince Regent
himself, had come to rest obscurely on the Continent. Here was one
less attraction waiting for Byron in his old world, one more reason
to remain comfortably where he was. He finally wrote to Hobhouse on
3 March 1820:

> the loss of Scrope is irreparable — we could have 'better spared' not only
> 'a better man' but the 'best of Men'. — Gone to Bruges — where he will
> get tipsy with Dutch beer and shoot himself the first foggy morning. —
> Brummell — at *Calais* — Scrope at Bruges — Buonaparte at St. Helena
> — you in — your new apartments[4] — and I at Ravenna — only think
> so many great men! — there has been nothing like it since Themistocles
> at Magnesia — and Marius at Carthage.

Nothing would entice him back to his homeland, not even the coronation of the new king after the death of George III on 29 January 1820. As a peer of the realm Byron was entitled to attend the coronation but declined: 'I shall let *"dearest Duck"* [Lady Byron] waddle alone at the Coronation — a ceremony which I should like to see and have a right to act Punch in — but the Crown itself would not bribe me to return to England — unless business or actual urgency required it.'[5]

And as ever, despite the social demands of his new city, Byron was composing prolifically. By December 1820 he had sent Cantos III, IV and V of *Don Juan* to England. Shelley was deeply impressed by Byron's new project and detected a new power in *Don Juan* that he had so sorely missed in the last canto of *Childe Harold*. With great pride in its accuracy and sensitivity, Byron also sent his translation of Pulci's *Morgante Maggiore*, a comic piece in the same vein as *Beppo*. In order to draw attention to his skill as a translator, Byron requested that it be printed alongside the Italian original. Early in the spring he sent a translation of the episode of Francesca of Rimini from Dante's *Inferno* and also the first four cantos of *The Prophecy of Dante*, a poem in the style of the great poet which had been requested by and was dedicated to Teresa, whose native city Ravenna held Dante's tomb.

Shelley himself had yet to achieve anything remotely comparable with Byron's literary celebrity; but Mary was more eager than ever that her husband should enjoy a critical success. The public seemed to favour a strong narrative line in their fiction and their poetry. She therefore urged Shelley to undertake more projects like *The Cenci* (1820), a drama that he had written more as a challenge to his talents than through natural inclination. Despite the inflammatory nature of the story — of rape, incest and murder — *The Cenci* had met with relative success; its first print-run of 500 sold out and a second edition was published. But when compared to *The Corsair* which, on its first day of publication, sold over 10,000 copies, 'success' was indeed a relative term. Nevertheless, the drama offered what to Mary's mind was missing from much of her husband's poetry, 'the delineations of human passion'.[6] Shelley was evidently hurt and annoyed by Mary's designs on his imagination and by the knowledge that in some respects she sympathized with his critics. The dedication to *The Witch of Atlas* acknowledges their differences:

> How, my dear Mary, are you critic-bitten,
>   (For vipers kill, though dead,) by some review,
> That you condemn these verses I have written,
>   Because they tell no story, false or true!
> What, though no mice are caught by a young kitten,
>   May it not leap and play as grown cats do,
> Till its claws come? Prithee, for this one time,
> Content thee with a visionary rhyme.

Shelley could not have been immune to feelings of despair when he compared his own professional obscurity with Byron's stratospheric popularity. Yet, as always, he expressed his anxiety in a creative way, continuing to urge Byron to strive for a greater and more profound success. On 16 April 1821 he wrote:

> You have now reached the age at which those eternal poets, of whom we have authentic accounts, have ever begun their supreme poems; considering all their others, however transcendent, as the steps, the scaffolding, the exercise which may sustain and conduct them to their great work. If you are inferior to these, it is not in genius, but industry and resolution. Oh, that you would subdue yourself to the great task of building up a poem containing within itself the germs of a permanent relation to the present, and to all succeeding ages!

Byron returned the compliment by praising *The Cenci*. But he responded to Shelley's undiminished cajoling more drily on 26 April: 'You want me to undertake a great Poem — I have not the inclination nor the power. As I grow older, the indifference — *not* to life, for we love it by instinct — but to the stimuli of life, increases.'

Byron enjoyed the winter and early spring of 1820 in his new provincial home at Ravenna, but in May Count Guiccioli suddenly became displeased with the arrangement that he had previously happily condoned. It was hardly surprising under the circumstances. Prepared to honour the rigid code of the *cavaliere servente* if observed to the letter, Guiccioli was outraged by its violation: arriving home at an inopportune moment he found his wife and his guest apparently *in flagrante delicto*, or, as Byron would have it, 'quasi in the fact'. He suggested that Byron should seek accommodation elsewhere. But ever determined to keep his daughter happy, Count Gamba, now a firm ally of the English lord, took her to his country home at Filetto and sought a legal separation for her from the Papal courts. The lovers would remain together after all, and in July, after the separation agreement was secured, Teresa was transferred to the sympathetic protection of her father. Byron established Allegra at a country home near the Gambas at Filetto and passed many pleasant summer days in the company of his mistress and her delightful father and brother.

But, during that summer, Byron too became caught up in the fever of revolution. With his growing affection for the Gambas, and his nagging desire to participate in some worthy or challenging activity — no doubt inspired by Shelley's example — he joined the clandestine Carbonari, one of the secret societies of aristocrats dedicated to the overthrow of Metternich and Austrian rule and to the liberalization of the Papal states. Byron could perhaps feel more sympathetic now towards Hobhouse (although his friend's association with the sullied underclass of the radicals was not, of course, the same thing as his own initiation into the élite society of the ancient families of Italy). He could also reactivate his old allegiance to the Whigs, take up the cause of political reform and reaffirm the supremacy of the aristocracy at the same time. 'It is a grand project,' he enthused in his Ravenna journal on 18 February, 'the very *poetry* of politics. Only think — a free Italy!!!' Byron participated in the February 1821 plot to cut off the Austrian artillery as it passed through Ravenna on its way south to crush the Neapolitan uprising. He grew nervous when his home was used to stockpile weapons. The plot failed, the Gambas were discovered and Byron's adopted family was sent into exile to Florence in the summer of 1821, where Byron and Teresa would soon follow.

Meanwhile, in Pisa, in the late autumn of 1820, the imaginative and emotional spell that Mary had cast over Shelley six years before had begun to wear thin. Shelley had been drawn to another woman. Emilia Viviani, the nineteen-year-old daughter of the Governor of Pisa, was beautiful, talented and victim of an irresistibly romantic fate; she had been effectively 'imprisoned' in a convent by her jealous mother (thirty years younger than her husband, Emilia's father), to be freed only at the time of her arranged marriage. The Shelleys had been fascinated by her plight (so too were others, Emilia had become something of a local tourist attraction): 'It is grievous to see this beautiful girl wearing out the best years of her life in a[n] odious convent where both mind and body are sick from want of the appropriate exercise for each,' wrote Mary to Leigh Hunt on 1 January 1821.

Shelley became infatuated with Emilia, endowing her, in his imagination, with literary genius and the beauty of a goddess. She inspired his long love poem *Epipsychidion*, which Shelley called 'an idealized history of my life and feelings',[7] and which reveals just how powerful was her hold on him, both emotionally and erotically:

Our breath shall intermix, our bosoms bound,
And our veins beat together; and our lips,
With other eloquence than words, eclipse
The soul that burns between them; and the wells
Which boil under our being's inmost cells,
The fountains of our deepest life, shall be
Confused in passion's golden purity,
As mountain-springs under the morning Sun.
We shall become the same, we shall be one
Spirit within two frames, oh! wherefore two?
One passion in twin-hearts, which grows and grew
Till like two meteors of expanding flame,

Those spheres instinct with it become the same,
Touch, mingle, are transfigured; ever still
Burning, yet ever inconsumable:
In one another's substance finding food,
Like flames too pure and light and unimbued
To nourish their bright lives with baser prey,
Which point to Heaven and cannot pass away:
One hope within two wills, one will beneath
Two overshadowing minds, one life, one death,
One Heaven, one Hell, one immortality,
And one annihilation.

The passionate sentiments expressed in the poem must have caused Mary pain. *Epipsychidion* was formally addressed to Emilia and Mary was well aware that she herself was identified with the figure of the Moon in the poem, the poet's first love who disappoints him, chilling him in her 'chaste cold bed'. Indeed, in her 1839 edition of Shelley's poems, *Epipsychidion* stands without comment, the only long poem for which Mary does not provide biographical information. Mary swiftly became disenchanted with the girl who addressed her as 'sister', and weary of her husband's enthusiasm. And Shelley too saw through the girl soon enough; the divine creature was not without guile and indeed she had been leading him on and subtly insulting Mary all the while. He was disillusioned when she entertained arranged suitors for her hand and later he successfully evaded her request for a substantial sum of money. Mary wrote to a friend about the affair:

The conclusion of our friendship *a la Italiana* puts me in mind of a nursery rhyme which runs thus —

As I was going down Cranbourne lane,
Cranbourne lane was dirty,
And there I met a pretty maid,
Who dropt to me a curt'sey;
I gave her cakes, I gave her wine,
I gave her sugar candy,
But oh! the little naughty girl!
She asked me for some brandy

Now turn Cranbourne lane into Pisan acquaintances, which I am sure are dirty enough, & brandy into that wherewithall to buy brandy (& that no small sum *pero*) & you have [the] whole story of Shelley['s] Italian platonics.[8]

Emilia left the convent to marry in September 1821 — 'we hear that she leads him & his mother (to use a vulgarism) *a devil of a life,*' continued Mary with not a little satisfaction. Shelley withdrew *Epipsychidion* from publication. Some years later, in her short story *The Bride of Modern Italy* (1824), Mary portrayed a character based on Emilia as fickle and vain, and that based on Shelley as gullible and absurd.

In August 1821 Shelley finally made his promised visit to Byron in Ravenna, alone as requested. He had not seen his friend since the autumn of 1818 and they were both eager for the reunion. Shelley found Byron much improved from the spiritual reprobate of Venice. He was fit and strong and, for the first time, his relationship with a woman appeared beneficial to his health and disposition; the Countess Guiccioli was good for him. The first night together they sat up talking until five in the morning, a relief for Byron from the quiet and conversation-starved life he had been leading in the provincial town. They wasted no time during Shelley's limited visit:

> Lord Byron gets up at *two*. I get up, quite contrary to my usual custom, but one must sleep or die . . . After breakfast we sit talking till six. From six till eight we gallop through the pine forests which divide Ravenna from the sea; we then come home and dine, and sit up gossiping till six in the morning. I don't suppose this will kill me in a week or fortnight, but I shall not try it any longer.[9]

But there was the matter of Allegra and Claire to be discussed. Shelley hoped finally to resolve the problem in Claire's favour but Byron had no intention of giving up his daughter to a woman who was the subject of five years of irrational hatred. She was still writing to him, begging for permission to see her daughter and provoking his rage:

> Clare writes me the most insolent letters about Allegra — see what a man gets by taking care of natural children! — Were it not for the poor child's sake — I am almost tempted to send her back to her atheistical mother — but that would be too bad; you cannot conceive the excess of her insolence and I know not why — for I have been at great care and expence — taking a house in the country on purpose for her — she has *two* maids & every possible attention. — If Clare thinks she shall ever interfere with the child's morals or education — she mistakes — she never shall — The girl shall be a Christian and a married woman — if possible. — As to seeing her — she may see her — under proper restrictions — but She is not to throw every thing into confusion with her bedlam behaviour. — To express it delicately — I think Madame Clare is a damned bitch . . . [10]

Unable to control the life of his own legitimate daughter, Byron seemed bent on subjecting Claire to the same cruelty that Annabella and her family had inflicted upon him in their sequestration of Ada. If he was powerless and could not see Ada, the very least he could do, in blind bitterness, was to impose his will upon Claire. He had placed the little girl in an isolated convent school at Bagnacavallo, just outside Ravenna.

Shelley was always shocked by the coldness of Byron's treatment of Claire and his daughter whilst, much as he admired Shelley, Byron disapproved of his political and philosophical convictions — 'Surely he has talent — honour — but is crazy against religion and morality.'[11] He could not forget the hotel registers in Chamonix where, over four years before, his friend had written 'atheist' beside his name. It could not be denied; Byron had been shocked, and even his own extravagant immorality could not obliterate his Calvinist upbringing. The poet certainly enjoyed outraging friends and critics and was not shy of taking potshots at the Church, but he did not accost the Christian God and religion with Shelley's dedicated vigour. Shelley's vegetarianism also annoyed Byron, though he evidently did not perceive that his own peculiar diet — one undertaken purely for the sake of vanity — was at least equally eccentric. In another vein, he tried unsuccessfully to get Shelley to accept Pope as England's greatest poet and the Augustan school as the only valid poetic model. As Byron ultimately resisted Shelley's Wordsworthian evangelism in Geneva, so Shelley remained unconvinced about his friend's chosen master.

And the complexity and paradoxical nature of Byron's character still troubled the younger poet. The quintessential conflict that he had defined and commented on at Venice and in the verses of *Julian and Maddalo* was no more resolved than it had been. Byron continued to be torn between the affectations of the Regency buck — a style that he had adopted after arriving in the capital from a largely provincial upbringing — and the rarefied feeling of the poet. The sophisticated and irreverent man about town demanded a jaded manner; he must eschew any display of emotional depth or sensitivity. He clung fast to the behaviour that had brought him such social success in his youth, both before and after the publication of *Childe Harold*. At the same time, Byron was genuinely moved by the human plight, almost as much as he was influenced by the eighteenth-century concept of 'sensibility' and its correspondingly extravagant display of the sensitivity of the feelings, as exemplified by Goethe's *Young Werther*. It is not surprising that Goethe deemed Byron the greatest poet of his day and helped to establish his considerable reputation on the Continent. Shelley must have been equally confused by Byron's paradoxical political attitudes — he was proud of his aristocratic background and sure that his class should rule, but at the same time he was also dedicated to the principle of reform and his irreverence for all established and venerable institutions was instinctive. Disappointed, Shelley wrote to Hunt at the end of August 1821, 'Lord Byron . . . has many generous and exalted qualities, but the canker of aristocracy wants to be cut out.'

Shelley was not alone in noticing the Byronic paradox. Moore was troubled by his confusing and contradictory behaviour and did not even attempt to account for it in his biography, where he endeavoured to rationalize so many of his friend's foibles. In her *Conversations*, Lady Blessington comments on Byron's eccentric manner:

> He adopts a sort of Johnsonian tone, likes very much to be listened to, and seems to observe the effect he produces on the hearer. In mixed society his ambition is to appear the man of fashion; he adopts a light tone of badinage and persiflage that does not sit gracefully on him, but is always anxious to turn the subject to his own personal affairs, or feelings, which are either lamented with an air of melancholy, or dwelt on with a playful ridicule, according to the humour he happens to be in . . . [he] seems to take a peculiar pleasure in ridiculing sentiment, and romantic feelings; and yet the day after will betray both, to an extent that appears impossible to be sincere, to those who had heard his previous sarcasms: that he is sincere is evident, as his eyes fill with tears, his voice becomes tremulous, and his whole manner evinces that he feels what he says . . . He talks for effect, likes to excite astonishment, and certainly destroys in the minds of his auditors all confidence in his stability of character.[12]

Byron was uncertain ground, a wild moor pocked with dark and uncharted pools. Lady Blessington put her finger on precisely that vexing characteristic of Byron's personality that has left its stamp on the slippery narrator of *Don Juan*. That man of the world we also have difficulty trusting, though he begs, demands and charms us for our confidence. Byron's true nature is not found in the romantic poems of his early fame, *Childe Harold, The Giaour, The Corsair* or *Lara* but in the poetry of his exile, in the wicked humour, the political and moral satire, and true pathos of *Don Juan, Cain, Heaven and Earth* and *The Deformed Transformed*.

But Claire was a stronger influence on Byron's ambivalent attitude to Shelley. Byron's vehement and irrational hatred of her had grown steadily over the years, and yet she was protected and loved by Shelley. Much as Byron admired Shelley, he could not forgive him for his stepsister-in-law and it is possible, as Claire the monster grew and mutated in his imagination, that he saw Shelley as the catalyst that had brought them together in the first place. Claire had claimed his notice through her associations with Godwin and the young poet, and it was under Shelley's care that she was brought to him in Switzerland. Byron could not help but be angry at Shelley for his kindness to the silly girl. If Byron also felt guilty about his conduct to Claire, just eighteen and so naïve at their first meeting, then Shelley's presence might also have seemed a reproach.

And before Byron's involvement with the Gambas and the Carbonari, and his contribution to the cause of freedom, he once again showed the shabby side of his nature. He picked up the shady story of the Neapolitan charge — that Shelley had had a child by Claire which he later abandoned — from the once-loyal Hoppners. The Hoppners had heard the tale from the nursemaid Elise, who for some unknown reason was bent on destroying her former employers. The Hoppners shared it with Byron who 'confirmed' the story and believed it for a time:

> The Shiloh[13] story is true no doubt — though Elise is but a sort of *Queen's* evidence — you remember how eager she was to return to them — and then she goes away and abuses them. — Of the facts however there can be little doubt — it is just like them. — You may be sure that I keep your counsel.[14]

Byron did not reveal the Hoppners' prejudice until Shelley's visit to Ravenna. Shelley immediately informed Mary of the Hoppners' deceit (naturally Byron did not reveal his part in the generation of the story) and she responded on 10 August, eloquently and with indignation, defending her husband and giving no indication of their discord:

> Before I speak of these falsehoods permit [me] to say a few words concerning this miserable girl. You well know she formed an attachment with Paolo when we proceeded to Rome, & at Naples their marriage was talked of — We tried to dissuade her; we knew Paolo to be a rascal ... An accident led me to the knowledge that without marrying they had formed a connection; she was ill we sent for a docter who said there was a danger of a miscarriage ... we had them married ... she left us; turned Catholic at Rome, married him & then went to Florence ... we have seen little of them; but we have had knowledge that Paolo has formed a scheme of extorting money from Shelley by false accusations — he has written him threatening letters saying that he w^d be the ruin of him ... And now I come to her accusations — I must indeed summon all my courage while I transcribe them; for tears will force their way, and how can it be otherwise? You knew Shelley, you saw his face, & could you believe them? Believe them only on the testimony of a girl whom you despised? ... I am perfectly convinced, in my own mind that Shelley never had an improper connexion with Claire — At the time specified in ... Elise's letter, the winter after we quited ... Este ... we lived in

lodgings where I had momentary entrance into every room and such a thing could not have passed unknown to me. The malice of the girl is beyond all thought . . . Claire had no child — the rest must be false — but that you should believe it . . . That my beloved Shelley should stand thus slandered in your minds . . . Need I say that the union between my husband and . . . myself has ever been undisturbed — Love caused our first imprudences, love which improved by esteem, a perfect trust one in the other, a confidence and affection, which visited as we have been by severe calamities (have we not lost two children?) has encreased daily and knows no bounds.

I will add that Claire has been separated from us for about a year — She lives with a respectable German family at Florence — The reasons of this were obvious — her connexion with us made her manifest as the Miss Clairmont, the Mother of Allegra . . . and solely occupied with the idea of the welfare of her child, she wished to . . . appear such that she may not be thought in aftertimes to be unworthy of fulfilling the maternal duties — you ought to have paused before you tried to convince the father of her child of such unheard of atrocities on her part — If his generosity & knowledge of the world had not made him reject the slander with the ridicule it deserved . . . what irretrievable mischief you would have occasioned her.

Those who know me . . . well believe my simple word . . . but you, easy as you have been to credit evil, who may be more deaf to truth — to you I swear — by all that I hold sacred upon heaven & earth by a vow which I should die to write if I affirmed a falsehood — I swear by the life of my child, by my blessed & beloved child, that I know these accusations to be false . . . You were kind to us, and I shall never forget it; now I require justice; You must believe me, and do me, I solemnly entreat you, the justice to confess that you do so.

But the Hoppners never responded to her bold defence. Mary's letter, which was sent care of Byron to be forwarded, probably never reached its destination — the testimonial of her fierce loyalty to her husband was discovered amongst Byron's papers after his death. Could Byron have simply forgotten to send the letter, or did Mary's remarks on his innocence in the matter deter him? Was the temptation to destroy Claire so great that it could overcome his loyalty to his friend?

Following the failure of the Carbonari plot and the Neapolitan uprising, the Gambas were to be exiled. After some indecision, they were persuaded by Shelley's invitation to Byron and his adopted family to join the Shelleys in Pisa. Byron happily accepted and, with the Gambas, moved into the Palazzo Lanfranchi, which Mary had already rented for him, in November 1821. One of the grandest and oldest palaces on the Arno — its magnificent staircase was reputedly the work of Michelangelo[15] — Lanfranchi was even more forbidding than Mocenigo. It had deep dungeons and cells hollowed out within the thick walls. It was rumoured that its former occupants had been driven out by its noisy ghosts and the loyal Fletcher, still attending Byron as valet, took fright. He demanded a different bedroom, only to find the second even more full of unquiet spirits than the first. Byron too was disturbed by bumps in the night, familiar after the 'haunted' bedroom at Newstead, and he was delighted. He settled in with a new billiards table and a suite of eight servants.

Byron and Shelley were once again in close contact — here was another opportunity to point the noble poet in the right direction, Shelley believed. They formed the sparkling centre of a lively constellation. Gathered around them were Englishmen and women in exile, all removed from their birthplace in order to live out the unconventional life-styles so impossible at the time in England. They gained intimacy with the notorious poets through the strength of their introductions. In January Thomas Medwin, Shelley's second cousin and childhood friend, arrived in Pisa with Jane and Edward Williams. Medwin bored Mary and Percy but he was tolerated. He 'is infinitely commonplace and is as silent as a firescreen but not half so useful; except that he sometimes mends a pen,' quipped Mary in a letter to Claire on 21 January 1821.

Jane and Edward's tale was almost as romantic as Mary and Shelley's own. Edward, a retired army officer on half-pay, was handsome, friendly and intelligent. He was a talented draughtsman and his drawings of the group (sadly none of Shelley survive) are full of character. He met Jane, beautiful and serene (a serenity chiefly due to dullness and shallowness of character) in India after she had fled from her cruel husband. Though they lived as husband and wife they were not married. After two years together their mutual passion was still strong and obvious — no doubt reminding Mary and Shelley, not without some pain, of the glorious early days of their own love. Like Claire, Jane had a sweet singing voice, and the couple endeared themselves to the Shelleys immediately. Edward's pleasure in sailing matched Shelley's own.

But one important star, who would have added to the brilliancy of the Byron-Shelley gathering, was missing. John Keats had died at Rome in February 1821 at the age of twenty-five. Shelley, who had met him at the Hunts' in Hampstead in December 1816, had invited him to Pisa. Keats would have come, but the consumption that had brought him reluctantly to the warmth of Italy, and away from his fiancée Fanny Brawne, was already well advanced. In fact, there had been no real chance of a recovery. In his sadness for the untimely death of a promising poet who had also suffered so undeservedly at the hands of the critics, Shelley wrote *Adonais*, the elegy, which, unbeknownst to them all, would serve for his own. But to Byron, sorry as he was at the young man's death, the deceased had been a low-bred Cockney poetaster who had defied the legacy of the great Pope. Johnny 'Piss-a-bed' Keats, as Byron called him, had allegedly been killed by a harsh review. Byron thought *Hyperion* admirable, but not particularly remarkable. It should be noted that Keats's great odes, those on which his reputation stands today, were still largely unread, though some had been published, at the time of his death.

Edward Trelawny, another friend of Medwin, arrived in Pisa at the beginning of 1822. Trelawny, a Cornishman, had served in the Navy. He was a self-styled adventurer who had carefully modelled his behaviour and 'career' on the figure of Byron's Corsair. He was certainly striking in appearance, outdoing the Corsair, the Giaour, or Byron himself for that matter with his Byronic looks, and it suited his romantic self-image to let his new friends believe that he might have at least a little Arab blood. Mary was especially pleased with his appearance and described him to her friend Maria Gisborne on 9 February 1822:

> a kind of half Arab Englishman ... he is six feet high — raven black hair which curls thickly & shortly like a Moors, dark, grey — expressive eyes — overhanging brows upturned lips & a smile which expresses good nature & kindheartedness — his shoulders are high like an Orientalist — his voice is monotonous yet emphatic & his language as he relates the events of his life energetic & simple — whether the tale be one of blood & horror or of irrisistable comedy His company is delightful for he excites me to think ...

Trelawny had been longing to meet Byron since the publication of *The Corsair* in 1814, and he believed, whole-heartedly, in the particular identity of the poet as portrayed in his fiction. It is hardly surprising that Byron did not live up to Trelawny's fantasies. He had long ago abandoned Harold for the sometimes cynical, sometimes sincere narrator of *Don Juan*, a persona that fitted him much better than many of his friends and admirers realized. Trelawny was disabused of his illusions about Byron but still managed to become his friend. The poet made him captain of his new boat, the *Bolivar*. But Trelawny attached himself unreservedly to Shelley, never doubting his integrity for a moment, and for the rest of his life, after a six-month friendship, would devote himself to Shelley's memory, even reserving the plot next to the poet's grave for his own. He would also devote himself, through a constant, changing narrative that grew ever more unreliable with the years, to elevating his own position in regard to the two poets and colouring his exploits in their company with spectacular vainglory.

He was also delighted with Mary, daughter of the famous Wollstone-craft, her 'calm, grey eyes' and her impressive facility of expression. But, with considerable artistic licence, he contrasted her charming practicality with Shelley's other-worldliness, laying the foundation for the creation of the 'Shelley myth': the poet as visionary and impractical, a misunderstood genius devoted to the mind and spirit. Trelawny described their first meeting in January 1822:

Swiftly gliding in, blushing like a girl, a tall thin stripling held out both his hands; and although I could hardly believe as I looked at his flushed, feminine, and artless face that it could be the Poet, I returned his warm pressure. After the ordinary greetings and courtesies he sat down and lis-tened. I was silent from astonishment: was it possible this mild-looking, beardless boy, could be the veritable monster at war with all the world? — excommunicated by the fathers of the Church, deprived of his civil rights by the fiat of a grim Lord Chancellor, discarded by every member of his family, and denounced by the rival sages of our literature as the founder of the Satanic school? I could not believe it; it must be a hoax. He was habited like a boy, in a black jacket and trowsers, which he seemed to have outgrown, or his tailor, as is the custom, had most shamefully stinted him in his 'sizings'. Mrs. Williams saw my embarrassment, and to relieve me asked Shelley what book he had in his hand? His face brightened, and he answered briskly.

'Calderon's Magico Prodigioso, I am translating some passages in it.'

'Oh, read it to us!'

Shoved off from the shore of common-place incidents that could not interest him, and fairly launched on a theme that did, he instantly became oblivious of everything but the book in his hand. The masterly manner in which he analysed the genius of the author, his lucid interpretation of the story, and the ease with which he translated into our language the most subtle and imaginative passages of the Spanish poet, were marvellous, as was his command of the two languages. After this touch of his quality I no longer doubted his identity; a dead silence ensued; looking up, I asked,

'Where is he?'

Mrs. Williams said, 'Who? Shelley? Oh, he comes and goes like a spirit, no one knows when or where.'

Presently he re-appeared with Mrs. Shelley. She brought us back from the ideal world Shelley had left us in, to the real one, welcomed me to Italy, and asked me the news of London and Paris, the new books, operas, and bonnets, marriages, murders, and other marvels. The Poet vanished and tea appeared.'[16]

Trelawny was not alone in his fermentation of the myth. Leigh Hunt also idealized Shelley to an astonishing degree in his memoirs, adding, he 'was like a spirit that had darted out of its orb, and found itself on another planet. I used to tell him that he had come from the planet Mercury.'[17] Modern critics have convicted Mary of sole responsibility for creating the 'Shelley myth', but the example was there before she even took up her own pen in reminiscence.

The tranquil life that Byron had grown accustomed to in Ravenna persisted in Pisa, but he shared it enthusiastically with the circle of friends. He even organized his friends to stage theatricals at Lanfranchi and brought his scheme to mount *Othello* for the Pisan public as far as rehearsals. He still breakfasted late, at around two in the afternoon, and at three or four was often joined by Medwin, Teresa's brother Count Pietro, Williams, Trelawny and Shelley. After a game of billiards, Byron set off in his carriage for the town gates where his horses waited — he was still the object of outraged curiosity and he went undercover through the town to avoid the stares of the English tourists. Meeting the others already on horseback, and often accompanied by Mary and Teresa in the carriage, they made for a farm where Byron had bought permission to shoot at targets. The two poets were both good shots and Byron revelled in his frequent successes, but a poor average for the day could send him home in a foul mood just before sunset. If he still felt buoyant after his exercise, the men gathered for dinner in the sumptuous rooms of his palazzo. Never 'did he display himself to more advantage than on these occasions,' reported Shelley, 'being at once polite and cordial, full of social hilarity and the most perfect good humour; never diverging into ungraceful merriment, and yet keeping up the spirit of liveliness throughout the evening.'[18]

As at Diodati in 1816, the women were not invited to these regular parties — even a grand feast held on Christmas day — and they spent much time together, Mary growing fond of Teresa. Byron and Shelley had resumed their former pleasure in one another's company, and Mary wrote to Maria Gisborne on 7 March 1822, for 'the present S. is entangled with Lord B. who is in a terrible fright lest he should desert him'. In contrast to Byron's routine, Shelley rose early, around six or seven, and read Spinoza, Plato or Sophocles while chewing dry bread, his favourite food. He then sailed on the Arno with Williams, book in hand. On the days that he didn't join Byron and the others he then retired into the forest or to the river bank to think and compose, returning in the evening to take his dinner at home or at Lanfranchi.

In March 1822, soon after Trelawny's arrival, the friends were involved in an incident which further antagonized the authorities towards Byron. The group was returning to Pisa in the evening from pistol practice, Mary and Teresa following in the carriage. As they approached the city gates on horseback, a soldier galloped through their ranks, jostling and frightening their horses. Refusing to suffer the insult, the men, no doubt still flushed with their success at the pistol range, pursued the soldier, Shelley in the vanguard. They demanded satisfaction, believing the drunken man to be an officer. He responded with curses and the threat of arrest. Byron laughed at this and the men rode at speed back to the city gates, the enraged soldier in pursuit. Byron and Gamba passed through but, unsheathing his sabre before Shelley, Captain Hay (a friend of Byron) and the others could follow, the soldier slashed madly, wounding Hay and causing Shelley to be thrown from his horse. He was unconscious for some time. The mêlée continued into the town, Byron challenging the soldier with a sword stick until one of his servants, thinking his master had been killed, wounded the soldier with a pitchfork.

The authorities in Ravenna had been powerless to react officially to Byron's participation in the Carbonari débâcle of July 1821, and could only remove him from the state by exiling the Gambas. When the English Milord became personally involved in an assault on an Italian soldier, the Pisan government, in turn, were determined to revenge the insult to their sovereignty and to rid themselves of the trouble-making foreigner by once again banishing the Gambas. For the rest of the spring and throughout the summer Byron waited to learn the Gambas' fate, and thus his own, as the two were now inextricably bound together. On 29 June the Pisan authorities banished the Counts Gamba from Tuscany. Byron would follow them to Genoa in September.

Soon after that event, in April, they learned of the death of five-year-old Allegra from typhus at her lonely convent outside Ravenna. Shelley had gone to see her in August 1821, and the girl had appeared happy. She was the favourite of the nuns and she took Shelley around her secluded home, showing him her favourite haunts. He had left reassured of her welfare (though later he and Mary would come to hear stories of food shortages in the area and that the austere convent school was known to be for families of the poor). They had not been informed, however, that by 1822 an epidemic of typhus was raging in the Romagna. They had trusted Byron to look after Allegra and he had failed them. But before they could bring themselves to tell Claire, still residing in Florence and enjoying an active role in high society there, the Pisan circle was broken up. The different households sought country retreats on the coast for the six months of summer and, though Byron and Shelley remained in close contact, their daily intimacy was at an end.

Plate 9 Anne Isabella Milbanke, Lady Byron.

*Plate 10 Countess Teresa Guiccioli, Byron's last and most enduring
mistress.*

Plate 11   Claire Clairmont, Mary Shelley's step-sister.

Plate 12 Edward John Trelawny, self-aggrandizing adventurer and friend of Byron and the Shelleys.

Plate 13 Leigh Hunt, *editor of the* Examiner *and friend of Keats, the Shelleys and Byron.*

Plate 14 Casa Magni at La Spezia, Shelley's last home, which was detested by Mary.

Canto 6th   1822.

1.

"There is a Tide in the affairs of Men
"Which taken at the flood" — you know the rest,
And most of us have proved it now and then;
At least one thinks so, though but few have guessed
The moment till too late to come again —
But no doubt every thing is for the best —
Of which the surest sign is, in the end,
When things are at the worst they sometimes mend.

2.

There is a tide too in the Affairs of Women
"Which taken at the flood or leads," — God knows where,
Those Navigators must be able Seamen
Whose Charts lay down its' currents to a hair;
Not all the reveries of Jacob Behmen
With its' strange whirls and eddies can compare:
Men with their heads reflect on this and that —
But woman with their hearts or Heaven knows what!

or,

Man with his head reflects — (as Spurzheim tells)
But woman with the heart — or something else. —

or,

Man's pensive part is (man & figure) the head —
But Woman's the heart — or anything instead.

Plate 16 One of the last portraits of Byron, taken from life just before his departure for Greece in 1823. The sketch is by Count D'Orsay, companion of Lord and Lady Blessington.

CHAPTER VIII

THE GULF OF SPEZIA AND DEATH

B Y THE END OF APRIL 1822 the Shelleys had settled with Jane and Edward Williams in a secluded house overhanging the sea in the sheltered and quiet Gulf of Spezia, about forty miles up the coast from Livorno. Mary hated her new home, the Casa Magni, its isolation, the barren scenery and the surliness of the Genovese peasantry. She must have missed Teresa Guiccioli with whom she had formed a close friendship, delighted and surprised by her sincerity, culture and genuine devotion to Byron.

To compound the sense of gloom that surrounded the Casa Magni for Mary, Claire came to spend a few days with them and they finally told her of Allegra's death. The grief that they had suffered so recently when they first learned the terrible news themselves, they suffered again with the mother. Years of separation during which Claire had planned and fantasized about a reunion with her daughter had ended abruptly in desolation. Mary was relieved when her devastated stepsister returned to Florence, clutching the small portrait of her daughter and a lock of her hair that Byron, with unexpected kindness, had finally sent.

Much as she liked them, Edward in particular, Mary felt crowded by the Williamses and their two children and resented their enforced intimacy; the house was small — a single storey over an unpaved ground floor — and their bedrooms adjoined one another around a large central dining-room. Housekeeping was difficult; the area was so impoverished that Mary and Jane had to travel for miles around to collect enough food. The servants of the two families, in the separate quarters behind the house, quarrelled incessantly. 'No words can tell . . . how I hated our house & the country about it,' she would later write.[1] The sea, which washed the lower floor, dominated all.

Though Mary so disliked Casa Magni and their situation, Shelley was delighted. He was free for the first time in many years from his chronic pains and he revelled in his favourite variety of landscape: the open, the wild and the desolate. He was at work on a major poem, *The Triumph of Life*,[2] evoking the spirit of Rousseau and, no doubt, the summer of 1816 and the excursion around the lake of Geneva with

Byron. To complete his joy, his own boat was moored on the beach below his home. He was concerned about Mary's latest depression, but he realized that there was little he could do for her. Wishing to spare her further grief, he kept Godwin's disturbing letters from her, with their urgent demands for funds and their descriptions of his continued financial distress. Mary had suffered a miscarriage on 16 June and had haemorrhaged severely. Shelley plunged her into a bath of ice water to arrest the flow of blood and when the doctor congratulated him on his quick thinking — he almost certainly saved her life — he was deeply gratified. Her physical recovery was slow, and her spiritual recovery still slower. Shelley grew impatient with her; her depression was starving him of the emotional support that he himself required. 'I only feel the want of those who can feel and understand me,' he wrote to his friend John Gisborne on 18 June, 'whether from proximity and the continuity of domestic intercourse, Mary does not. It is the curse of Tantalus, that a person possessing such excellent powers and so pure a mind as hers, should not excite the sympathy indispensable to their application to domestic life.'

Shelley was also disturbed by visions and nightmares. One night he terrified Mary by his screams and apparent sleepwalking as he rushed into the room where she lay ill. In panic when she could not rouse him, she hurried to the Williamses for help. Later, when he recovered his senses, Shelley described his vision to Mary, insisting that it was no dream:

> lying as he did in bed Edward & Jane came into him, they were in the most horrible condition, their bodies lacerated — their bones starting though their skin, the faces pale yet stained with blood, they could hardly walk, but Edward was the weakest & Jane was supporting him — Edward said — Get up, Shelley, the sea is flooding the house & it is all coming down'. S. got up, he thought, & went to the . . . window that looked on the terrace & the sea & thought he saw the sea rushing in. Suddenly his vision changed & he saw the figure of himself strangling me . . . [3]

Shelley's seemingly prophetic dreams and visions were catching. He himself had others — he saw the infant Allegra dancing over the waves and his own image greeted him with the words, 'How long do you mean to be content?' Even the unimaginative Jane swore that she saw Shelley's *Doppelgänger* pass twice along the terrace.

But Shelley, like Byron, sought solace and rejuvenation in love and he had already chosen a new object to fascinate him — the agreeable but otherwise ordinary Jane Williams. She had a fine singing voice and Shelley gave her a guitar with which to accompany herself. She inspired some of Shelley's most beautiful poems and lyrics, such as 'To Jane, The Recollection' and 'To Jane, The Invitation' and 'With a Guitar', but it was rather the intense love that she and Edward shared that so fascinated him. He and Mary had shared such a love, and now it seemed to be gone.

Not surprisingly, Shelley's poems to Jane are characterized by a yearning for communion, but at the same time show his painful knowledge of exclusion from that ideal. This is particularly striking in 'The Serpent I Shut Out from Paradise' (Byron's new nickname for Shelley was 'the snake' — a relation, they both jested, of the snake which had tempted Eve in the Garden of Eden):

VI

The crane o'er seas and forests seeks her home;
No bird so wild, but has its quiet nest,
   When it no more would roam;
The sleepless billows on the ocean's breast
Break like a bursting heart, and die in foam,
   And thus, at length, find rest:
Doubtless there is a place of peace
Where *my* weak heart and all its throbs will cease.

Jane, for her part, was deeply in love with Edward. Though in later years she made much of her ascendancy over the poet — primarily to hurt Mary, it seems — she was too shallow, as Emilia Viviani had been, truly to understand him. Indeed, like many of his critics and most vicious enemies, she was profoundly baffled by his behaviour. One day, while she was sitting on the beach with her children, Shelley persuaded her to join him in the small and treacherous skiff that Edward had recently built. Shelley passed many hours drifting idly in the shallows, thinking and composing, in what amounted to little more than a large waterproof basket. Nevertheless, as soon as Jane and her two babies had settled themselves into the wicker-framed boat, he rowed straight out from the beach into deep water. Jane was terrified, too terrified to protest in fact, and stared death in the face as Shelley suggested that they 'solve the great mystery' together. If Shelley was half in love with death, Jane Williams was decidedly repelled by it. She suggested that they should postpone the investigation as she hadn't dined yet, and her children were hungry. Shelley, sadly, made for shore. She told her bewildered husband that she would never again get into a boat with Shelley. Her appreciation of the other-worldly poet would only go so far.

Trelawny, meanwhile, sailed regularly between Lerici and Byron's Villa Dupuy at Montenero, just south of Livorno. Byron had moved there in May, finding nothing suitably grand for a summer residence in the poor, undeveloped neighbourhood of his friends up the coast. Trelawny had taken command of the schooner *Bolivar*, which Byron had lost interest in as soon as it was delivered from the shipbuilders in Genoa. Anticipating the arrival of the ever-growing Hunt family with its six children, Byron and Shelley had devised a new journal that the accomplished literary editor was to run. *The Liberal* would give a voice to the spirit of the South and its literary views on the eagerly anticipated surge forward in political reform. The first offerings in the journal's very short life were from its proprietors. The first edition, published on 15 October 1822, consisted mainly of writing by Hunt, while Byron offered *The Vision of Judgement*, a politically satirical prose piece, and some epigrams, and Shelley contributed a translation in verse from Goethe's *Faust*.

Shelley was excited by the venture, Byron less so (though both had sent money for the Hunts' passage to Italy). Byron began to withdraw from the project almost as soon as Hunt arrived. He insulted Hunt openly and in letters to England. He regretted his role in bringing the hapless man and his family to Italy where they were now his responsibility. Shelley, not surprisingly, was angered by Byron's change of heart. Less than eight months earlier he had been full of hope for his friend, but now the patrician poet had disappointed him again.

After his visit to Ravenna in August 1821 Shelley had been recharged with his original enthusiasm for Byron; he seemed to be fulfilling Shelley's designs for his artistic career. As the great poem took shape, he grew more and more hopeful for *Don Juan*. He read Cantos III–V and he was awed by their power and reassured that they would not repeat the mistakes of the first two cantos. He wrote, full of praise, contrasting Byron's latest efforts with his earlier: 'The few passages which any one might desire to be cancelled in the 1st & 2nd Cantos are here reduced almost to nothing.' Shelley's reservations dissolved. He wrote to Byron on 21 October 1821:

> This poem carries with it at once the stamp of originality and defiance of imitation. Nothing has ever been written like it in English — nor if I may venture to prophesy, will there be; without carrying upon it the mark of a secondary and borrowed light — You unveil & present in its true deformity what is worst in human nature, & this is what the witlings of the age murmur at, conscious of their want of power to endure the scrutiny of such a light. — We are damned to the knowledge of good & evil, and it is . . . well for us to know what we should avoid no less than what we should seek . . . The fifth canto, which some . . . said was *dull*, gathers instead of loses, splendour & energy — the language in which the whole is clothed . . . is such as these lisping days could not have expected, — and are, believe me, in spite of the approbation which you wrest from them — little pleased to hear.

Shelley's praise had been sincere. He was almost satisfied. Byron had finally begun to exercise his full powers, but Shelley maintained his vigilance:

> This sort of writing only on a great plan & perhaps in a more compact form is what I wished you to do when I made my vows for an epic. — But I am content — You are building up a drama, such as England has not yet seen, and the task is sufficiently noble & worthy of you.

But the highpoint of *Don Juan* was succeeded by disappointment. Now Byron had veered from the path again in his rejection of Hunt and Shelley was out of patience. 'I detest all society — almost all,' he wrote, 'and Lord Byron is the nucleus of all that is hateful and tiresome in it . . . [He] is so mentally capricious that the least impulse drives him from his anchorage,' he wrote to John Gisborne on 18 June 1822. The 'canker of aristocracy' had not left Byron's soul, as far as Shelley could tell, and he seemed further away than ever from the project that the younger poet determined he should undertake. Indeed, in the interval, for nearly a year, Teresa had actually succeeded in persuading Byron to give up writing *Don Juan* and to cease upsetting the establishment at home in England. Shelley's enthusiastic approbation had obviously meant nothing, he discovered. To add to his gall, he could not help but resent the more famous poet's success even more: 'I do not write — I have lived too long near Lord Byron & the sun has extinguished the glowworm.'[4] He knew that he and Byron were more divided than ever — 'there is a great gulf fixed, which by the nature of things must daily become wider.'[5]

Shelley's greatest pleasure and preoccupation that summer was his new boat: he could forget about the recalcitrant Byron and the brooding Mary with his new occupation. As a boy he had dreamed of owning his own ocean-going boat, spending hours floating small paper vessels down the streams and rivers of England, imagining high winds in the Mediterranean or the Atlantic. On 12 May 1822, he took delivery of his boat. 'Shelley's boat is a beautiful creature,' wrote Mary. But the beauty had a blemish. When her construction was to have been a partnership between Williams and Trelawny, Trelawny named her *Don Juan* in honour of Byron. When Shelley took on the expense of her construction by himself, he wished to rename her *Ariel*, and informed her builders of the change. But when she arrived from the boatyard in Genoa, 'Don Juan' was painted in huge red letters across the sail. Byron had learned of Shelley's intention and had insisted on the original name. For 'days and nights full twenty one did Shelley and Edward ponder on her anabaptism, and the washing out the primeval stain,' wrote Mary to Maria Gisborne on 2 June, much amused. They scrubbed at the offending words without success and finally cut out the piece and grafted in a new patch of sail. They were satisfied, but the boat remained the *Don Juan* and Shelley gave up his *Ariel*.

It hardly mattered. Shelley was perhaps happier than he had ever been, relinquishing his ambition and anxieties. He sailed every day in the Bay of Spezia and further out into the Gulf of Genoa. He sailed down to Livorno, less than a day's journey, and travelled frequently to Pisa. Even Mary took pleasure in her voyages with Shelley. The boat had been expensive — £80 — but was well worth it. Shelley wrote to John Gisborne on 18 June:

> it is swift and beautiful, and appears quite a vessel. Williams is captain, and we drive along this delightful bay in the evening wind, under the summer moon, until earth appears another world. Jane brings her guitar, and if the past and future could be obliterated, the present would content me so well that I could say with Faust to the passing moment, 'Remain, thou, thou art so beautiful.'

The sailors planned visits to islands in the Gulf, and even talked of voyages in the vast and threatening Atlantic.

But it was clear that Shelley and Williams, even though the latter had served two years in the Navy, overreached themselves in a boat that was ill-designed and difficult to handle in seas considered capricious by even the most seasoned sailors of the Mediterranean. It was twenty-four feet in length but completely undecked. It required two tons of ballast to sit securely and drew four feet of water, so that it was impossible to bring it in close enough to the beach — hence the construction of the equally unseaworthy skiff. The boat was extremely fast, not least because she carried far too much sail for her size. Trelawny had advised that they should employ a crew of three, but they made do with Charles Vivian, the boy whom Trelawny had originally sent with the boat from Genoa. When Trelawny accompanied the two enthusiastic but largely unskilled sailors into the Bay, he was considerably alarmed. Shelley tried to read the whole time, even with one hand on the tiller. He didn't listen to the commands of Williams, the nominal commander, and laughed with pleasure when they bungled a basic manoeuvre. Trelawny cautioned Williams:

> You will do no good with Shelley ... until you heave his books and papers overboard; shear the wisps of hair that hang over his eyes; and plunge his arms up to the elbows in a tar-bucket. And you, captain, will have no authority, until you dowse your frock coat and cavalry boots. You see I am stripped for a swim, so please, whilst I am on board, to keep within swimming distance of the land.[6]

Though Trelawny's *Recollections* were written with richly embroidered hindsight and the determination to present himself in a masterly and heroic light throughout, it was clear that Shelley, completely unqualified, was seduced by the threatening sea.

On 1 July Shelley and Edward set sail in the *Don Juan* for Livorno to meet the Hunts, who had sailed from Genoa on the last leg of their long and gruelling journey from London. Marianne had been ill during the voyage, as she so often was, and Shelley, who always had the name of a good doctor, accompanied them to Pisa. Dr Vacca, greatly respected by the English community (indeed, Shelley had settled near Pisa to be close to him) offered on this occasion an erroneous diagnosis — Marianne's death was imminent, he declared sadly. In fact Marianne would live for another thirty-five years and bear more children, but Shelley was concerned for Hunt and what he supposed would be his motherless brood. Eager to get his latest project under way and make the editor of *The Liberal* as comfortable as possible, Shelley helped to settle the family into the ground-floor apartment at the Palazzo Lanfranchi, where he had selected simple, inexpensive furniture, paid for by Byron. Before Hunt realized that the furnishings had been Shelley's choice, he complained about Byron's meanness and the magnificence of his host's rooms as compared to his own.

Shelley returned to Livorno and the *Don Juan* and prepared to sail home to Casa Magni on 8 July, just a few weeks before his thirtieth birthday. Edward was restless to return to Lerici and Jane and would not be delayed any longer. Trelawny had intended to leave port on the *Bolivar* in convoy with his inexperienced friends, but at the last minute he was stopped by the customs officials and ordered back to port for papers. The *Don Juan* would press on, despite Trelawny's advice that they wait out a line squall, just visible on the horizon. They left port, followed by Trelawny's spyglass, until they disappeared from his view in a sea mist. Very soon a violent storm swept over the harbour. Fishing boats and fellucas sped into the safety of port, sails were furled, masts struck, second anchors dropped. Trelawny was immediately concerned for the *Don Juan*. He was sure that Shelley and Williams would turn back to the harbour, and his anxiety grew as boats returning over that day and the next reported no sighting of the English vessel. Trelawny was alarmed. He knew that had the boat foundered, no one would have come to its rescue:

> So remorselessly are the quarantine laws enforced in Italy, that, when at sea, if you render assistance to a vessel in distress, or rescue a drowning stranger, on returning to port you are condemned to a long and rigorous quarantine of fourteen or more days. The consequence is, should one vessel see another in peril, or even run it down by accident, she hastens

on her course, and by general accord, not a word is said or reported on the subject.[7]

And ominously, one of Trelawny's sailors swore that he saw an English-made oar from the *Don Juan* on the deck of one of the new arrivals.

On the third day Trelawny rode into Pisa and to Byron's home, hoping for a letter from Casa Magni with news of the sailors' safe return. Byron too was alarmed, 'his lip quivered, and his voice faltered'. Trelawny dispatched the *Bolivar* to patrol the coast and he himself rode north along the sea. Maybe the *Don Juan* had made for Elba or Corsica in the storm and he would receive some word soon.

Meanwhile, on 12 July, Mary and Jane received a letter from Leigh Hunt in Pisa, inquiring whether the men had returned safely. The *Don Juan* had left Livorno on the 8th; the men were four days overdue on a voyage of less than seventy-five kilometres, a day's sail. Mary was still sick with depression and the effects of her miscarriage but her premonition of evil was too strong, she could no longer simply wait at home for news. She and Jane Williams left the Casa Magni immediately and set out for Pisa, arriving in the middle of the night at the Palazzo Lanfranchi. Hunt was asleep, but Byron and Teresa received the two women. The poet was deeply struck by Mary's terror and told Lady Blessington, the following year, about her dramatic entrance:

> I never can forget the night that his poor wife rushed into my room at Pisa, with a face pale as marble, and terror impressed on her brow, demanding with all the tragic impetuosity of grief and alarm, where was her husband! Vain were all our efforts to calm her; a desperate sort of courage seemed to give her energy to confront the horrible truth that awaited her; it was the courage of despair. I have seen nothing in tragedy on the stage so powerful, or so affecting, as her appearance, and it often presents itself to my memory.[8]

Finally, ten days later Trelawny confirmed their fears. At Viareggio, half-way between Livorno and Lerici, he learned that some bottles, a water-keg and a familiar small skiff had been washed ashore. And then two bodies were discovered on the beach, one at Viareggio and the second three miles away. Identification was not immediate but, inevitably, it came. Mary and Jane, having lived for so long in a horrifying limbo, knew at last that they were widows. Williams's body was identified by a black silk kerchief. Shelley's body, almost as badly decomposed and fish-eaten as Williams's, was found with a book of Keats's poems in the pocket, bent back upon itself as if stuffed hurriedly away with the approach of the high winds. Weeks later, further down the coast, the remains of Charles Vivian were also found.

The myth that sees Shelley as romantically embracing his own destruction — gathered into the storm — reaches its apotheosis in the story surrounding the wreck of the *Don Juan* and the funerals. Shelley's careless attitude to his own death, first expressed when he and Byron nearly drowned on the Lake of Geneva in 1816, has no doubt fed the erroneous notion of high romance surrounding his eventual death in similar circumstances — a man too spiritual to further sustain a corporeal presence on earth, Shelley sailed purposely into the eye of a Mediterranean storm to greet death. The reality is somewhat more banal: poor and inexperienced seamanship, a badly designed boat and a disregard for local weather conditions caused not only his own death, but that of two others. Byron harboured no such fantasies about the beauty and seductiveness of death. He is said to have remarked upon the remains of Williams as they were removed from the sand:

> What *is* a *human* body! Why it might be the rotten carcase of a sheep for all I can distinguish! . . . Look an old rag retains its form longer than he who wove it. What an humbling and degrading thought that we shall one day resemble this![9]

Trelawny escorted the traumatized widows back to Pisa and, with their blessing, took it upon himself to arrange the funerals, with an eye towards drama and the gory detail. The strict laws of quarantine forbade the transportation of a corpse for any distance and Trelawny decided practically, but also one imagines with some satisfaction, to cremate the bodies, with Homeric ritual, at the places where they were found. It was with the utmost difficulty that he obtained permission to exhume the bodies, buried in the sand immediately after their discovery, and to burn them on the beach. Under the careful eye of Pisan soldiers dispatched to oversee the proceedings, Trelawny executed his spectacle. Mary and Jane could not bring themselves to attend the ceremonies, but waited anxiously for an account of the funerals.

It took the officials some time to locate Shelley's body in the sand on 16 August and finally, with the hollow clunk of the shovel, they realized that they had struck the skull of the corpse. Quicklime had speeded up the process of decomposition; the friends must have been disturbed by what they found. Byron, as usual in moments of stress or discomfort, was flippant and Trelawny, with his usual elaboration of such events, 'remembered' years later that Byron asked him for the poet's skull. Citing the story of the monk's head drinking cup of Newstead, Trelawny refused (or simply included this exchange in his memoirs the better to show himself off as the protector of Shelley's sacred memory). The body was removed to a cast-iron bier built to Trelawny's order. An enormous fire was kindled beneath and, as the flames grew high, wine, oil, salt and frankincense were poured upon the burning corpse. They waited and watched as the body burned. Hunt recalled:

> the flame of the fire bore away towards heaven in vigorous amplitude, waving and quivering with a brightness of inconceivable beauty. It seemed as though it contained the glassy essence of vitality. You might have expected a seraphic countenance to look out of it, turning once more, before it departed, to thank the friends that had done their duty.[10]

Trelawny was more prosaic and decidedly ghoulish in his observations:

> The heat from the sun and fire was so intense that the atmosphere was tremulous and wavy. The corpse fell open and the heart was laid bare. The frontal bone of the skull, where it had been struck with the mattock, fell off; and, as the back of the head rested on the red-hot bottom bars of the furnace, the brains literally seethed, bubbled, and boiled as in a cauldron, for a very long time.[11]

Byron was appalled by the hideous mortality of his friend. He had witnessed the exhumation of all three corpses and human decay struck him so forcibly that, as Williams's remains were removed from the sand, he struck his man-of-fashion pose and joked with hollow dispassion on death. But he was deeply moved. Not waiting for the completion of Shelley's cremation, he removed his clothes and swam out from the beach, in the direction of the moored *Bolivar*. Trelawny, meanwhile, noticed that the heart did not burn. Unable to resist the romantic potential of such a phenomenon, he reached into the dying flames and plucked it out with his bare hands, burning them severely in the process. The fire died down, the ashes and fragments that remained were gathered into a box and brought aboard the *Bolivar*. Everyone returned to their homes and Trelawny arranged for the ashes to be transported to the Protestant cemetery at Rome and buried next to the remains of little William, in the shadow of the Cestius pyramid. The preserved heart that Trelawny snatched from the bier was eventually given to Hunt. Only after considerable quarrelling would Hunt finally give it to Mary, and it would not be laid to rest until 1851.

Mary's journal of that summer stopped abruptly on Monday 8 July 1822. Two hundred and twenty-six empty pages followed. With the exception of a meticulous, detailed account of her bleak summer and the shipwreck, sent as a letter to Maria Gisborne, Mary's pen was silenced by shock and grief; her 'blank moral death' had begun. All the premonitions of doom that had haunted her since her happiness with Shelley began — a happiness that began to grow and appear unclouded in retrospect — seemed to be fulfilled. The deaths of the premature baby, of Clara and of William had all been leading up to this greatest of abandonments. The very centre of her life was obliterated. She was instantly overcome with loneliness.

Mary's grief at Shelley's death would remain a theme that dominated the rest of her life. She poured out her loneliness and despair in her new journal — 'The Journal of Sorrow —/ Begun 1822/ But for my Child it could not/ End too soon'. She began on 2 October:

> I have now no friend. For eight years I communicated with unlimited freedom with one whose genius, far transcending mine, awakened & guided my thoughts; I conversed with him; rectified my errors of judgement, obtained new lights from him, & my mind was satisfied. Now I am alone! Oh, how alone! The stars may behold my tears, & the winds drink my sighs . . . no eye answers mine . . . my voice can with none assume its natural modulation, all is shew — & I but a shadow — What a change! Oh my beloved Shelley — It is not true that this heart was cold to thee. Tell me, for now you know all things — did I not in the deepest solitude of thought repeat to myself my good fortune in possessing you? How often during those happy days, happy though chequered, I thought how superiorly gifted I had been in being united to one to whom I could unveil myself, & who could understand me. Well then, I am reduced to these white pages which I am to blot with dark imagery.

Mary's shame and regret, for her own depression and emotional withdrawal from her husband just before his death, was her continual penance. For Shelley would become her religion, the establishment of his reputation and the veneration of his memory, the substance of her worship. She would devote the following years to the collating and editing of his poetry and prose and, ironically, find some solace in that activity for, as she recorded in her journal on 5 October, 'Literary labours, the improvement of my mind, & the enlargement of my ideas are the only occupations that elevate me from my lethargy.' Within weeks of the funeral she was writing to England, asking Peacock to gather Shelley's letters, papers and first editions from his publisher so that she could begin the enormous task.

Byron's feelings about Shelley's death were indeed strong but, characteristically, conflicted. It is true that, like Mary, he was perhaps sorry for occasionally wronging his friend, but his letters immediately after the funeral are largely preoccupied with business, only mentioning the deaths and the distress of the widows in passing. He did offer a tribute in a letter to John Murray on 3 August, however, defending his dear friend: 'You are brutally mistaken about Shelley who was without exception — the *best* and least selfish man I ever knew. — I never knew one who was not a beast in comparison,' He likewise defended him to his friend Douglas Kinnaird, who thought that Shelley was a destructive influence, and continued in the same vein to Thomas Moore: 'he is, to my knowledge, the *least* selfish and mildest of men — a man who has made more sacrifices of his fortune and feelings for others than any I ever heard of.'[12]

Byron was genuinely saddened by Shelley's death and he must have felt, even more strongly than he felt when he returned to England from the Ottoman Empire in 1811, that he was doomed to see his loved ones die before him: Matthews, Edleston, his mother, Allegra, and now Shelley, were lost to him for ever. But at the same time, Byron was now free of the best and least selfish man he ever knew. Shelley's outstanding example of altruism and integrity must have been galling for a man like Byron whose temperament was so volatile and whose desires so changeable. Indeed, the two poets were often compared by their friends and acquaintances, and usually to Byron's disadvantage. Where Shelley was described as self-effacing, self-denying and compassionate, Byron was judged to be vain, materialistic and uncaring. Hunt was the most extreme in his disparate views of the two men, but as the poets became linked together after their deaths, such juxtapositions of character were not uncommon.[13] In fact, Shelley was often portrayed as an angelic figure with a soul so rarefied that it was in danger of ascending with its owner at any moment. Byron may have been the more famous, perhaps even the superior poet, but Shelley was seen, sentimentally, to be the better man.

Shelley had long tried to persuade Byron to give in to his better self and to toss aside the disguise of unworthiness that he assumed. Perhaps it wasn't a disguise and Byron was indeed guilty of all those faults alleged against him, but Shelley would not accept such blanket criticism of his friend and, still more vexing, would not allow *him* to accept it. Byron's gadfly was gone, but his influence was still potent.

Nine months earlier Shelley had been greatly encouraged by Byron's work on *Don Juan*. But during the last months of his life he had become increasingly disappointed with Byron's recalcitrant character — the older poet was cruel to Hunt, cruel to Claire, and, there could be no denying it, largely responsible for his daughter's death. Byron must have known that Shelley was angry with him. Did he also know that Shelley had been disappointed? Did he feel a nagging doubt about the unachieved project, just possibly taking shape as *Don Juan*? He had resumed work on the poem in April and, by May, seemed to understand what Shelley had found so unsatisfactory about his old goals and his old style:

> The only literary news that I have heard of the plays ... is that the Edinburgh R[eview] has attacked all three[14] ... Murray writes

discouragingly — and says 'that nothing published this year has made the least impression' ... You see what it is to throw pearls to swine — as long as I wrote the exaggerated nonsense which has corrupted the public taste — they applauded to the very echo — and now that I have really composed within these three or four years some things which should 'not willingly be let die' — the whole herd snort and grumble and return to wallow in their mire. — However it is fit that I should pay the penalty of spoiling them — as no man has contributed more than me in my earlier compositions to produce the exaggerated & false taste — it is a fit retribution that anything [like a?] classical production should be received as these plays have been treated.[15]

The old productions no longer satisfied him and, with or without Shelley's help, he had come to realize that his true voice lay with *Beppo* and the poems that came after. But would he press on, now that Shelley was dead, to 'some greater enterprise of thought'?[16]

Byron must now have been left with the uncomfortable thought that he must act decisively if he were ever to eradicate the 'canker of aristocracy' that ate at his soul. His dissolute, aimless life-style, coupled with his cynical pose of world weariness, prevented him from producing his best work. Shelley was no longer there to press him, yet to satisfy his friend's ghost Byron would still have to compel his genius to one more task; he was not unconvinced that Shelley might have been right about him after all. He would select an arena for some noble purpose and follow up his tentative dip into the world of freedom-fighting — his vain attempt to cripple tyranny with the incompetent Ravennese Carbonari — by striking out on some glorious campaign, a natural extension of his own desire to fight the good cause.

CHAPTER IX

AFTER SHELLEY

I N THE MONTHS FOLLOWING SHELLEY'S DEATH Byron turned his attention to business, to publishing and to his remaining estates at home. He also attended to Mary, determined to offer her help and comfort. He declared that she should consider him her banker and have no fear of straitened means, despite the fact that he was trying to curb his own spending.

In mid-September, isolated and lonely, Mary moved to a suburb of Genoa, to the Casa Negroto. Claire left for Vienna to join her brother Charles, and Jane Williams, to whom Mary had grown deeply attached in their mutual sorrow, returned to England. At the beginning of October Byron arrived in Genoa. Mary had rented the Casa Saluzzo for him, about a mile away from her, and he settled in with the Gambas. Once again his establishment was sufficiently large for each family to have complete privacy. Indeed, Byron often communicated with Teresa by letter. Saluzzo could also easily accommodate his menagerie; his pet geese, originally intended for a Christmas feast, wandered freely with the rabbits, cats, monkeys and dogs.

Hunt and his family followed Byron, now that their champion, Shelley, was gone. Hunt was determined that the source of their sporadic income should not disappear, but this time they shared Mary's large house. Byron had had enough of unruly children. The Hunt offspring, all between the ages of one and ten years, had occupied the ground-floor apartments of the Palazzo Lanfranchi in Pisa. Hunt believed that children should not be chastised before they were old enough to be reasoned with and their mother was almost constantly indisposed. As a result, the children were out of control — they scribbled on the palace walls and disturbed Byron with their clamour. Leaving his own private apartments one day, Trelawny noted that the poet's ferocious English bulldog, Moretto, guarded his door. Byron reached down to pet the animal and said, 'Don't let any Cockneys pass this way.'[1] In purchasing one of Shelley's sofas, he rescued it from the children's destructive clutches:

> I have a particular dislike to anything of S[helley]'s being within the same walls with Mr. Hunt's children. — They are dirtier and more mischievous than Yahoos ... what they can['t] destroy with their filth they will with

their fingers ... Poor Hunt with his six little blackguards ... was there ever such a *kraal* out of Hottentot Country before?[2]

In fact, Byron had had enough of Hunt himself. He was already bored with *The Liberal* and concerned that he was being associated with the 'Cockney' poets — Hunt and Keats — back in England. Indeed, the first edition of the journal, which included Byron's controversial *The Vision of Judgement*, led to its publisher's prosecution. That publisher, none other than John Hunt, Leigh's brother, was eventually fined £100 for sedition; he had libelled the memory of George III. The unseemly association with the brothers Hunt and the uproar over the poem caused a significant and worrying censure of Byron and his work. What is more, the great number of pirated editions of the early part of *Don Juan* (Cantos I–V), as well as his other poetry, were severely undercutting Murray. The hitherto generous publisher claimed that he could not afford to pay the huge copyright fees that Byron had enjoyed in the past. With Canto XII Byron had brought Don Juan triumphantly to London and into the glittering social scene of his own youth, but he had not yet arranged the bulk sale of the copyright of the cantos that he had completed since selling I–V to Murray for such a high price. The Cockney connection could only damage his chances for a good sale.

Leigh Hunt was not unaware of Byron's anxiety about money and his blatant new rapacity — 'I loves lucre,' Byron wrote to Kinnaird in January. Hunt was still borrowing money from the poet and was worried that this support would be withdrawn. The two men would never be at ease together and Byron was only too willing to quarrel in the hope of severing ties for good. 'I cannot describe to you the despairing sensation of trying to do something for a man who seems incapable or unwilling to do anything further for himself,' Byron wrote to Moore on 2 April 1823, of Hunt. It 'is like pulling a man out of a river who directly throws himself in again'.

Hunt knew that he was disliked, but held his fire to prevent alienating his patron altogether. Only after Byron's death would he freely express his animosity — he had nothing good to say about him in *Lord Byron and Some of His Contemporaries* (1828). He was particularly cruel about Byron's appearance, pointing out his effeminate features, his tendency to plumpness, his inability to grow a beard, his handful of rings and the white handkerchief that he habitually carried to show off his 'delicate white hand'. The 'remnant of his hair [was] oiled and trimmed with all the anxiety of a Sardanapalus'.[3] And Hunt was even more vicious about Teresa, who, he believed, shared no real love with her poet: 'In a word, Madame Guiccioli was a kind of buxom parlour-boarder, compressing herself artificially into dignity and elegance, and fancying she walked, in the eyes of the world, a heroine by the side of a poet.'[4] Hunt's condemnation of Teresa is much harder to understand than his attack on the poet — she went to great lengths to patch up his squabbles with Byron and to ease their differences over money. Teresa's 'foreignness' may have disturbed Hunt; he was a dedicated xenophobe. He never took to Italy nor did he ever properly master the language as his friends had done.

By contrast, for Mary, Byron had nothing but good will for the moment — she was, after all, a link with his vanished friend. He now wished to express his appreciation of Shelley by looking after his widow; she had no income, save the cash recovered from the salvaged *Don Juan* and a fraction of the price of the boat's sale. *The Liberal* would bring in a small sum and Mary wrote a 'Tale of the Passions' in October 1822 for the second number. Byron was one of the executors of Shelley's will (along with Thomas Love Peacock) and, initially, he exercised his responsibility with gravity and generosity. He graciously turned down the £2,000 that Shelley had left to him.[5] His first practical act of kindness was to buy Shelley's furniture from his widow, consisting of dozens of chairs of different descriptions, tables, beds and lamps. He could hardly have needed so much. His own collection was considerable, and the complicated business of moving his enormous household from Pisa to Genoa — dealing with customs as he crossed state boundaries was just one of the many complexities that the move entailed — caused him considerable upset.

Mary clung to the man who had been her husband's friend and had shared her greatest periods of happiness. She was able to feel something of Shelley's presence in her talks with Byron and to experience again the height of the happiness they had had at Geneva in the summer of 1816. In the middle of October 1822, she wrote in her journal:

> I do not think any person's voice has the power of awakening melancholy in me as Albe's — I have been accustomed when hearing it to listen & to speak little; — another voice, not mine, ever replied, a voice whose strings are broken; when Albè ceases to speak I expect to hear *that other* voice, & when I hear another instead, it jars strangely with every association. I have seen so little of Albe since our residence in Switzerland, & having seen him there every day his voice, a peculiar one, is engraved on my memory with other sounds and objects from which it can never disunite itself . . . since incapacity & timidity always prevented my mingling in the nightly conversations of Diodati — they were as it were entirely tête-a-tête between my Shelley & Albe & thus I have said — when Albe speaks & Shelley does not answer, it is as thunder without rain, The form of the sun without heat or light, as any familiar object might be shorn of its dearest & best attribute — & I listen with an unspeakable melancholy — that

> yet is not pain ... when in company with Albe, I can never cease for a
> second to have him [Shelley] in my heart & brain with a clearness that
> mocks reality, interfering even by its force with the functions of life ... [6]

Byron, for a moment, could restore to her her husband. She was reluctant to leave Italy, the country that they had both so loved, and reluctant to lose Byron's company. He easily persuaded her to remain for the moment. She made herself indispensable as his amanuensis and in some way perpetuated the relationship that her husband and Byron had shared. Mary's friendship offered Byron the luxury of dominating an intelligent but naturally submissive personality and he indulged his patrician penchant for protecting and befriending those weaker and more vulnerable than himself. Though Mary was keenly aware of Byron's tastes, knowing how to stroke his vanity and praise his talents when appropriate, their new friendship was perhaps more satisfactory and quietly productive than had been her husband's with Byron before her.

Byron, as he repeatedly mentioned, had opened his purse to Mary. In order to avoid the stigma of charity that his free-flowing funds would impose, she would once again undertake the chore that he found so tedious — the copying-out of his poetry from his difficult autograph drafts. Mary had already proved to be of great value: she had worked on his dramas *Sardanapalus*, the story of the fall of the magnificent Assyrian king; *Mazeppa*, the tale of the transgressor lashed to a wild horse; *The Two Foscari*; and *Werner*, among other things. But now began her intensive work on *Don Juan* and her new relationship with the poet. Starting with Canto VI, she fair-copied each succeeding canto, regularizing Byron's punctuation, his use of capitals and in some cases, as her confidence in his regard grew, offered her advice on matters of 'taste' and the selection of a particular word or rhyme. Mary's fair copies were then checked and corrected by Byron — who progressively allowed her alterations to stand — and were then sent to Murray for printing. In most cases, Byron then received the proofs some months later for inspection. By the middle of October he had already completed Canto X and had decided to switch publishers. He had grown impatient with Murray's timidity in the face of public outcry and had reluctantly turned *Don Juan* over to the eager John Hunt.

But Mary was to become disenchanted with the complicated man who had so exasperated Shelley. In January 1823 Byron wrote to Sir Timothy Shelley on her behalf, hoping that the widow and oprhan might receive at least some of the allowance that had automatically ceased with Shelley's death — all Mary desired was a small 'Italian maintenance'. But Sir Timothy was adamant in his animosity towards his second daughter-in-law: Percy Florence would be provided for and given a privileged education, but he must be relinquished completely into the care of a designated party in England. Mary was outraged. Under no circumstances would she be parted from her child and Sir Timothy's cruel offer stung her deeply. What hurt still more was Byron's recommendation that she should accept the cold-hearted scheme. 'I literally writhed under the idea that one so near me should advise me to a mode of conduct which appeared little short of madness & nothing short of death,' she wrote to Jane Williams on 7 March 1823.

Byron's powers of conjuring up Shelley's comforting ghost had been on the wane for some time. 'Lord Byron reminds me most of Shelley in a certain way, for I always saw them together,' she wrote to Maria Gisborne on 22 November 1822. 'But this must wear off — & there is so little resemblance in their minds, that LB. seldom speaks to me of him without unwittingly wounding and torturing me.' Mary was remarkably sensitive about Shelley's memory and was offended by what she felt were Byron's insults: she could not enjoy, as the two men had done, the intellectual combat that had characterized their friendship. She may well have been hurt by Byron's pompous and patently unsupportable distinction between his true friendships and 'man of the world' friendships. The former he maintained he felt for only one man, Lord Clare, a friend of his schooldays whom he saw fleetingly and only once or twice as an adult. He said that not even Shelley could be counted amongst this exclusive set, but one need only read his affectionate letters to Hobhouse, Kinnaird and Moore to see just how expansive and profound was Byron's capacity for friendship and that his treatment of Lord Clare, whose aristocratic background no doubt enhanced his suitability as the one chosen friend, was hopelessly tinged with nostalgia and runaway romanticism.

Mary may have been hurt by Byron's insensitive comments about her dead husband, but she understood, just as Shelley had, the fundamental differences between the two poets' characters as well as their poetic style and intent. She was remarkably critically perceptive and shared Shelley's evaluation of Byron's early work in relation to *Don Juan* and the late verse dramas. After she had finished copying Canto XI and the satirical verse drama *The Deformed Transformed* for Byron in November, she commented, 'I delight in your new style more than in your former *glorious one*, & shall be much pleased when your fertile brain gives my fingers more work.'[7]

In the flush of her growing resentment, instigated by Hunt's tactlessness and misunderstanding of Byron, Mary also began to think less of Teresa. As she took Hunt's side in the fight with Byron over funds that he had promised to them both, she became aware of Teresa's 'unamiable jealousies & falsehoods', where before she had found her a sympathetic friend. Hunt's bitter opinion of Byron and his lover began to infect

Mary as well — she did not realize that Hunt was taking advantage of her, nor did Byron realize that much of the money he gave to Mary was subsequently turned over to the ever-needy Hunt. With Hunt's prompting, Mary grew more suspicious of Byron's kindness. She wrote to Jane Williams on 8 April: 'He piques himself on giving good advice & I must follow it, or lose my credit with him — which stands greatly I believe on my known admiration of his writings and my docility in attending to him.'

But Mary was dissatisfied above all by Byron's inability to offer her what she so missed. 'For eight years,' she wrote, 'I communicated with unlimited freedom with one whose genius, far transcending mine, awakened & guided my thoughts; I conversed with him; rectified my errors of judgement, obtained new lights from him, & my mind was satisfied. Now I am alone!'[8] She was desperate not only for the emotional closeness that she had taken for granted with Shelley, but for the intellectual partnership that had, above everything else, characterized their relationship. She was fiercely attached to her child, but he was, after all, only a baby.

Trelawny's antics began to annoy even her, though he was still some comfort. He offered his money and services and the kindness of his manner as he told her of Shelley's death had touched her deeply: 'I feel so deep a gratitude towards him that my heart is full but to name him. He supported us in our miseries ... & when I shake his hand I feel to the depth of my soul that those hands collected those ashes.'[9] What is more, she could indulge her grief by talking eagerly for hours with him about her lost lover. But Trelawny did not stay in one place for long and he was occupied elsewhere, hunting, sailing and entertaining his mistresses. Though she spent evenings with the Hunts gathered round the one fireplace in the house that didn't smoke, devoted herself to their children, walked regularly into Genoa, and gradually saw more of Byron and Teresa as her resentment faded, Mary was intensely lonely. She even missed Claire, bound for Russia as companion to the daughter of a wealthy St. Petersburg minister. She hated Genoa and the weather, a winter as wet and cold as England's. There were no pleasant walks near by, just sunken lanes within high enclosing walls. The sea was too close. She was tortured by the sound of the murderous waves as she tried to sleep, stirred by the relentless sirocco. She often dreamed, asleep and awake, that she met her lost Shelley. She saw a white sail on the horizon — his sail — and almost called to be taken out to it. Shelley's voice spoke her name in the night as she sat at her desk, working through the confusion of his scraps of poems, drafts and notebooks.

In company she was as composed, calm and efficient as ever. She nursed Marianne through another illness, brought on by inevitable pregnancy — her seventh. But in her journal she poured out her grief in endless paragraphs of woe, unlike any of her previous records. She addressed the journal entries to 'my own Beloved', 'my lost Angel', focusing on her loneliness. Were it not for her fatherless child, she would surrender to death. She was also tortured by the notion that her coldness, her 'moon-shine', had contributed to Shelley's unhappiness before his death. When challenged by Mary for his evident ill-will towards her, Hunt savagely accused her of having been a poor wife, because of her own bad temper and impatience, to a quietly suffering Shelley. (Meanwhile, her beloved Jane Williams was propagating this idea back in England.) And Mary had no image of Shelley. Besides a pencil sketch of Edward's that Jane had taken back to England, only one existed. She spent the next two years trying to obtain it from Amelia Curran in Rome. The portrait was poor and they had all agreed that it was an inaccurate likeness. Still, Mary was desperate for the comfort that she was sure it would bring. She begged Curran for the picture and also asked her to purchase from one of the shops in the Piazza di Spagna two mosaic stones depicting the pyramid of Cestius and a pansy, or 'heart's-ease', a flower that Shelley had adopted as a symbol of memory. She would fashion a locket, and enclose a lock of his hair. She had begun to assemble the holy relics of her grief.

Don Juan and the steady love of Teresa Guiccioli were not enough for Byron and if Mary's reports of his home life were true, that he was 'kept in excellent order, quarrelled with & hen-pecked to his heart's content',[10] then he was surely tiring of his role as *cavaliere servente*. He was becoming bored with the quiet domesticity that the frenzied years of his youth had given way to. His passion for his young mistress had died down — in her uncharitable moments Mary believed it dead and cold — and Teresa shared his company only by invitation. When Teresa received word of her sister's death, he wrote her a formal letter of condolence and did not see her for four days. He felt the old urge to travel and to seek adventure, but he had not yet hit on a plan of action; this time there should be some design in his travels. Perhaps he would go to America, a nation that even the most decorous liberals admired and none more so than Byron. In the stream of strangers who came to his door, hoping for an audience, he would always find time for the American visitor who had been seduced by the *Childe* or the *Corsair*. He loved to listen to the sound of the American voice. Perhaps he and Trelawny — ever willing to remain near that steady source of income — would cross the Atlantic together to experience this young and promising republic. Or perhaps he would buy a province in Peru or Chile, or mine copper in Mexico.

Meanwhile, in January 1822, Byron's mother-in-law, Lady Noel, had died. By the ruling of his complicated marriage contract, settled so long ago during the snowy winter of 1814, he inherited her distinguished family name and half of her fortune, shared equally with his wife. His income was increased by £2,500 a year. With some embarrassment, but with altogether more pride, he began to sign his letters with the ancient name; 'Noel Byron' was his new incarnation and with it he doubled his previous income. The money that he had been earning from his poetry since resident in Italy, coupled with the Noel fortune, made him rich and comfortable by the standards of the day (especially in Italy), though he had already taken to hoarding his money and living more frugally, selling some of his horses and laying off servants.

And Byron was no longer young, nor did he have the heroic beauty of his youth. At thirty-five his famous head of dark heavy curls was greying and thinning, inching back from his high forehead. His dress, so meticulous when he had associated with the dandies and beaux of his youth, appeared to his English visitors as at best ill-fitting, at worst shabby — though he still indulged his penchant for an abundance of pristine linen. Lady Blessington, who spent some time in Genoa with her husband during Byron's last months there, saw him nearly every day. After his death she published her *Conversations of Lord Byron*, evidently with a view to deflating the Byron myth. She elaborated on his appearance at the time. She was disappointed in his less than magnificent presence and with his unaristocratic flippancy. In trying to make him appear human, she often reduced him to the ridiculous, vain and petty, and nowhere more so than in her description of him on horseback, in a costume which she painted as extravagant and absurd:

> The saddle was à la hussarde with holsters, in which he always carried pistols. His dress consisted of a nankeen jacket and trousers, which appeared to have shrunk from washing; the jacket embroidered in the same colour, and with three rows of buttons; the waist very short, the back very narrow, and the sleeves set in as they used to be ten or fifteen years before; a black stock, very narrow; a dark blue velvet cap with a shade, and a very rich gold band and a large gold tassel at the crown; nankeen gaiters, and a pair of blue spectacles, completed his costume, which was anything but becoming.[11]

This ensemble was occasionally altered by the addition of a green tartan jacket and this, coupled with what Lady Blessington judged his poor horsemanship, deflated the image of the dashing Harold. He was the parody of Napoleon crossing the Alps in David's painting.

By the late spring of 1823 Byron was thin again after a winter of dieting and purging with vinegar and salts. He was also weak. He was even more susceptible to fever — the blistering sunstroke and subsequent illness that had seized him after his three-mile swim out to the *Bolivar* and back on the day of Shelley's funeral seemed to have broken his health. But he was always more pleased to be thin than robust and at last his restlessness had given way to a plan of action. Perhaps he could make some impression on the Greek struggle for independence which had begun two years before with the spontaneous massacre of thousands of Turks by their Greek neighbours in the Peloponnese, a series of slaughters that were matched by equally savage Ottoman reprisals. European Philhellenes — lovers of the idea of classical Greece — who included sophisticated Greeks educated in the West, were committed to the erroneous idea that the modern Greeks were direct descendants of the ancient, and they envisioned a new golden age for a country that was, in the 1820s, hopelessly backward. A sundering of centuries-old shackles was all that was required, they believed, to 'restore' liberty and enlightenment to the land made sacred by the classical heroes who had dominated their European educations. The Greek Orthodox Christians of the Ottoman Empire revolted against the authorities, but not in order to restore a European ideal of high classical culture; that idea came strictly from a Europe intoxicated by the romance of the Athenian ideal.

Byron, like so many others, was not yet aware of the discrepancies between his ideal of the Greeks and the reality of that country's natives. He was prepared to champion the Greek cause as so many German, Swiss, French and British volunteers had already done and sail once again to the Ionian and Aegean Seas where the most carefree and vigorous days of his youth had been spent. In April, Edward Blaquiere, one of the founders of the London Greek Committee, dedicated to the liberation of Greece from the Turks, was passing through Genoa with a representative of the Greek revolutionary government on their way to witness the war. Hobhouse, another active member of the Committee, had suggested that Blaquiere should meet his friend. An English peer who had so enthusiastically demonstrated his devotion to Greece in his best-selling poetry would be a great asset to the cause. Hobhouse wrote and told Byron of their visit. They arranged to meet, and Byron wrote to Blaquiere on 5 April:

> I shall be delighted to see you and your Greek friend — and the sooner the better . . . I cannot express to you how much I feel interested in the cause — and nothing but some Italian connections which I have formed in Italy — connections also in some degree referring to the political state of this country — prevented me from long ago — returning to do what little I could as an individual — in that land which is an honour even to have visited.

Byron had decided: he *would* go to Greece. Once the decision had been made, he grew more excited — and confident. He would be a hero with a purpose, the noble man that Shelley had always demanded he should be. Perhaps he might be able to return to England to reclaim his reputation, his daughter, maybe even his wife. Byron committed himself formally to the cause and waited impatiently for his assignment from the Committee. He was elected a member of the Committee and finally, in May, after he had begun to regret his early enthusiasm, his contribution was decided. He consolidated his own funds with the help of his agents in England and by selling off some of his valuable possessions. He would fit out a ship and carry arms, ammunition, provisions, medical supplies and cash to the independence fighters. He and Pietro Gamba, wild with enthusiasm for the adventure, would command their little army. A ship, the *Hercules*, was engaged and fitted with the two one-pound cannons from the *Bolivar*, which Byron had already arranged to sell for £400 to Lord Blessington. Horse boxes were built on the ship and Byron acquired yet another enormous dog of the Newfoundland breed named Lyon. He had many new suits of clothes and boots — the right ones carefully fitted with inserted insoles to compensate for his limp — made for the journey. He would be resplendent on arrival in Greece in brightly coloured costumes, cut and gold-braided in the military style. But his most stunning contribution to the outfitting of the expedition was the splendid Homeric helmets that were made for himself, Pietro and Trelawny. Crested and plumed, they bore his family motto, 'Crede Byron'. Pietro was delighted, Trelawny scoffed retrospectively; needless to say, they were never worn.

Yet Byron's doubts about the expedition still lingered. He had a taste of the incompetence that would characterize the entire campaign when he learned that the revolutionary leaders were at odds with one another, and were vying for control of his resources. He had also anticipated, with some eagerness, a short trip to England before his voyage east and was almost disappointed when the complications surrounding his business interests there were resolved without his presence being required. Despite his need for privacy and domestic freedom, he had also become undeniably attached to Teresa. He was genuinely worried that she might prevent his going. She grew more agitated as his departure neared, especially when he suggested she should return to her husband, who was evidently ready to forgive her and take her back. He also began to believe that he would never return from Greece. His health was poor; perhaps he was physically incapable of such an undertaking. But Trelawny had agreed to join the expedition. This news convinced Mary that, despite his misgivings, Byron would go to Greece. He 'hates Genoa', she wrote. 'Pierino is half mad with joy at the very idea — because Greece has many charms for him, & his pride will also be gratified.'[12] In a moment of indignant, ungenerous anger she also wrote, 'LB. is fixed on Greece — he gets rid of two burthens; the G —13 & the Liberal.'14

As the date for Byron's departure approached, he had a complete falling-out with Hunt, grew impatient with his duties as Shelley's executor and nearly lost Mary's friendship as well. She was embittered by what Hunt had told her of Byron's harsh words about her and Shelley, and determined not to take a penny from him for her journey home. She would rely on Trelawny's offer to pay for her passage back to England. She wrote constantly to Jane Williams, complaining of Byron's duplicity, and attacking his character. She even took out her anger on Teresa: 'He talks seriously of returning to her,' she wrote, 'and may if he finds none of equal rank to be got as cheaply — She cost him nothing & was thus invaluable.'15 But it was Teresa who engineered Mary and Byron's reconciliation. She sent conciliatory letters and, at Byron's request, Mary was on hand to comfort the Countess on the evening that she took leave of her lover. But Mary did not see Byron to say goodbye and to clear up the sad misunderstandings that, exacerbated by Hunt, had so distressed their last months as friends. Yet Mary, in her later reminiscence, was to remember Byron with fondness and affection.

On 13 July 1823, Byron left Teresa in the evening and went to spend the night on the *Hercules*, in preparation for an early start the next day. The next morning Teresa left with her father for Bologna; his exile from the Romagna had been revoked. She was still only twenty-three and, because of her illicit domicile with Byron, had been deprived of all the social occupations that would otherwise have filled her days. But she was in despair and would gladly have renounced a glittering social life to remain in seclusion with her ageing poet.

The crew of the *Hercules* woke to find themselves becalmed in Genoa's harbour. Deflated, Byron went back to Saluzzo to bathe. The next day saw further delay, and the next a storm which forced them back into port. A further day was spent repairing the damage done by the panicked horses which had been stabled on deck. Byron was cheered by the foul weather — he loved being on deck in wild weather. 'I have always looked upon a storm as one of the sublimest spectacles in nature,' he told Pietro Gamba.16 Finally, on 17 July they were away, the sluggish and heavy vessel sailing slowly down the coast.

Mary knew that she too must leave her beloved Italy, the country that sheltered the remains of her love and her youth, and return to a cold and resentful England, where no comfort could be found in her father's penurious and frenetic household. Godwin had successfully brought her novel, *Valperga*, to publication after taking considerable liberties in editing it, but she had after all given him its copyright as a gift. She probably still smarted from the terrible letter that he had written on Shelley's death, one to rival in its insensitivity his 'condolence'

letter for the loss of William. Having hounded her and her husband for
money throughout her marriage and before, Godwin wrote soon after
the news of the drowning reached London at the beginning of August:

> I looked on you as one of the daughters of prosperity, elevated in
> rank & fortune; & I thought it criminal to intrude on you for ever the
> sorrows of an unfortunate old man & a beggar. You are now fallen to
> my own level.[17]

Mary had no choice but to return, however, and Byron too believed
that it was now time for her to go. Percy Florence, who spoke only
Italian, must be given a proper English education and Mary determined
that it would be as fine and as expensive as his father's. To provide for
her son she would become a professional woman of letters and scratch
out an income with her pen. Such a career could only be conducted in
London. She would dedicate her life to her child, to her literary endeav-
ours, and to the sanctified memory of Shelley. She left Italy on 25 July
1823, just a few days after Byron sailed for Greece, determined to give
direction to his own life. Thanks to Trelawny's loan Mary arranged her
travel home by coach, in comparative comfort. The Italian enchantment
was ended, the mortal remains of her life's focus left behind in the soil
of Rome.

CHAPTER X

GREECE AND DEATH

When a man hath no freedom to fight for at home,
  Let him combat for that of his neighbours;
Let him think of the glories of Greece and of Rome,
  And get knock'd on his head for his labours.

To do good to mankind is the chivalrous plan,
  And is always as nobly requited;
Then battle for freedom wherever you can,
  And, if not shot or hang'd, you'll get knighted.

THE *HERCULES* MADE SLOW PROGRESS down the coast of Italy. After two days in port at Livorno, where it took on more supplies and volunteers for the cause and where Byron received a packet from Goethe — stanzas full of praise for the misunderstood master-poet of England — it was finally heading for Greece. Byron had judged it more prudent, however, to delay his appearance on the mainland until his role in the conflict could be more clearly defined and his influence exercised to the maximum. He chose the Ionian island of Cephalonia for his first headquarters. The Ionian Islands, which included Corfu, Santa Maura, Zante and Ithaca, were a British Protectorate and had been under French rule before their effective annexation by Britain. They had never been part of the Ottoman Empire and their Greek inhabitants were well educated and westernized, a very different group from the Ottoman Greeks of the mainland. The Greeks of the Ionian Islands, like other Europeans, were Philhellenes, enamoured of the impossibly romantic notion of the renaissance of the glory of ancient Greece.

The British government had officially assumed neutrality on the issue of the Greek war. However, the British officers on Cephalonia were themselves Philhellenes. When Byron arrived on 3 August with his heavily laden ship to set up his headquarters, the military officials turned a blind eye to his real intentions, but with full knowledge of the significance of his cargo.

In fact, Byron was pleasantly surprised to find such a warm welcome from the English contingent — Colonel Charles Napier, the British Resident on the island was, despite his official role, a staunch Philhellene and an avid supporter of the Greek cause. Even more surprisingly, the British officers were delighted to meet the poet and invited him to a mess supper. Byron had expected continued ostracism by his countrymen and was moved by their kindness and warmth.

Less favourable was his immediate impression of the state of the cause and of the character of the Greeks. He arrived to discover the war at stalemate — both sides disorganized and reluctant to move. He also found complete dissension among the leading Greek factions and a stubborn unwillingness to see the common ground of their supposedly glorious war. Every group, each nothing more than a tribal faction with a warrior chieftain at its head, was eager to seize power and take the leading role in the new order that they believed would follow the destruction of their Ottoman rulers. Each saw Byron's money and influence as the means to that end. As Pietro Gamba, who quickly came to abhor the Greeks, described in his narrative of the Greek adventure:

> As soon as it was known that an English nobleman of great fame, and — what acted not less powerfully on the imagination of the Greeks — of great wealth — exaggerated, notwithstanding his efforts to undeceive them — was at Cephalonia, is easier to conceive than to relate the various means employed to engage him in one faction or the other; letters, messengers, intrigues, and recriminations; — nay, each faction had its agents, exerting every art to degrade its opponent.[1]

From the moment that he landed on Greek soil Byron was besieged by the war lords supplicating for his already legendary resources, lying and displaying dishonesty to a degree that astonished him. The *Hercules* had brought with it 10,000 Spanish dollars in cash, and bills of exchange for 40,000 more — and clearly, the purveyor of such riches was fair game. 'Against the intrigues of the very persons he came to help and benefit he was obliged to be constantly on his guard; and while he necessarily opened his purse for their service, he was exposed to be made their prey.'[2]

Byron brushed aside his disillusion and chastised himself with the reality of the situation; romantic dreams about a reincarnated golden age were absurd. The effects of generations of 'slavery', he rationalized along with many other disappointed European volunteers, had already bitten too deeply into the Greek character to be expunged at the first taste of freedom, an insight that his own poem, *The Prisoner of Chillon*, had taught him — and Shelley, too — in 1816. He would stand by his commitment. He would not succumb to disappointment.

In fact, Byron thrived during his months in Cephalonia. The voyage from Italy had revitalized him — he had spent most nights on deck. His health was improved and the pain of leaving Teresa rapidly diminished. Indeed, his only communications with her were as postscripts to Pietro's letters. His new project and the renewal of the happy scenes of his youth were taking her place in his busy mind and emotions.

He was pleased with the island and swam, rode and shot pistols daily and the English officers had little trouble persuading him to dine at their lavish table. He was even happy to rise to the challenge of the island's resident theologian and argue religion. Remembering the savage glamour of the Albanian warriors that he had encountered on his first trip to Greece, he hired a band of rough Suliote fighters, refugees from southern Albania, as a personal bodyguard. Their picturesque attire and reputation for bravery and loyalty appealed to him but in practice they were impossible to manage. They demanded not only pay for themselves but a maintenance for their families as well. They were aggressive and easily provoked and fought frequently amongst themselves. From time to time they unilaterally elevated their own military rank and demanded more pay. Finally, in disgust, Byron disbanded them, but he had to pay still more to get rid of them.

He remained resolutely settled in the Ionian islands, visiting nearby Ithaca on an outing where he dispensed alms and 'adopted' a destitute family, taking its young son Loukas as his page. But in Greece Byron changed the habits of a lifetime. Not only did he live frugally and abstemiously, but his habit of rising late was over, and he was at his desk, writing letters and attending to dispatches, by nine o'clock. He bided his time on Cephalonia, determined to wait before plunging his person and his resources into the battles ranging fitfully and ineffectually across the mainland, just a day's sail to the east. Pietro, ever loyal, praised his caution and explained the thinking behind it:

> He carefully avoided every appearance of ostentation, and had a great dread of being taken for a searcher after adventures. By perseverance and discernment he hoped to assist in the liberation of Greece: to know and be known was consequently, in the outset, his principal object.[3]

Besides, the London Greek Committee, in reality a small organization, with very little influence, had not yet raised the all-important loan that would help to finance the war for the Greeks. (The Committee's money would also reimburse Byron for his own personal loan, paid in cash directly to the revolutionary government.) And Byron was playing a vital role by simply establishing himself in Greece. He was an important asset — other Englishmen and Philhellenic Europeans would contribute their own time and money more generously if they saw the great poet personally involved in the cause. Byron prepared to make himself more comfortable for his indefinite stay. He moved from his cramped quarters on the *Hercules* where he had lived for a month and took up residence with Pietro in a pleasant villa in the sunny village of

Metaxata, with its fine views, and waited for news from England and from the mainland. Behind his back, Trelawny accused him of idleness, indecision and inertia. For his own part, Trelawny could wait no longer. In September Byron made the restless man his personal emissary on the mainland. He carried Byron's letters to the revolutionary government but soon joined the retinue of the factional leader Odysseus and, dressed in scarlet and gold, sabre at his side and attended by two servants, he lived out his exotic fantasy.

Byron had written almost no poetry since leaving Italy. He added nothing to the fourteen stanzas of Canto XVII of *Don Juan*; indeed, he never would. Instead, his days were filled placating unruly soldiers and chieftains and with the complicated business of exchanging bills from his bank in England for instantly negotiable Spanish dollars. Occupied with important matters of business outside his own interests for the first time in his life, Byron appeared to have forgotten his artistic calling altogether. He had found a second and more satisfying one. 'Poetry,' he told Pietro, 'should only occupy the idle. In more serious affairs it would be ridiculous.'[4] He had become a man of action after all. Shelley would have been surprised by his abandonment of his art, but proud of his friend's noble commitment. The significance and scope of that commitment were to grow, in direct proportion to the frustration and seeming hopelessness of the political and military situation as it revealed itself to Byron over the coming months.

Meanwhile, good news arrived from England in November. Colonel Leicester Stanhope, another passionate Philhellene, had been deputed by the Committee to work with Byron and he brought news that their cause was finding increasing favour at home; the completion of the loan could not be long hence. Byron was made the European representative of the Committee in Greece, an honour bestowed probably in order to maintain the commitment of their single most important member. In his new official capacity he addressed the general revolutionary government. The legislative and executive bodies were at odds and Byron wrote on 30 November stating his position with regard to the division in their ranks:

> Unfavourable rumours of new dissensions in the Greek government, or rather of the civil war, have reached here. I hope with all my heart that they are false or at least exaggerated, since I could not imagine any calamity that is to be more feared for you than this. I must admit to you frankly that if some kind of order and union is not confirmed, all hopes for a loan will be lost, — any assistance that Greece might expect from abroad, which certainly would not be inconsiderable nor contemptible, will be suspended, and maybe even stopped, and what is worse is that the great Powers of Europe, of which none was an enemy of Greece,

and which seemed favourably inclined to agree with the establishment of an independent Greek state, will be persuaded that the Greeks are not capable of governing themselves and will cut short all your most noble hopes, and all those of your friends.

Allow me to add this once more and for always: I want what is good for Greece and nothing else: I will do everything in my power to insure this: But I do not consent, nor will I ever consent to permit the Public or private English citizens ever to be deluded about the true state of things in Greece. The rest depends on you, Gentlemen.

There were no stars before Byron's eyes. His approach to the complicated enterprise signalled a new development in his character. He was now prepared to face disappointment stoically. His new sense of responsibility was sorely tested, however; he was disgusted to learn that the Greek fleet had attacked a small and helpless Turkish vessel run aground on Ithaca. This violation of the British neutrality of the Ionian island was bad enough but, in their quest for booty, the Greeks had massacred the entire crew. Byron was perhaps unaware, like other Europeans, that such massacres of Turks by Greeks, in a completely random fashion, had characterized the earliest days of the revolution in 1821. Greeks in the Peloponnese murdered their Turkish neighbours in huge numbers, and they themselves were subject to the same treatment when the Ottoman government in Constantinople executed the Patriarch of the Greek Orthodox Church and commanded Turkish citizens likewise to slaughter Greeks. There were countless massacres on both sides, resulting in the deaths of tens of thousands.[5]

With Byron's long-delayed move to the garrison town of Missolonghi on the mainland at the end of December 1823, his spirits sank despite himself. The town was already devastated by previous Turkish attack and its fortifications were in an abysmal state. It was low-lying and swampy, its streets nothing more than muddy tracks and it rained excessively throughout the winter and early spring. Byron's retinue had arrived in two boats, after some difficulty evading the Turkish fleet — Pietro and his heavily laden vessel were even taken into custody for two days. Byron was welcomed, along with his already legendary cargo of cash and supplies, with great ceremony and celebration. The unruly soldiery — Suliotes again — saluted their new leader in traditional fashion. They fired their muskets wildly into the air, and wasted precious cannon fire, barely missing the bows of Byron's boat. In fact, whenever they showed their appreciation, the exuberant Greeks were in danger of killing their hero.

Byron shared the largest house in the town with Colonel Stanhope. It stood at the end of a soggy spit of land jutting into the shallow lagoon. Byron had two rooms on the second floor hung with weapons like an armoury; guns, swords, carbines and daggers left barely enough room for his books. His sixty-five-strong new Suliote bodyguard shared a large, open shed on the ground where they ate, slept and amused themselves while off duty. Byron frequently strolled amongst them with his dog Lyon on the many days when he was confined to home because of the weather and he enjoyed their rough ways, though when the young daughter of his regular laundress took on the task of collecting and delivering the bodyguard's laundry, he warned the girl's mother of the certain danger of sending her alone among his savage tribesmen.

Byron's arrival in Missolonghi also meant that he would finally meet Prince[6] Alexander Mavrocordato, who had become Mary Shelley's close friend in Pisa in December 1820. Mavrocordato was urbane, intelligent and highly educated. He had been biding his time in Italy, exiled from his country, waiting for the revolution to begin. He had returned to his homeland at the start of the war in the summer of 1821 and had been elected Prime Minister at Athens. (By the time Byron arrived in Greece, however, a rival faction had challenged and successfully put paid to Mavrocordato's premiership.) In exchange for Greek lessons, Mary had taught Mavrocordato English (a study in which he was evidently well advanced before he met the attractive Englishwoman) and, as their friendship developed through the spring of 1821, she began avidly to follow the campaign that he helped to lead for a liberated and revivified Greece. It is clear that a measure of flirtation characterized the friendship of Mary and the Prince. They spoke and corresponded in French and Mavrocordato flattered her extravagantly. 'Do you not envy my luck,' she asked Maria Gisborne on 14 February, 'that having begun Greek, an amiable, young, agreeable and learned Greek prince comes every morning to give me a lesson of an hour and a half.' Shelley had also caught the fire of Greek independence from the Prince and his band of Greek aristocrats in exile. He had not been personally enamoured of the dapper statesman — perhaps he had resented the easy, warm relationship that Mavrocordato shared with his wife — but he dedicated his great poem of liberty, *Hellas*, to him.

Mavrocordato left Pisa for the Greek mainland in June 1821, eager to join the fight. Mary was sorry to lose his delightful daily company, but they maintained a lively correspondence long after his departure and for many years later. What is more, her admiration for the Prince, coupled with the recommendations of others of his honour and intelligence, established him as Byron's chief contact with the revolutionary Greek government. Despite his sometimes passive or hesitant handling of difficult situations, Mavrocordato worked well with Byron and soon became the only Greek that the disillusioned Englishman would trust.

At Missolonghi Byron realized that his irregular army put the Greek cause at a considerable disadvantage. None of the Suliote chieftains would accept the overall command of another Greek who was their social equal. Thus, for practical reasons, it was agreed that Byron himself should take military command of 600 men, personally financing 500 of them. On 5 February William Parry, 'fire-master', a military engineer hired by the Committee, finally arrived with his anxiously awaited supplies. He was to establish a munitions laboratory for the construction of artillery and rockets, guns and fortifications. He would oversee the technical side of all military matters. But, when he landed, the Greeks refused to unload his heavy equipment. In despair with the rain soaking through the precious stores of gunpowder that Parry had brought, Byron himself hauled cases and crates on to the beach. Only by that example could he persuade the Greeks to help. The unloading and setting up of the laboratory took several days, and was only possible when the Suliotes had been persuaded to vacate the premises of the old seraglio that Parry had been promised for his workshop.

Parry was a great comfort and encouragement to Byron. He took over the drilling of the troops. He was joined by Byron every day on the parade ground and instructed him in the 'mechanical arts of war'.[7] Together they watched the army take shape. Byron had in mind the attack of Lepanto, another garrison town in Turkish hands which he discovered from various sources would be an easy target. Encouraging the obstreperous Suliotes into action and securing a morale-boosting victory was essential and Parry recognized this as no one else. He became Byron's confidant at Missolonghi. He was a practical man — not of the officer class — but he showed the leadership and energy that had been so sorely lacking in the whole enterprise. Byron eventually entrusted him with the disbursement of his funds. Parry became strongly attached to the poet and echoed Pietro's devoted words:

> He was ready, like some general of old Rome, to share the privations of the meanest soldier; and he shewed, both by what he submitted to, and by the dangers he braved, that his love of liberty and of the good cause of mankind was not limited to writing a few words in their favour from a comfortable well-warmed library; or to sending from a table, smoking with all the superfluities of French cookery, a small check on his banker. The propriety and utility of some of his measures may possibly admit of a doubt, as, in fact, they have been censured; but of the purity of his intentions, and the intenseness of his zeal, the dangers he encountered, the privations he submitted to, the time and money he bestowed, and the life forfeited, there are such proofs as no other man in this age and country has given.[8]

By contrast, Colonel Stanhope was preoccupied with his printing press, brought out from England by the Committee at great expense, and he devoted all his energies to publishing a newspaper for the cause. Byron called him the Typographical Colonel and was amused to find himself, a man of letters, more eager for the fight than the trained soldier.

Throughout the winter the weather in Missolonghi, never pleasant, was especially wet and cold. Riding was prohibited because of the weather and boredom and disappointment began to chip away at Byron's enthusiasm. His spirit dwindled as Loukas Chalandritsanos, his page-boy, became the subject of an unrequited romantic yearning, alluded to in one of the last poems that he wrote. 'On This Day I Complete My Thirty-Sixth Year' was found amongst Byron's papers and describes his feelings of emptiness and futility when he discovers himself unable to inspire love:

> 'Tis time this heart should be unmoved,
>   Since others it hath ceased to move:
> Yet, though I cannot be beloved,
>   Still let me love!
>
> My days are in the yellow leaf;
>   The flowers and fruits of love are gone;
> The worm, the canker, and the grief
>   Are mine alone!

His diet was even more restricted and Pietro reported that he ate 'nothing but fish cheese and vegetables; having regulated his table so as not to cost more than forty-five paras. This he did to show that he could live on fare as simple as that of the Greek soldiers.'⁹ Parry was shocked at how little Byron ate, particularly his abstinence from meat, and was even more dismayed when his doctors and colleagues did not see how weakened and debilitated he was becoming.

On 15 February 1824, Byron complained of feeling ill. In the evening, in the company of Parry and another officer, he collapsed and was shaken by convulsions for some time. He regained consciousness and was taken to bed, disoriented and afraid for his health — he was worried that he might be epileptic and that the seizures would return. Pietro reported his anxiety: '"Let me know," he said to his doctor, "Do not think I am afraid to die — I am not."'¹⁰ His Italian physician, Dr Bruno, in consultation with Dr Millingen, an English physician sponsored by the Committee, applied leeches to his temples. When the leeches were removed the nervous doctors could not staunch the flow of blood and their helpless patient fainted.

The next day Byron was somewhat recovered and, soon after, began to go about his business. He was as usual visited by the clergy

of Missolonghi who, as was their custom, thanked him, praised him
— then asked for more money. Such routines began to depress him
even more and compounded his anxiety over his physical weakness.
Still more problems arose. The German officers, 'soldiers of etiquette',
refused to serve under the practical and experienced Parry because of
his inferior rank. The Suliote troops were up to their old tricks. They
fought with the town residents, with foreigners and amongst themselves
and constantly threatened mutiny, as they demanded more pay. They
had not yet engaged in a single battle under their present command.
What is more, six of Parry's well-trained engineers decided to return to
England. They were frightened after the murder of one of the German
officers by a raging Suliote and demanded to be returned to safety. 'I
begin to fear,' Byron told Pietro, 'that I have done nothing but lose
time, money, patience, and health; but I was prepared for it: I knew
that ours was not a path of roses, and that I ought to make up my
mind to meet with deception, and calumny, and ingratitude.'[11]

Parry too believed that his friend despaired of ever making a difference
in Greece: 'He might put a good face on the matter to others, because
he would not be thought Quixotic or enthusiastic; he might even be,
as in fact he sometimes was, the first to laugh at his own difficulties,
to prevent others laughing at his folly; but in his heart, he felt that he
was forlorn and forsaken.'[12]

But spirit enough remained for Byron to revel in some practical
jokes at his friends' expense. The company had been terrified by a
severe earthquake on 21 February (they had experienced an equally
violent one at Cephalonia) and Parry in particular showed considerable
fear of a repetition. One night Byron arranged for some of his guards to
tramp on the ceiling above Parry's room and to roll cannon-balls across
it in a barrel. The terrified man fled from the room screaming for his
life. He was deeply humiliated when he discovered that he had been
duped, as was the amorous Fletcher, when Byron, in another jape, sent
a young soldier disguised as a village virgin to his room.

Byron was also temporarily heartened when news came that the
Committee was about to secure the loan that it had been trying to
raise for so long, and that the desperate quest for funds might soon
be alleviated. But he was further frustrated when floods prevented him
from travelling to Salona where Trelawny and Odysseus, to whom the
adventure-seeking buccaneer had become aide-de-camp, had invited him
to a conference of all the factions in an effort to unify the forces of eastern
and western Greece. As Byron's hopes were raised, they were inevitably
quashed.

On 9 April he could not bear to be house-bound any longer. Lack of
outdoor exercise contributed to his depression, and he finally insisted on
riding. Accompanied, as always, by his Suliote guard on foot, he and his

retinue, in bright uniforms, made a colourful spectacle. Parry was exasperated by the Greeks (no less than the London Greek Committee), but he showed a grudging admiration of the Suliotes' show: 'They were tall men, and remarkably well formed; and perhaps, take them altogether, no sovereign of Europe can boast of having a finer set of men for his body-guard.'[13]

But returning from the ride Byron and Pietro were caught in a shower and after leaving their horses on the firm ground, to be led back through the rutted, impassable streets, they travelled by open boat across the shallow lagoon in the cool of evening. Soaked with rain and heated by exercise, Byron complained of pains. The next day he stayed at home and Parry observed that he shivered involuntarily and his speech wandered. Alarmed, Parry urged him to go to the island of Zante to consult its resident doctor who had a high reputation. On 12 April, according to Pietro (an assertion contradicted by Parry), Byron rode out again, and realized only later that his groom had put the same wet saddle on his horse. He returned in the afternoon, more sick than ever, and on the following day a storm prevented his sailing for Zante where he had resolved to go for medical advice. By the 14th he was confined to bed and sometimes delirious.

Byron himself knew that his illness was serious but the doctors, still urging him to be bled, were not alarmed by his condition. Parry seems to have been the only one of those surrounding Byron who was aware of the danger and of his severely debilitated state. He alone sided with the patient against the doctors' demands for still more blood-letting. Dr Millingen, a young English physician sent by the Committee for the benefit of the Greek forces, was most confident in his diagnosis and treatment and bolstered the more timorous Bruno. Millingen worked on the weakened man to break down his will:

> I laid aside all consideration for his feelings, and solemnly assured him how deeply I lamented to see him trifle with his life in this manner. I told him, that his pertinacious refusal to be bled had caused a precious opportunity to be lost; that a few hours of hope yet remained; but that unless he would submit immediately to be bled, neither Dr. Bruno nor myself could answer for the consequences. He might not care for life, it was true; but who could assure him, unless he changed his resolution, the disease might not operate such disorganization in his cerebral and nervous system as entirely to deprive him of his reason. I had now touched the sensible chord; for, partly annoyed by our increasing importunities, and partly convinced, casting at us both the fiercest glance of vexation, he threw out his arm, and said, in the most angry tone: 'Come; you are, I see, a d — d set of butchers. Take away as much blood as you will; but have done with it'.[14]

Threatened with his worst nightmare, madness, Byron submitted to one of the few therapies available to doctors of the day. On 16 April the doctors opened his arm and drained away 'two pounds' of his blood. But, Millingen reported, 'the relief, obtained, did not correspond to the hopes we had anticipated.'[15] From that time Byron's periods of delirium began to overcome those of lucidity. The doctors' belief in the efficacy of their treatment did not falter. Parry stood by helplessly as they alternated blood-letting with the administration of violent purgatives, no doubt accelerating his already severe dehydration.

As Byron realized what was happening, his need to express his many wishes and instructions grew more desperate. He had called out before for 'My wife! My Ada! My country!' according to Parry,[16] but now he tried to explain what he wanted for his family and his dependants, loans that needed to be raised and money sent. He reeled off names — Augusta, Ada, Hobhouse, Kinnaird and even Claire[17] — and tried to explain to Fletcher that he and Tita, his faithful Venetian gondolier, must be provided for, that he must tell Lady Byron all. Pietro, listening, recorded the distressing exchange of 17 April:

> He then said, 'Now I have told you all.'
>
> 'My Lord', replied Fletcher, 'I have not understood a word your Lordship has been saying.'
>
> Lord Byron looked most distressed at this, and said, 'Not understand me? What a pity — then it is too late — all is over.'
>
> 'I hope not,' answered Fletcher; 'but the Lord's will be done.' Byron continued, 'Yes, not mine.'[18]

The delirium continued into the night and the following day. By now Byron was too ill to read the cheering news that had just come from the Committee and from Hobhouse, who was preparing to join his old friend in Greece. Speaking half in English, half in Italian, Byron was tortured by a mass of instructions that he could not give, a life of remembrances that he could not pay tribute to:

> 'Poor Greece! — poor town! — my poor servants ... Why was I not aware of this sooner? ... My hour is come! — I do not care for death — but why did I not go home before I came here?' At another time he said, 'There are things which make the world dear to me [*Io lascio qualche cosa di caro nel mondo*]: for the rest, I am content to die.' He also spoke of Greece, saying, 'I have given her my life! — what could I do more?'[19]

On the 18th, at six in the evening, the desperate hours of semi-coherent speech ceased. Byron slipped into unconsciousness, leeches silently draining his white temples. A rattle growing in his throat, he lay still for twenty-four hours until, on the following evening at six, he abruptly opened his eyes, then closed them for ever.

On the night that he died Missolonghi was subjected to a storm of thunder and lightning that few could compare to any other. Its spectacle lit up the sky, just as the Jura and Lake Geneva had been illuminated in summer almost eight years before. Parry took note of the extraordinary circumstances:

> At the very time Lord Byron died, there was one of the most awful thunder storms I ever witnessed. The lightning was terrific. The Greeks, who are superstitious, and generally believe that such an event occurs whenever a much superior, or as they say, a supreme man dies, immediately exclaimed, 'The great man is gone!'[20]

By the following day the Greeks were aware of their loss. The great man's papers were sealed and his belongings gathered together by his band of grieving friends and servants. Fletcher, ever loyal in his duty to his master, now doubly venerated in death, dispatched a letter to Augusta:

> I am sorry to be under the Painfull Obligation of wrighting to you the Most Disagreeable letter that I ever to this unfortunate moment Had ever to write, not only for *me* or *you* But for all the world in General.[21]

The doctors, meanwhile, unconvinced that they had hastened the poet's death, could not resist the temptation, in the ostensible guise of embalming the body, of performing an autopsy. This they did and, by crudely hacking at the head and chest, discovered almost nothing and left little information in their rudimentary notes on which subsequent doctors in later years might make any adequate diagnosis of the malady that had killed Europe's most famous poet. A chronic inflammation of the brain, aggravated by harsh living conditions, is perhaps the best suggestion modern medicine can provide by way of putative diagnosis. The body of the great poet, lover, friend was laid open to curious eyes, just as the fiercely burning body of Shelley had been laid open by the flames on the beach at Viareggio as his companions looked on. Trelawny arrived in Missolonghi too late to bid farewell to his commander, but he too could not resist a close scrutiny of the famous deformed leg, and he joined a host of others who attempted to describe the mystery. Needless to say, none of these descriptions, from the sensational to the prosaic, corroborate one another. Trelawny, with characteristically implausible elaboration, found *both* feet clubbed and the legs startlingly deformed.

Byron's corpse was spared few indignities, despite the loyalty and affection of his survivors.

Meanwhile, Greece prepared to do Byron homage in Missolonghi and, with a new and surprising unity, on the mainland as well. Mavrocordato had arranged a hero's funeral and, with a decisiveness and efficiency that had heretofore eluded all Greek commanders, he issued a proclamation: thirty-seven guns were to be fired, one for each year of Byron's life; public offices were to be shut for three days; all shops were to be closed and Easter celebrations were to be postponed; general mourning for twenty-one days was called and prayers for the dead man's soul and funeral services were to be held in all the churches. On 22 April the coffin, a hastily constructed rough wooden box, was brought to the main church in Missolonghi and a black pall was laid over it, topped by a helmet, sword and crown of laurels. Soldiers crammed the church and spilled out into the streets. On the following day the body was taken back to the house where Byron had lived. Many came to gaze on the famous face which, Pietro recorded, 'seemed gradually to soften; for when I took a last look at him, the expression, at least to my eyes, was truly sublime'.[22]

Finally, on 25 April, the lid of the coffin was nailed shut, the Greeks clamouring not just for the remainder of his dollars, but for a part of Byron's body as well — some of the poet's viscera were left in Greece for the veneration of the people that, to their dismay, he had sacrificed his life to save. Holes were drilled in the sides of the coffin and it was placed within a larger cask of spirits in order to preserve the body for the long voyage back to England, where, at the poet's request, his remains were to return. On 2 May, guns firing in salute, a procession of mourners carried the coffin to the harbour and Byron's remains left Missolonghi, just days after the *Florida* had arrived in Zante from England with the first instalment of the loan from the Greek Committee. That same vessel was to bear the remains of Byron, his two dogs Lyon and Moretto, his servants Tito and Fletcher, Stanhope and Dr Bruno back to England. Pietro, loyal and discreet, sailed in a different ship, not wishing to remind those waiting in England of the nature of Byron's relationship with his sister. Trelawny remained with the Greek fighters, struggling to obtain Byron's resources for his hero Odysseus.

The convoy left the Greek islands on the morning of 25 May 1824, despite Stanhope's attempts to have the new Greek hero transferred to Athens for interment. The *Florida* reached the mouth of the Thames a month later, on 29 June, and there it paused before its slow, final progress to London. How would the hallowed remains, those of the saviour of Greece, be received on their native soil, just eight years after the poet had so dramatically hastened away?

ENGLAND

M ARY SHELLEY LEARNED OF BYRON'S DEATH at Missolonghi at the beginning of May 1824. When she discovered that his body would be 'lying in state' at the home of a friend, after being denied burial in Westminster Abbey (John Cam Hobhouse, deeply shocked and grieved by Byron's death, had applied rather optimistically on his friend's behalf), she hurriedly arranged to see it. At two o'clock on Friday 9 July, she went to Great George Street to gaze on the ruined face of her once beautiful friend and to listen to Fletcher,[1] hovering about the body, telling and retelling the story of the poet's last days. The coffin, draped in black velvet and surmounted by the Byron coronet and escutcheon, was opened for the benefit of close friends, relatives and the sensation-seekers who managed to gain access to the house. But few could recognize the familiar beauty, the face once celebrated as the epitome of the classical ideal, in the rigid, sunken lines of the three-month-old corpse with its long moustache. The *Morning Chronicle* could not resist a poetic effusion on the less-than-sublime experience of peering at the dead:

> I went to look
> On Byron's awful *manes*; — 'twas a sight
> Which all my spirit to its centre shook —
> Grand, glorious, passion-moving, still — the blight
> Of death was there; but who could bear or brook
> Such a sun, clouded in so dark a night?
> Not I — I gazed upon his fearful sleep,
> And tried to weep; but O! I could not weep
>
> Yet he was pale and ghastly! — nought was left,
> But that high intellectual forehead, crown'd
> With a few dark grey hairs — his lips bereft
> Of all their bitter scorns! — his eyelids bound
> In mists, and all his glories chilled and cleft . . .[2]

On 12 July Mary watched from her window above Highgate Hill as the funeral cortège passed beneath on its way north to the Byron family vault at Hucknall Torkard Church near Newstead Abbey. Hobhouse, smarting from the rejection by Westminster Abbey, had designed a funeral of magnificence — the undertaker's bill alone was for over £1,000.[3] According to one newspaper report, a hundred carriages[4] followed the hearse with its six black-plumed horses. Where the cobbles of London ended, the procession was abandoned by the empty coaches sent by the few great families — the Duke of Bedford, Lord Melbourne, Lord Holland, the Earl of Jersey, Earl Grey and the Earl of Carlisle among many other members of the Whig aristocracy — former friends and hosts of the poet. Not bold enough to attend Byron's funeral in person, they would go so far as to present their servants in their easily recognized livery, but their own persons were still not proof against the scandal that yet clung to the dead nobleman. Indeed, the *Nottingham Review* complained that only the common people joined the cortège as it passed through villages on its four-day journey north, lying in state each night at designated inns along the way, and that none of the noble families whose homes lined the long route joined the procession as it passed their estates.[5] It also noted that the new — seventh — Lord Byron, Captain George Anson Byron, did not attend the funeral, nor did any representative from Lady Byron's family. And not one Tory of consequence felt inclined to attend either.

Augusta could not bear to take her seat in the chief mourner's carriage and sent her husband instead. Though she was by now in thrall to Lady Byron, self-appointed as her redeemer, she none the less still loved her sinful half-brother. She would spend the rest of her life under Annabella's thumb trying, and always failing, to expiate her sin of incest to her sister-in-law's satisfaction. Until her death in 1851 Augusta outwardly tried to please her persecutor. She gratefully accepted Annabella's loans — Colonel Leigh's gambling still left the household resources drained — but she always cherished Byron's memory.

In John Cam Hobhouse Byron had a truly disinterested champion who was now thrust into a maelstrom of competing claims on the poet's memory. As soon as word reached London of Byron's death, Hobhouse received messages from countless women anxiously asking for the return of their letters. Chief among them was Lady Caroline Lamb. Her life since Byron's marriage and departure from England in 1816 had been one of unhappiness and psychological instability. As her husband William soared politically, so Caroline declined in health and spirits. After a failed love affair with the young novelist Bulwer Lytton, and an inevitable, acrimonious split with her husband followed by an eventual reconciliation, she died, aged forty-two, in 1828.

Hobhouse's first move on behalf of his friend's reputation was to ensure that Fletcher's account of his master's last days, making much of the fact that he had kept the Bible by him at all times, should not be circulated. Detractors would seize on such information to claim that the demonic poet had died a hypocritical coward, embracing the hope of Christian salvation after all. Hobhouse knew that this was not the case, but that the Bible had been a parting gift from Augusta. He was determined, despite the insurmountable odds, to control the Byron industry and to make sure that his position, as the poet's best friend, was firmly established.

Hobhouse's next project was also well-meaning and sincere, but an aggressive act of literary vandalism none the less. The newspaper reports of the poet's death had been largely sympathetic (with some exceptions, most notably *John Bull*, a resolutely conservative paper), many being willing to celebrate his artistic achievement and pardon his immorality. On 15 May 1824, *The Times* wrote:

> There are individuals more to be approved for moral qualities than Lord Byron — to be more safely followed, or more tenderly beloved; but there lives no man on earth whose sudden departure from it, under the circumstances in which that nobleman was cut off, appears to us more calculated to impress the mind with profound and unmingled mourning.
>
> Lord Byron was doomed to pay the price which Nature sometimes charges for stupendous intellect, in the gloom of his imagination, and the intractable energy of his passions. Amazing power, variously directed, was the mark by which he was distinguished far above all his contemporaries. His dominion was the sublime — it was his native home; at intervals he plunged into the lower atmosphere for amusement, but his stay was brief . . .[6]

Hobhouse was eager for this favourable pattern to continue. With Murray and Lady Byron's lawyers in agreement, and Moore protesting (Moore and Murray had complicated financial stakes in the manuscript), the memoirs that Byron had begun in Venice were burned on 17 May 1824 in the drawing-room of the premises of John Murray, the publishers, in Albemarle Street, before the poet's body had reached England. Though Byron had given his journal to the frequently hard-up Moore to do with as he liked after his death, no portion of the manuscript was saved. Many over the years had been allowed to read it but Hobhouse (one of those who did *not* read it) was certain that if the journal survived — recounting, as he was sure it did, the feverishly promiscuous days in Venice — it would render the effort of cleansing his friend's name utterly futile. It did not take the newspapers long to learn of the destruction of the memoirs, and the flames of Byronomania were stoked still higher; Hobhouse could only be engulfed in the conflagration.

If Shelley's rehabilitation and reputation were built slowly and steadily over the years, and Mary gave only pertinent biographical details in her notes to her comprehensive edition of the poems, the voracious industry that fed on the notorious life of Lord Byron was running at full speed before his body even came home. Try as he might, Hobhouse could not stop the rash of biographies written by opportunistic acquaintances and 'friends' eager to cash in on the hungry market. R. C. Dallas, to whom Byron had made a gift of the copyright of the first two cantos of *Childe Harold* in 1811, was the first to announce publication of letters from the poet to his mother, with notes on his life. The boring but industrious Medwin quickly followed with Pisan 'recollections' shamelessly fabricated or inaccurately paraphrased. He did, however, provide a useful service to Mary, striving in comparative obscurity to raise the name of Shelley; for the first time, in Medwin's *Conversations*, the two poets were linked as friends and, more importantly, as artistic equals. Relaxed in its tone and intimately revealing, it proved to be one of the most popular of the biographies, much to Hobhouse's annoyance.

Pietro Gamba, with the full endorsement of Hobhouse, gave his measured and respectful version of Byron's last year in Greece. Published in 1825, his book was simultaneously translated into English by Hobhouse. Pietro did not live to enjoy its relative success, however. He returned to Greece to continue his fight for the cause (and Byron's memory) and died there, of typhoid, in 1827. Brave, honest and gentlemanly, Pietro was one of those few friends who never sought to profit financially or personally from their association. His motive for hurrying into print was to provide an accurate, unsensational account of Byron's efforts in Greece.

Moore's biography was not published until 1830 but it had the unique advantage of intimate, personal recollections of the summer of 1816 — Mary anonymously contributed her descriptions of life at Diodati. But between the poet's death and Moore's work over seventeen biographies, memoirs or reminiscences were published, in addition to countless essays, reviews and pamphlets.[7] When Teresa Guiccioli came to visit London in 1832, she was the subject of tremendous curiosity. She charmed many with her own undeniably compelling personality, but it was her attachment to Byron that riveted the attention of drawing-rooms and salons across the capital. She was taken up by the socially ruthless Lady Blessington whose own journal of conversations with the poet would have deeply offended the ever-loyal Teresa. Lady Blessington was not overly concerned about hurting Teresa's feelings, however; she was fond of mocking her foreign guest behind her back. But Teresa was largely immune. When she later married the Marquis de Boissy after the death of Guiccioli, her new husband delighted in introducing her as the *ancienne maîtresse de Byron*.

Byron's death was an emotional set-back for Mary Shelley, compounding the feeling of loneliness and isolation that already overwhelmed her. She had long thought of him as a comfort, as a solid link between her present and past, between the living Shelley and his memory. When she learned of his death and its circumstances from Trelawny, still at the side of the wily Greek chieftain Odysseus in Greece, she was plunged deeper into melancholy and introspection. She wrote in her journal on 15 May:

> Byron has become one of the people of the grave — that innumerable conclave to which the beings I best loved belong. I knew him in the bright days of youth, when neither care or fear visited me: before death had made me feel my mortality and earth was the scene of my hopes — Can I forget our evening visits to Diodati — our excursions of the lake when he sang the Tyrolese hymn — and his voice was harmonized with winds and waves — Can I forget his attentions & consolation to me during my deepest misery?
> — Never.
> Beauty sat in his countenance and power beamed from his eye — his faults being for the most part weaknesses induced one readily to pardon them. Albe — the dear capricious Albe has left this desart world.
> What do I do here? Why am I doomed to live on seeing all expire before me? God grant I may die young ... At the age of twenty six I am in the condition of an aged person — all my friends are gone ...

Indeed, the news of Byron's death only confirmed Mary's sense of impending doom. She felt herself 'the last relic of a beloved race' and had recently begun her most ambitious and gloomy novel, *The Last Man*. Characters based on Byron, Shelley, Claire and herself (characters that she would use again in subsequent novels) see the world's population destroyed by a relentless plague. She now knew how Byron had periodically felt for most of his adult life — that he was weary, that his life had sped faster than most and that, though young in years, he was profoundly old in spirit.

Mary also felt bereft of Byron's special regard, both personal and professional. The hideous months that had followed Shelley's death had only been relieved by Byron's attentions, in particular that honour that he bestowed upon her with *Don Juan*. Her work for him had been exemplary and he had returned her dedication by acknowledging the remarkable intellectual powers, clear-eyed judgement and skilful editorial insights that her extensive copying work had manifested. When he left for Greece in July 1823, he left instructions with his publisher that Mrs Shelley's fair-copy of Canto XVI should be considered the printer's copy. Byron himself would not need to see the proofs. Mary must have felt that Byron considered her within his own intellectual orbit. He had had little patience with the 'Bluestockings'; he saw the women intellectuals of London high society as too self-conscious in their literary ambitions.[8] They hosted literary salons and kept their wealthy husbands firmly in check. He lampooned them in *Don Juan*: ' . . . oh ye lords of ladies intellectual! / Inform us truly, have they not henpecked you all?' He had earlier written, even more candidly, 'Of all bitches dead or alive a scribbling woman is the most canine.'[9] Mary, along with Madame de Staël, was the only forthright woman of letters to whom Byron gave his approbation and for whom he expressed his admiration. The unpleasantness of the last weeks in Genoa, where quarrels over money had marred Byron's departure for Greece, had not left a lasting impression on Mary, and what little displeasure remained was purged by the shocking news of his death.

Mary had arrived in London on 25 August 1823, just five days before her twenty-sixth birthday and just as Byron was settling into his life on the island of Cephalonia. She clung tightly to her young son, and for the rest of her life refused to let him go, searching hopelessly in his placid, stolid countenance for some spark of his magnificent father. They briefly returned to the care of Godwin and, with a kind of desperation, Mary tried to re-establish the filial tie that she had so mortally ruptured when she had fled into the night with her lover nine years before.

But she could not, despite herself, retreat into anonymity. *Frankenstein* had made her famous — far more famous than her husband had ever been — and her first pleasurable evening in England was a night at the theatre where *Presumption; or the Fate of Frankenstein*, a very free adaptation of her celebrated novel, was played to a delighted public.[10] Mary's spirit, despite its depressive nature, craved intellectual stimulation and debate, as well as the reassurance of old and warm friendships. The Hunts returned to England in October 1825 and Mary saw much of them. Leigh continued to edit journals, and produce essays and poetry, some of it meeting with considerable success. In 1847 he received a Civil List pension, and with the annuity that he had been collecting from Mary — without any pangs of conscience — he and his family finally lived in some comfort.

Claire would never provide friendly solace, however, and Mary was happy for her to be far away. She came back to England from Russia in 1829, eagerly anticipating Sir Timothy's death and the legacy from Shelley which would free her from the life of genteel service which she felt to be so beneath her. Disappointed that the old man was still vigorous, she took a position in Dresden. She finally received her fortune in 1844 and returned to England, squandering all of the £6,000 legacy. She lived until 1879, plaguing and embarrassing Shelley's son Percy Florence, who hated her. He rejected his father's letters that Claire offered to sell him and refused to consider her a relative.

Mary would be thwarted in friendship by others. Jane Williams, whose husband had shared Shelley's tragic fate, turned out to be all the things that her shallow nature had presaged. On her return to England she formed a secret romance with Thomas Jefferson Hogg, whom she later married. She spread malicious rumours of Mary's inadequacy as a wife, and exaggerated her own position in Shelley's regard at the end of his life. Mary had counted on Jane to share her misery for ever, that they would be bound together by the circumstances of their widowhood. But Mary's pretty friend had other plans. She was determined to live as happily as she could.

None the less, as a celebrity Mary discovered a wide circle of friends and an active life in London writing, visiting, play-going and sharing stories about her famous friends with her new ones. She was admired for her beauty, gentle charm and intelligence. She was warmly welcomed into the homes of Mary and Charles Lamb and the young poet Thomas Beddoes. Coleridge, an old friend of her father, played host on a number of occasions. She became a close friend of the American dramatist John Howard Payne and even held some hope of a romantic relationship with his friend, the novelist Henry Irving. In later years Disraeli would join her circle, as would Prosper Mérimée, whom she met on a highly successful trip to Paris in 1828. Though only twenty-four to her thirty, the young poet fell in love with her. Mary might easily have remarried — she was not short of offers. But the one or two men that she entertained romantic feelings for did not return them in any obvious way and she would never have pressed her suit.

Despite her celebrity Mary Shelley was fastidiously excluded from that very stratum of society to which she craved admission. She had been the close friend and confidante of a peer of the realm of ancient name, the wife of a baronet's son of similar venerability: now suddenly she was simply a widow, and one with a questionable past. She had renown certainly, but she was the daughter of disreputable parents who had outraged society in their own day, and had not had the benefit of nobility to balance their scandalous behaviour. Mary remained simply middle class, her interested and interesting friends were middle-class writers, journalists, musicians and artists. She rarely had enough money and, even after Sir Timothy finally granted his grandson an annual allowance of £200, she was constantly engaged in cost-cutting and never stopped soliciting for literary commissions. She would never be lionized, as Byron had been, and as her husband might have been, in the great homes of the Hollands, the Jerseys or the Melbournes. Glittering fragments of her former life fell about her after the cataclysmic deaths of Shelley and Byron, fragments sufficient to make her heart bleed for the privilege of her former days, but not enough to encircle her with a glory sufficiently potent to elevate her above her class or away from the very public sins of her youth.

In reality she was not only a literary widow, but a widow who was herself a legend. Yet her position was profoundly ambiguous, the future direction of her life so uncertain. Not until many years later, when Percy Florence inherited the baronetcy after Sir Timothy's much belated death at the age of ninety,[11] married a woman of Mary's choosing, and settled into the ranks of the obscure gentry, could she herself relax into the new role of dowager. But on her return to England she was only twenty-six, and still beautiful. Her life might have been on its threshold, but she felt old, played out, eager to join the dead.

Yet Mary would pluck an active vocation out of a life that she knew was over. Many besides Hobhouse would see to the rehabilitation of Byron's character — Sir Walter Scott eulogized his literary compeer with great eloquence and Goethe said that, excepting Shakespeare, England had produced no poet to rival Byron — but even the zealous and loyal Hobhouse could not match the fervour of Mary Shelley when she dedicated her life to the foundation of her husband's name and reputation. Her task, to ensure that Shelley's genius was universally accepted before his memory was lost to the public, would not be easy. Byron's posthumous reputation had its own relentless momentum, but Mary started pushing her massive boulder from the very bottom of the hill. The 1821 pirated publication of *Queen Mab* had revived the public ire against Shelley's radical notions, conflating the events of his life with the poem's explicit and objectionable philosophy. In fact, the public was more willing to forgive Byron his notorious lechery, or uncontrollable 'passions', than they would be to forgive Shelley for proclaiming himself an atheist so many years before.[12] What is more, Mary's own story of illicit love was known. Though that story and its tragic outcome lent her an air of romantic authenticity — her own feminine and demure looks adding considerable poignancy to the heady aura — there were none the less many who could never forget her irredeemable fall and her husband's role in it. The obituaries of Shelley that had appeared in the newspapers following his death two years before had ranged from the perfunctory to the cruel. The *Courier* had written, 'Shelley, the writer of some infidel poetry, has been drowned, *now* he knows whether there is a God or no.'[13]

Despite the colossal challenge, Mary persevered. In June 1824, before the return of Byron's body, she published *Posthumous Poems* after an exhausting and painstaking examination of the drafts, first editions, notebooks and fragmentary scrawls that made up the core of Shelley's *oeuvre* — poems that he himself rarely bothered to punctuate. She presented sixty-five formerly unpublished poems as well as those that were no longer in print or had received only the most limited exposure in journals or single sheets. The project left her exhausted for many years to come, she told friends, but the book was quickly suppressed by Sir Timothy, still active and unforgiving, after only 200 copies had been sold. He refused to allow his miscreant son's name to appear yet again before the public. Undaunted, Mary gave her secret assistance to other editors pirating volumes of Shelley's poetry. Four different editions appeared in Britain and France between 1826 and 1836, spreading the evidence of Shelley's genius. Slowly, painstakingly, his reputation was in the making.

Finally, in 1839, and only after Sir Timothy's final consent, Mary published a four-volume edition of Shelley's poetry and prose. Since 1824 she herself had written and published four three-volume novels, many short stories and reviews, and, in the years after 1839, she produced another travelogue and contributed seventy portraits to a popular and critically acclaimed encyclopaedia of biography. She also worked hard for other people, editing works by her father and by Trelawny.[14]

Gradually, Shelley had become a subject of sufficient public interest to ensure the enterprising biographer (and publisher) a financial reward. Though few had had the opportunity to read it, *Posthumous Poems* none the less made a certain impact. Medwin,[15] never one to waste time when money could be made, discovered a market for Shelley. In 1832, he produced a series of memoirs for *The Athenaeum*, including several unpublished Shelley poems. In the same year, Thomas Jefferson Hogg also wrote a series for the *New Monthly Magazine* on 'Percy Shelley at Oxford'. At the same time Hunt finally published Shelley's satirical poem *The Masque of Anarchy* (something that he had been asked to do ten years earlier but delayed in order to avoid further attacks on his friend's character and morals), and he included a lengthy preface with much biographical material.

Shelley's reputation was eventually taken up and celebrated by those who had not known him in life. At Cambridge, the young poets and critics Tennyson, Arthur Hallam and Richard Milnes (who was to write a life of Keats) 'discovered' the new poet. When Mary's four-volume and later one-volume editions of the collected works came out in 1839, in the new climate of comparative government liberality, the world appeared to be ripe for Shelley. The times had finally caught up with him. In that context Mary's efforts, in her extensive notes and commentary on the poetry, to make Shelley an appealing poet for a God-fearing public, do not seem so far-fetched. With her occasional willingness to explain away the many cases of Shelley's vehement radicalism as the product of immaturity, she cooled the fiery red rebel to a comfortable warmth more acceptable to a general readership. Contemporaries — Trelawny and Hogg — bitterly accused her of undermining, even betraying Shelley, but she was convinced of the urgency of her mission and neither man contributed much in the way of truth about the poet in their respective works. Mary's imperative was to create a great poet; explain his growth and development and emphasize his emotional, political and spiritual

maturation. It is worth while remembering that without Mary's comprehensive edition Shelley might not be read today. What is more, her
approach — presenting a relatively unknown poet in a complete edition as if he were already a member of the established canon — was
unprecedented.

With the completion of what Mary regarded as her life's work,
she could finally relax. Her great effort of love had somehow assuaged
the profound guilt she still felt about her own crippling depression and
alleged emotional abandonment of Shelley just before his death. The idea
that she might have been responsible for causing her husband pain had
haunted her. That he was often responsible for *hers* seems to have been
forgotten in the fervour of her remorse and devotion. She expressed her
sense of shame at the depression which had caused her withdrawal in
her autobiographical poem, *The Choice*:

> It speaks of cold neglect, averted eyes,
> That blindly crushed thy soul's fond sacrifice: —
> My heart was all thine own, — but yet a shell
> Closed in it's core, which seemed impenetrable,
> Till sharp-toothed misery tore the husk in twain,
> Which gaping lies, nor may unite again.
> Forgive me! let thy love descend in dew
> Of soft repentance and regret most true;[16]

Shelley's son, Sir Percy Florence, and his wife Jane readily received
Mary's devotional torch. She charged them with the duty of enhancing
and celebrating Shelley — in a large measure hiding his shortcomings and
censorable activities. As Byron's transgressions were discussed, exposed
and argued over by the world at large, as well as by his own descendants,
well into the twentieth century, Shelley's were obliterated by his select
votaries. Jane and Percy Florence controlled their legacy of papers and
memorabilia with punctiliousness. In their choice of official biographer
they made certain that Shelley, his second wife and family were nearly
deified and that their sins — the desertion of Harriet and her children and
her consequent suicide, Mary and Percy's co-habitation before marriage,
the ambivalent position of Claire in their household — were glossed or
passed over in silence. In fact, it was Jane who was largely responsible
for the blackening of Harriet's name and the fomentation of the idea
that she pre-empted Shelley in unfaithfulness.

As the biographies of Byron and Shelley continued to appear the two
were inevitably linked. After the publication of Hunt's *Lord Byron and
Some of His Contemporaries* in 1828, in which Byron is damned and
Shelley praised in contradistinction, the life stories of the two poets were
inextricably bound together. But not until 1837, with the publication of

Benjamin Disraeli's[17] novel *Venetia*, do we see a complete and passionate apologia for the faults and presumed sins of both Byron and Shelley together. The book's moody protagonist, based on Byron, is a misunderstood genius whose faults of unruly passion and occasional violence are the result of a childish and immoderate mother. Disraeli even goes out of his way to celebrate his character's fidelity and chastity. His friend, exiled from England for his advanced beliefs, is obviously indebted to Shelley's biography and the ignominy which he suffers in the novel is shown by Disraeli to be wholly undeserved.

As Mary grew older and her loneliness became less acute, her memories of Italy grew more golden, more enchanted, as if she looked backward towards paradise rather than forward to the one to come. She dreamed of returning there with Percy Florence to visit, perhaps even to settle. 'Then I might live,' she confided to her journal on 26 February 1841, 'as once I lived — hoping — loving — aspiring — enjoying.' Though she had found a purpose to her life and a kind of contentment since Shelley's death, she would always focus her emotional energies on the past, even coming to fear that Percy Florence would die in the same way as his father — a passion for boating was one of the few things that the boy had inherited from the poet.

Mary's desire to return to the Continent, to Italy, was fulfilled. Travel, as it had been for Byron, was the antedote to her melancholy and dissatisfaction. In 1842 and 1843 she visited Shelley's grave for the first time and took nearly a year to journey even further south than she and Shelley had ever been in their travels together — as far as Sorrento. But she had taken an earlier trip. In 1840 Mary's European journey was shorter and kept to a more northerly route. She began her excursion into the past with her son beside her, visiting again Lake Como, Milan and Florence. But when Percy returned to Cambridge for the start of the autumn term, Mary went on to delve further into her past life than she had ever dared before. She drew up at the very shrine of her youth.

Mary arrived at Geneva at the beginning of October and went immediately to revisit the setting of those days which saw the beginning of her life's adventure:

> At length, I caught a glimpse of the scenes among which I had lived, when first I stepped out from childhood into life. There, on the shores of Bellerive, stood Diodati; and our humble dwelling, Maison Chapuis, nestled close to the lake below. There were the terraces, the vineyards, the upward path threading them, the little port where our boat lay moored; I could mark and recognize a thousand slight peculiarities, familiar objects then — forgotten since — now replete with recollections and associations. Was I the same person who had lived there, the companion of the dead? For all were gone: even my young child, whom I had looked upon as the

joy of future years, had died in infancy — not one hope, then in fair bud, had opened into maturity; storm, and blight, and death, had passed over, and destroyed all. While yet very young, I had reached the position of an aged person, driven back on memory for companionship with the beloved; and now I looked on the inanimate objects that had surrounded me, which survived, the same in aspect as then, to feel that all my life since was but an unreal phantasmagoria — the shades that gathered round that scene were the realities — the substance and truth of the soul's life, which I shall, I trust, hereafter rejoin.[18]

Mary had already lived more than twice as long without Shelley as she had with him, and she would live for another ten years, dying in 1851 at the age of fifty-three. Those years were active and productive. Her devoted son was a source of joy, though his lack of direction and ambition worried her. Ironically, the tranquillity that she had so desired in her life with Shelley she largely achieved. She was occasionally disturbed in middle age by reminders of her former transgressions and her health declined steadily. But she was never morose in company, nor was she ever accused of self-pity. Still, she would always look backwards to her years with Shelley, her lover and her husband, and to Byron, her friend. Those years together would remain the focus of her life and, as she admitted, existed in her memory as a more authentic reality than any time since. In those years, sitting by the fireside at Diodati, or on the windswept lake, Mary's imagination expanded with the richness of overheard conversation, to give birth to a creative work which has become better known than anything that either of those two great voices of the nineteenth century ever wrote.

As Mary stood on the shore before the Maison Chapuis and climbed the steep path to the Villa Diodati in 1840, we can imagine her longing, her loneliness, her regret at the passing of time. But she must also have felt an overwhelming gratitude for the magnificent legacy that was left her, that she was the direct beneficiary of a love and of a friendship of such potency and richness that, even while it still flourished, was beginning to take on the luminosity of legend.

NOTES

CHAPTER I
Geneva

1. Shelley, a keen amateur chemist, may have been aware of the effects of volcanic activity on global climate. In 1783, while serving as American ambassador to France, Benjamin Franklin observed that the summer and subsequent winter of 1784 were exceptionally cold and unusually foggy. He attributed these anomalies to the inability of the sun to penetrate the ash and dust clouds present in the atmosphere, those resulting from eruptions in Iceland and Japan. It is not inconceivable that Shelley was aware of the paper that Franklin published on this theory. Franklin was a pioneer in linking volcanic activity to climate.

2. *The Diary of Dr. John William Polidori, 1816*, ed. William Michael Rossetti (London: Elkin Mathews, 1911), p. 99.

3. Thomas Moore, *Life of Lord Byron* (London: John Murray, 1851), Vol. III, pp. 280–1.

4. Ibid., Vol. III, p. 281.

5. Ibid., Vol. III, p. 280.

6. Accounts vary as to the actual number. Murray reported that he sold 10,000 copies on the first day of publication.

7. Moore, Vol. III, p. 280.

8. Rossetti, pp. 1–2.

9. Polidori committed suicide by poison in 1821, long after his dismissal from Byron's employ.

10. Mary Shelley and Percy Bysshe Shelley, *History of a Six Weeks' Tour through a Part of France, Switzerland, Germany and Holland* (London: T. Hookham, 1817), pp. 128–30.

11. *Letters of Samuel Taylor Coleridge*, ed. E. L. Griggs (Oxford: O.U.P., 1956–71), Vol. I, p. 527.

12. Moore, Vol. III, pp. 271–2.

13. *The Works of Percy Bysshe Shelley*, ed. Mary Shelley (London: Edward Moxon, 1854), Vol. I, p. 96.

14. Moore, Vol. III, pp. 271–2.

15. George Paston and Peter Quennell, *To Lord Byron: Feminine Profiles* (London: John Murray, 1939), pp. 211–12.

CHAPTER II
Mary and Percy

1. T. J. Hogg, *Shelley at Oxford* (Methuen and Co., 1904), p. 108.

2. Ibid., pp. 32–3.

3. *The letters of Percy Bysshe Shelley*, ed. Frederick Jones, 2 Vols. (Oxford: O.U.P., 1964), letter to Godwin, 3 January 1812.

4. William St. Clair, *The Godwins and the Shelleys* (London: Faber & Faber, 1989), p. 238.

5. Mary Jane did not begin to call herself Clara or Claire until 1815 but, for the sake of clarity, I shall call her Claire throughout.

6. *Letters of Percy Bysshe Shelley*, Vol. I, p. 421 n.

7. *The Journals of Claire Clairmont*, ed. Marion Stocking (Cambridge, Mass.: Harvard

University Press, 1968), p. 8.

8. Coffee-houses were exclusively male preserves. Mary requested Shelley to meet her in the doorway of the predetermined coffee-house on the day in question, as it was 'disagreeable to go into those places' [*The Letters of Mary Wollstonecraft Shelley*, ed. Betty Bennett, 3 Vols. (Baltimore: The Johns Hopkins University Press, 1980–8), letter to Shelley dated 25 October 1814. Mary was equally shy of 'walking up and down in a public place' (letter to Shelley, ?2 November 1814). She was acutely aware of her already compromised position.

9. 4 November 1814.

10. *Shelley's Prose*, ed. David Lee Clark (London: Fourth Estate, 1988), p. 115.

11. *The Journals of Mary Shelley*, ed. Paula Feldmand and Diana Scott-Kilvert, 2 Vols. (Oxford O.U.P., 1987). 16 November 1814. This edition is used throughout.

12. Letter, 13 August 1814.

13. Several years later Hogg was to make do instead with Jane Williams, the widow of Edward Williams who had drowned at sea with Shelley. She was also, significantly, the object of Shelley's latest infatuation immediately before his death.

14. Letter to Howard Payne, 27 September 1825.

CHAPTER III
George Gordon

1. The house still stands today, about half-way down Piccadilly, and maintains its original number.

2. Thomas Medwin, *Conversations of Lord Byron* (London, 1832), pp. 82–3.

3. *Byron's Letters and Journals*, ed. Leslie Marchand, 2 Vols. (London: John Murray, 1973–81), letter to Henry Drury, 3 May 1810.

4. Ibid., Vol. I, p. 207, n.1.

5. Leslie Marchand has indicated that 'antiques' refers to the ancient Greek custom of boy love.

6. To Francis Hodgson, 25 June 1809.

7. Medwin, p. 163.

8. Moore, Vol. II, p. 196.

9. To Catherine Gordon, 28 June 1810.

10. Byron objected vehemently to the 'despoilation' of Greece and attacked Elgin in his poetry. He wrote, 'I oppose, and will ever oppose, the robbery of ruins from Athens, to instruct the English in sculpture (who are as capable of sculpture as the Egyptians are of skating).' (*Letters and Journals*, Vol. II, p. 66 n.)

11. 19 June 1811.

12. To Francis Hodgson, 10 October 1811.

13. Jerome McGann, *Byron, The Complete Poetical Works* (Oxford: O.U.P., 1980–6), Vol. I, p. 459.

14. Leslie Marchand, *Byron: A Biography*, 3 Vols. (London: John Murray, 1957), Vol. I, p. 279.

15. Moore, Vol. II, p. 138.

16. To Lady Caroline Lamb, ? April 1812.

17. Paston and Quennell, p. 49.

18. After a two-year battle the lawyers managed to retain £25,000 of the original down-payment of £28,000.

19. Byron 'could only ever love' a number of people, among them Augusta, Mary Chaworth and his Harrow friend Lord Clare.

20. Ethel Colburn Mayne, *The Life and Letters of Anne Isabella, Lady Noel Byron*

(New York: Scribner's Sons, 1929), p. 160.

21. He had 'had Lady B on the sofa before dinner' in any case, he apparently related. (Marchand, Vol. II, p. 510.)

22, Marchand maintains that the presence of a lady's maid was denied by both Annabella and Hobhouse.

23. Medwin, pp. 44–5.

24. Ibid., pp. 55–7. Medwin's *Conversations* with Byron, it should be noted, were not taken down verbatim and were most likely paraphrased. He may even have made up some of the passages which he attributes, without qualification, to his subject.

25. St. Clair, p. 401.

26. R. Glynn Grylls, *Claire Clairmont: Mother of Byron's Allegra* (London: John Murray, 1939), p. 55.

27. At this period correspondence in London could be as efficient as the telephone is today. With several posts a day, an invitation and acceptance could be exchanged in a single afternoon. After their marriage William Godwin and Mary Wollstonecraft maintained independent households but habitually invited one another to breakfast on the same morning.

28. Paston and Quennell, pp. 202–3.

29. Ibid., pp. 211–12.

30. To John Cam Hobhouse, 27 April 1816.

31. The circumstances of Lady Byron's departure from the marital home and Byron's from England were just beginning to be the subject of gossip. The controversy surrounding the exact nature of Byron's cruelty to his wife did not surface immediately. It began with Annabella's constant justifications of her ultimate rejection of her husband. She suggested, as her lawyer later reiterated, that at the same time as she became aware of the nature of Byron's relationship with Augusta, she was also forced into sodomy by her husband and that, in her extreme innocence, she was not aware that the act was 'unnatural'. The question of Byron's proclivities and Annabella's outraged innocence still quietly simmers as something of an irrelevant sideline in studies of Byron's life.

CHAPTER IV
The Enchantment Ends

1. Mary Shelley's 1831 Introduction to *Frankenstein*.

2. Paston and Quennell, p. 225.

3. *The Journals of Mary Shelley*, Vol. I, p. 139 n.

4. Mark Twain, 'In Defense of Harriet Shelley', in *In Defense of Harriet Shelley and Other Essays* (New York: Harper & Bros, 1918), pp. 55–6.

5. The marriage actually took place on the 30th.

6. *The Letters of Percy Bysshe Shelley*, Vol. I, p. 525 n.

7. Journal entry, 1 December 1813.

8. Letter to Maria Gisborne, 16 November 1819. Shelley was reading Calderon at the time and was particularly impressed by the dramatist's portrayal of an incest scene.

9. Mary wrote a note to the famous novelist thanking him for his review and acknowledging her authorship — Scott too had believed it to be Shelley.

10. Moore, Vol. III, p. 281.

11. Paston and Quennell, p. 79.

12. Teresa Guiccioli, *My Recollections of Lord Byron* (London: Richard Bentley, 1869), p. 4.

CHAPTER V
Venice

1. A London opera box could be an efficient and profitable investment. In her middle age Mary purchased one and negotiated vigorously to sublet it a season at a time and to sell it on at a profit. In her case, however, the venture was not a financial success.
2. To John Murray, 26 April 1817.
3. To John Murray, 9 May 1817.
4. To J. C. Hobhouse, 11 November 1818.
5. Godwin had inspired Byron's respect long before he met Shelley and Mary. In January 1816 he had proposed to Murray that Godwin, whom he knew to be in financial difficulties, should be sent the sum of £600, a portion of the copyright that Murray was to pay Byron for two poems. Byron had refused the money himself on principle and wished to send it to the destitute author of *Political Justice*. Godwin never received a cheque from Murray.
6. To John Murray, 30 May 1817.
7. Moore, Vol. II, pp. 144–5.
8. To John Murray, 1 August 1819.

CHAPTER VI
Reunion: *Julian and Maddalo*

1. English ties, especially Annabella.
2. Moore, Vol. IV, p. 112.
3. Ibid.
4. To James Wedderburn Webster, 8 September 1818.
5. Composed in 1807, but not published until 1830.
6. Paston and Quennell, p. 231.
7. To Mary Shelley, 24 August 1818.
8. From *Julian and Maddalo*.
9. To Maria Gisborne, 2 November 1818.
10. To Thomas Love Peacock, 8 October 1818.
11. To Hobhouse, 11 November 1818.
12. The vitriolic dedication to Southey was not published until 1833.
13. Later, Shelley composed 'Ode to the West Wind', perhaps his most famous poem, inspired by images of the sunken villas of Baiae:
    ' . . . old palaces and towers? Quivering within the wave's intenser day,/ All overgrown with azure moss and flowers.'
14. To Amelia Curran, 27 June 1819.
15. *The Works of Percy Bysshe Shelley*, Vol. I, p. 252.
16. Ibid., p. 250.
17. Second husband or *cavaliere servente*.
18. Shelley had left a considerable sum of money to Claire in his will. Predeceasing his father, however, he inherited none of the fortune that he had so long anticipated and could therefore pass none of it on. Claire was destitute (or rather, dependent on Mary) and Byron refused resolutely to give her any money. When Mary and Shelley's son Percy Florence finally inherited from Sir Timothy many years later, they honoured all Shelley's legacies.

CHAPTER VII
Pisa

1. Medwin, Vol. II, pp. 1–2.
2. *The Works of Percy Bysshe Shelley*, Vol. I, p. 320.
3. To Charles Ollier, 15 December 1819.
4. Byron believed that Hobhouse was still incarcerated in Newgate gaol at this time.
5. To John Cam Hobhouse, 3 March 1820.
6. *The Works of Percy Bysshe Shelley*, Vol. I, p. 160.
7. Letter to John Gisborne, 18 June 1822.
8. To Maria Gisborne, 7 March 1822.
9. Shelley to Thomas Love Peacock, ?10 August 1821.
10. To William Hoppner, 10 September 1820.
11. Ibid.
12. Countess of Blessington, *Conversations of Lord Byron with the Countess of Blessington* (London: Henry Colborn, 1850), pp. 24, 45.
13. 'Shiloh', an alternative name for the Messiah, was Byron's ironic nickname for Shelley.
14. To Richard Hoppner, 1 October 1820.
15. Sadly, this is not the case.
16. Edward Trelawny, *Recollections of the Last Days of Shelley and Byron* (London: 1858), pp. 20–2.
17. Leigh Hunt, *Lord Byron and Some of His Contemporaries with Recollections of the Author's Life, and of his Visit to Italy* (London: Henry Colburn, 1828), p. 177.
18. Moore, Vol. V, p. 358.

CHAPTER VIII
The Gulf of Spezia and Death

1. To Maria Gisborne, 15 August 1822.
2. *The Triumph of Life* would remain unfinished and, though in a very rough state, was included by Mary, who imposed some order on it, in her 1824 edition of Shelley's poems.
3. To Maria Gisborne, 15 August 1822.
4. To Horace Smith, 21 May 1822.
5. To Claire Clairmont, 30 May 1822.
6. Trelawny, p. 104.
7. Ibid., p. 118.
8. Blessington, pp. 75–6.
9. This incident occurs in but one version of Trelawny's narrative, copied into Mary's journal (Vol. I, p. 423). He was to write ten accounts of the ceremony, and each from an increasing distance of years.
10. Hunt, *Lord Byron and Some of His Contemporaries*, pp. 200–1.
11. Trelawny, p. 134.
12. To Thomas Moore, 4 March 1823.
13. Hunt modified his views of Byron much later in his life and publicly apologized for his early pronouncements on his character.
14. *Cain, Sardanapalus* and *Marino Faliero*.
15. To Shelley, 22 May 1822.
16. Letter from Shelley to Byron, 29 September 1816.

CHAPTER IX
After Shelley

1. Trelawny, p. 100.
2. To Mary Shelley, 4 October 1822.
3. Hunt, p. 91.
4. Ibid., p. 40.
5. It should be pointed out that Shelley's fortune would only have come to him at his father's death. His beneficiaries, of an estate already vastly encumbered by the borrowings that Shelley had made against it at outrageous rates throughout his life, therefore had to wait for that event.
6. I have not indicated, as have the editors of the journal, Mary's crossings-out or super-script writing.
7. To Byron, 16 November 1822.
8. Journal entry, 2 October 1822.
9. To Jane Williams, 22 November 1822.
10. To Jane Williams, 5 December 1822.
11. Blessington, p. 55.
12. To Jane Williams, 10 April 1823.
13. Teresa Guiccioli.
14. To Jane Williams, 31 May 1823.
15. To Jane Williams, 23 July 1823.
16. Pietro Gamba, *A Narrative of Lord Byron's Last Journey to Greece* (London: John Murray, 1825), p. 12.
17. As quoted by Doris Langley Moore in *Lord Byron: Accounts Rendered* (London: John Murray, 1974), p. 291.

CHAPTER X
Greece and Death

1. Gamba, pp. 38–9.
2. William Parry, *The Last Days of Lord Byron* (London: Knight and Lacey, 1825), p. 27.
3. Gamba, pp. 35–6.
4. Ibid., p. 48.
5. William St. Clair, *That Greece Might Still Be Free: The Philhellenes in the War of Independence* (London: Oxford University Press, 1972).
6. 'Prince' was a title given by the Turkish government to local Greek rulers.
7. Parry, p. 37.
8. Ibid., pp. 79–80.
9. Gamba, p. 177.
10. Ibid., p. 176.
11. Ibid., pp. 192–3.
12. Parry, p. 28.
13. Ibid., p. 77.
14. Julius Millingen, *Memoirs of the Affairs of Greece* (London: John Rodwell, 1831), p. 132.
15. Ibid., p. 133.
16. Parry, p. 121.
17. Mary, given the news in London by Fletcher, was satisfied that Byron made mention of his former mistress, but Byron had probably been thinking of his schoolboy friend Lord Clare.

18. Gamba, p. 263.
19. Ibid., pp. 264–5.
20. Parry, p. 128.
21. *Lord Byron's Illness and Death as described in a letter from William Fletcher to The Honorable Augusta Leigh, Missolonghi, April 20, 1824,* (Nottingham: Privately Printed, 1920).
22. Gamba, pp. 277–8.

EPILOGUE
England

1. Fletcher, along with Byron's steward-secretary Lega Zambelli, acquired from Count Guiccioli's household in 1819, established a macaroni factory in London. The business failed and both men lost their savings. Lega, who lived and died in England, gradually cleared his debts, but Fletcher remained generally impecunious and dependent on those who could still be persuaded to take an interest in him and his long history with Byron.
2. From *Lord Byron Painted by His Compeers* (London: 1869), p. 71.
3. Lady Byron had been asked for her wishes regarding the disposal of her husband's body but left all to Hobhouse, co-executor with Hanson of Byron's estate.
4. Doris Langley Moore, in *The Late Lord Byron,* records that forty-seven carriages followed the hearse to the outskirts of London, and Leslie Marchand does not list as many great families as having sent representation.
5. One aristocrat who did encounter the cortège on its way north, though accidentally, was Lady Caroline Lamb, staying at her husband's estate, Brocket Hall in Hertfordshire.
6. Doris Langley Moore, p. 54.
7. It should be noted that even after 1830 Byronomania had not died down. Still more biographies and memoirs poured out of publishing houses — Murray printed countless editions of Byron's works. There were also many spurious, anonymous and falsely attributed works purporting to tell of Byron's secret love life, and several, such as the underground poem *Don Leon,* were pornographic.
8. Byron admired nonchalance in his great literary figures. He consistently praised Walter Scott, noting in particular his strikingly unpretentious and very 'unliterary' character.
9. To John Cam Hobhouse, 17 November 1811.
10. Several other productions based on *Frankenstein* were also staged in London — and Paris — around this time.
11. Shelley's eldest son, Charles Bysshe Shelley, Harriet's child, died in 1826, leaving the title free for Percy.
12. The poem did gain more publicity for Shelley however — this time it received nine reviews.
13. Quoted in Newman Ivey White, *Shelley* (London: Secker and Warburg, 1947), Vol. II, p. 391.
14. Trelawny finally settled down to publish, with Mary's help, the highly successful *Adventures of a Younger Son* (1831), but not before many more self-aggrandizing adventures. He remained in Greece after Byron's death, securing all the munitions of Missolonghi for his champion Odysseus and the fortification of his own private stockade. He married the robber-chieftain's thirteen-year-old sister and shortly thereafter Odysseus was found to have betrayed his fellow Greeks by an alliance with the Turks. He was taken prisoner and a nearly successful attempt was made on Trelawny's life. Trelawny divorced his Greek wife in 1828, proposed to both Claire and Mary, and returned to England in 1832. He travelled in America and on the Continent and finally settled in England in

1835, where he was lionized for his colourful life and much embellished relationship with the poets. He married many times and had many mistresses and daughters. He published his *Recollections* of the poets in 1858, and again in 1878, and died in 1881, lauded as the spirit of two ages.

15. Medwin, with greater luck than he deserved, married a Swedish baroness and deserted her after spending her fortune. In later years he attempted to bribe Mary with the threat of a biography of Shelley which would have meant the severance of her small annuity from Sir Timothy.

16. Mary Wollstonecraft Shelley, *The Choice, A Poem on Shelley's Death*, ed. Buxton Forman (London: Privately Printed, 1876), p. 8.

17. Disraeli was a Byron enthusiast and even managed to acquire Tita, Byron's Venetian gondolier and favourite servant, for his own. Tita had acted as domestic to Hobhouse before returning to Greece to join the cause. He came back to England, however, destitute, and was hired by the young Disraeli. He also served as messenger at the Indian Office.

18. Mary Shelley, *Rambles in Germany and Italy in 1840, 1842 and 1843* (London: Edward Moxon, 1844), Part I, pp. 139–40.

BIBLIOGRAPHY

BIOGRAPHIES

Shelley: The Pursuit, Richard Holmes (London: Weidenfeld and Nicolson, 1974).
Byron: A Biography, Leslie Marchand (London: John Murray, 1957), 3 volumes.
The Godwins and the Shelleys, William St. Clair (London: Faber & Faber, 1989).
Mary Shelley: Romance and Reality, Emily Sunstein (London: Little, Brown, 1989).

CONTEMPORARY ACCOUNTS

Conversations of Lord Byron with the Countess of Blessington, Lady Blessington (London: Henry Colburn, 1850).
A Narrative of Lord Byron's Last Journey to Greece, Count Peter Gamba (London: John Murray, 1825).
Shelley at Oxford, Thomas Jefferson Hogg (London: Methuen, 1904).
Lord Byron and Some of His Contemporaries with Recollections of the Author's Life, and of his Visit to Italy, Leigh Hunt (London: Henry Colburn, 1828).
Conversations of Lord Byron, Thomas Medwin (London, 1832).
The Last Days of Lord Byron, William Parry (London: Knight and Lacey, 1825).
The Diary of Dr John William Polidori, 1816, ed. William Michael Rossetti (London: Elkin Mathews, 1911).
Recollections of the Last Days of Shelley and Byron, Edward Trelawny (London, 1858).

THE WORKS OF MARY SHELLEY

The works of Byron and Shelley are well known; however, those of Mary Shelley are less familiar:

Mary Shelley: Collected Tales and Stories, with Original Engravings, ed. Charles Robinson (Baltimore: Johns Hopkins University Press, 1976; rpt. 1990).
Falkner (London: Saunders and Otley, 1837).
Frankenstein (Oxford: O.U.P., 1969; rpt. 1984). First published 1818.
The Last Man (London: The Hogarth Press, 1985). First published 1826.
Lodore (London: Richard Bentley, 1835).
Mathilda (Chapel Hill, North Carolina: University of North Carolina Press, 1959).
Perkin Warbeck (London: Routledge, 1857). First published 1830.
Valperga, or the Life and Adventures of Castruccio, Prince of Lucca (London: G. and W. B. Whittaker, 1823).

INDEX